SOCIAL PSYCHOLOGY
Conflicts and Continuities

AN INTRODUCTORY TEXTBOOK

Dennis Howitt (editor), Michael Billig, Duncan
Cramer, Derek Edwards, Bromley Kniveton,
Jonathan Potter, and Alan Radley
(*The Loughborough University Social
Psychology Group*)

OPEN UNIVERSITY PRESS
Milton Keynes · Philadelphia

Open University Press
12 Cofferidge Close
Stony Stratford
Milton Keynes MK11 1BY

and
242 Cherry Street
Philadelphia, PA 19106, USA

First Published 1989

British Library Cataloguing in Publication Data

Social psychology: conflicts and continuities:
an introductory textbook
1. Social psychology
I. Howitt, Dennis
302

ISBN 0-335-09883-5
ISBN 0-335-09882-7 Pbk

Library of Congress Catalog number available

Typeset by Scarborough Typesetting Services
Printed in Great Britain by
St Edmundsbury Press, Bury St Edmunds, Suffolk

CONTENTS

THE AUTHORS

Michael Billig *(BA, Ph.D., Professor of Social Sciences)* was a student at Bristol University where he took a joint honours degree in philosophy and psychology and later gained his doctorate. Following a further period as a research fellow at Bristol, he was a lecturer in the Department of Psychology at Birmingham University for eleven years. He has been Professor of Social Sciences at Loughborough since 1985. He was awarded the Erik Erikson Prize for distinguished contribution to Political Psychology. His research interests include political psychology, ideology, social psychology of rhetoric and arguments, social and political attitudes of adolescents, intergroup relations and prejudice. He has written several books including *Social Psychology and Intergroup Relations* (Academic Press, 1976), *Fascists: A Social Psychological Analysis of the National Front* (Harcourt Brace Jovanovich, 1978), *Ideology and Social Psychology* (Blackwell, 1982); and *Arguing and Thinking* (Cambridge, 1987); and *Ideological Dilemmas* (Sage, 1988) written with other members of the Discourse and Rhetoric Group.

Duncan Cramer *(B.Sc., Ph.D., A.F.B.Ps.S., Chartered Psychologist, Lecturer in Social Psychology)* studied psychology at University College, London and went on to the Institute of Psychiatry in London where he completed his doctoral thesis on Eysenck's theory of personality. He lectured in psychology at Queen's University, Belfast before moving to Loughborough. His main research interests include the nature of effective psychotherapy, the supportive role of personal relationships, the influence of beliefs on emotional distress, and the nature of love. He has a number of publications in these and other areas, and is on the Editorial Board of the *British Journal of Medical Psychology*.

Derek Edwards *(BA, D.Phil., Senior Lecturer in Social Psychology)* was an undergraduate and postgraduate student at Sussex University and his interest in the development of language dates from that time. After completing his doctoral research, he moved to Loughborough University to lecture in social psychology. Along with Michael Billig, Jonathan Potter and other members of staff, he is a member of the Discourse and Rhetoric Group in the Department. His principal research interests are early language development, the social and conversational basis of memory and remembering in adults and children, and discourse and knowledge in educational contexts. Amongst his publications is the book *Common Knowledge: The Development of Understanding in the Classroom* (Methuen, 1987) and *Ideological Dilemmas.*

Dennis Howitt *(B.Tech., D.Phil., A.F.B.Ps.S., Chartered Psychologist, Senior Lecturer in Social Psychology)* was a student on the sandwich course in psychology at Brunel University. He then went to Sussex University and completed his doctoral thesis on the relationship between emotion and attitudes. For several years he was research officer at the Centre for Mass Communications Research at Leicester University where he carried out research on topics such as the effects of media violence and the role of the media in the lives of pre-school children. He has done research for a number of organizations including the Council of Europe, the British Board of Film Censors and the Home Office. His main research interests are violence, mass media, communications in crisis situations, pre-school children and television, crime, behavioural measures of attitude, social studies of psychology as a science, law, race, race awareness training. Books which he has written are *Mass Media Violence and Society* (Elek Science, 1975) and *Mass Media and Social Problems* (Pergamon, 1982).

Bromley Kniveton *(BA, Ph.D., A.F.B.Ps.S., Chartered Psychologist, Senior Lecturer in Social Psychology)* obtained his BA in psychology from Queen's University, Belfast and his Ph.D from Nottingham University. He then went on to be research fellow for the Mental Health Trust and Research Fund and a research officer in the Industrial Relations Unit at Nottingham University before becoming a lecturer at Loughborough. His research interests include the interactions of children with their environment with particular reference to the imitation of others; the influence of peers and the school milieu and bargaining at a personal level and within organizations. Books which he has written are *Training for Negotiating* (Business Books, 1978) and *The Psychology of Bargaining* (Gower, to be published in 1989).

Jonathan Potter *(BA, MA, D.Phil., Lecturer in Social Psychology)* studied psychology at Liverpool University and then went on to take an

MA in the philosophy of science at the University of Surrey. His doctoral research was undertaken at York University where he studied the techniques scientists use to argue with one another at scientific conferences. He lectured for a time in psychology at the University of St Andrews, Scotland before becoming a lecturer at Loughborough in 1987. His main research interests include discourse analysis in the areas of science, riots, racism, and current affairs television. He has published many scholarly articles and is joint author of two books – *Social Texts and Context: Literature and Social Psychology.* (Routledge and Kegan Paul, 1984) and *Discourse and Social Psychology: Beyond Attitudes and Behaviour* (Sage, 1987).

Alan Radley *(B.Tech., Ph.D, A.F.B.Ps.S., Senior Lecturer in Social Psychology)* studied psychology at Brunel University and went on to study for his Ph.D. at the Middlesex Hospital Medical School in London. His main research interests are in the area of health and illness where he has examined the situation of families where one member is to receive heart surgery. Other interests include the place of physical objects in the lives of people, and the role of the body in social behaviour. Before coming to Loughborough he worked for the Medical Research Council on a project studying schizophrenic patients. Included in his publications is *Prospects of Heart Surgery: Psychological Adjustment to Coronary Bypass Grafting* (Springer-Verlag, 1988) and *Ideological Dilemmas.*

Acknowledgements

While this book is the work of a collection of individuals who form the Social Psychology Group at Loughborough University, none of it is the work of one individual. Each of the chapters has been altered and revised in the light of various suggestions. Furthermore, in order to iron out stylistic differences, each chapter has been thoroughly rewritten by the editor and the original author. However, for the record, given that the final academic responsibility was left with the original author, the preliminary draft of each chapter was the work of the following:

Chapter 2 Derek Edwards, Chapter 3 Alan Radley, Chapter 4 Bromley Kniveton, Chapter 5 Duncan Cramer, Chapter 6 Dennis Howitt, Chapter 7 Michael Billig, Chapter 8 Jonathan Potter, Chapter 9 Michael Billig, Chapter 10 Dennis Howitt

The patience and skill of Cathie Ward and Gwen Moon of the Department of Social Sciences at Loughborough University were invaluable in the preparation of the manuscript.

1

INTRODUCTION

This book sets down a challenge, in that we want to make the reader approach social psychology as something to be thought about and questioned, not as something to be skimmed through, taking a few notes on the way, a collection of facts to be memorized at a later date. More than most disciplines, social psychology has the potential to be taken as an intellectual debate from the moment it is first studied.

But in order to throw down this challenge it has been essential to change the priorities of social psychological textbooks and replace them with something a little more risky. Normally textbooks tend to present a bland and, to a degree, patronizing face to the discipline. The underlying assumptions appear to be that the reader merely has information to absorb and, without a host of cartoons and the like, will quickly get bored. Ignoring the lack of faith in the intellectual substance of the discipline that these assumptions imply, the insult to the reader is obvious. Many introductory social psychology textbooks lack academic depth. Words like 'condescending', 'superficial', 'gimmicky', and the like are used by both teachers and students to describe virtually all of them. Perhaps more tellingly, phrases like 'too American' are also mentioned in European circles. This is a criticism not of things American, but of a discipline which has allowed itself to become almost ethnocentrically the product of one nation in terms of its contents but also in terms of its teaching materials. Cultures differ and different cultures do things differently, including education. So what may work in one educational system may not be right in another one.

There is more to it than that. The question arises of what one wishes social psychology to be, what priorities are to be established. This might at first seem to a newcomer to social psychology a strange thing to write, but it is not. Intellectual activity is as much a question of making choices as any other human enterprise. Social psychology is not simply a self-generating body of knowledge, since it is the product of the social world of which it is part. Consequently it cannot be detached from the environment which created it. Social psychology from North America is North American social psychology and is a response to the demands of that culture as much as anything. This does not make it necessarily good or bad but it does provoke the question of whether or not it is well suited for other cultures. The answer to that question, however, is not a ready-made or slick 'yes' or 'no' but can only come from a careful evaluation of such social psychological knowledge. While, in later chapters, North American social psychology is not dismissed out of turn, there is a considerable amount of social psychology which has its roots in Britain and continental Europe, much of it very recent. This material does not generally find its way into North American textbooks so its presence in later chapters provides a more European stamp to this book than is typical. This also seems to enable a more *social* social psychology and, one might venture, a more mature outlook on the social world.

It is possible to criticize most social psychology textbooks from another stance. They seem to conspire to present social psychological knowledge as unproblematic, almost as a closed book. Reading many of them is quite comforting in that there seems to be consensus of proven facts which can be noted down for handy reference to tackle social situations. But this does not match very well with social psychology as we experience it as members of the discipline. Social psychology is the focus of any number of conflicts and controversies so that to smooth them away is not to promote some of the most substantial and interesting aspects of the discipline. Without them, social psychology is dull. There are fundamental disagreements about what sorts of theory, what sorts of research method, what sorts of issue, what sorts of question, and what sorts of answer are right for a social psychology. They are not trivial hiccups in an otherwise well-oiled machine, they are the flesh, blood, bones and sinew of a more organic entity which changes and moulds itself in response to its internal and external dynamics. This book is not subtitled *Conflicts and Continuities* for nothing. However, you will not find that it deals with these conflicts by explaining that Professor X says one thing but Professor Y said quite the opposite. That is merely to turn controversy into yet one more fact to learn. Instead, the conflicts are built into an argumentative structure – that is, we see the task as being one of taking positions and arguing those positions. It is not intended that what is written down should be universally acceptable to social psychologists. It is intended that the text makes arguments which reflect points of view rather than reviewing, in a sterile fashion, what social psychologists have written.

So, throughout, points of view are taken. They tend to be those that the authors share as members of the same social psychology department, but that was not a criterion. Having adopted this strategy, one other very important feature of the book was necessary. No attempt has been made to fill the book with detail from a large number of studies on a particular theme, as is often the case. What we have done is to present material where especially interesting theoretical themes are to be found. This provides the framework for an evaluative approach to the material which we feel is essential in an educational process. The ratio of evaluative discussion to description of research and theory is comparatively high in the following chapters. This is not because criticism as an end in itself is highly valued, but because the ability to evaluate material is one of the most important skills a social psychologist can have and it needs to be taught. The evaluations are not there to be learnt off pat, but to show how social psychologists go about making evaluations. Some of the material discussed is included primarily because it highlights problematic issues in social psychology, not because the material in itself demonstrates substantial social psychological gains.

A further feature characterizes this book – there has been no attempt at all to cover every single conventional topic of social psychology textbooks. Some topics have been deliberately omitted. One such omission is the area of body language or non-verbal communication. This tends to be a highly popular topic among laypeople, to whom the idea that people communicate their 'true feelings' through gesture, posture and other signals is very familiar. Obviously people do communicate non-verbally, and there has been a considerable number of investigations into the topic. However, in our view, this has been an area where the theoretical issues have been relatively poorly developed, at least in comparison with other areas of social psychology which have been more intellectually stimulating.

Not all social psychology is worthwhile. This is not because it is old or has become outmoded. Often the reverse is true. Much of what follows pays more than lip-service to the classic contributions to social psychology. A book which emphasizes ideas cannot avoid a debt to the original thinkers of the discipline who laid down the issues and approaches of social psychology. Sometimes their contributions have never been bettered by later writers but, at times, they have sent social psychology along paths which led nowhere. Admiration does not have to take the form of besottedness. So while later chapters open up a view of the directions in which social psychology might do well to go, frequently they look back to the major figures for ideas.

A final feature of the following chapters warrants highlighting. That is the emphasis on change in society which is not at all typical of social psychological writing, let alone introductory textbooks. Social life changes and it is the duty of social psychologists to explain how change is possible. It is simply unsatisfactory to use explanatory concepts which concentrate on how social life is held firmly together without at the same time looking to see how changes in society can occur. Without such an emphasis, social psychology appears to have a static quality which contrasts markedly with the dynamic discipline which we think it needs to be. Obviously, the possibilities for doing this are to a degree constrained by what is available by way of existing theory, but the issue of change is faced head-on at appropriate points. This perspective ties in well with the view of a changing discipline which we present.

So this is a textbook with a serious intent. The challenge is a reasonable one but easily avoided. Not to accept it, however, is to miss much of what social psychology can offer.

2

BECOMING AN INDIVIDUAL IN SOCIETY:
Social development through language

How an infant learns about the social nature of its environment is an essential step in becoming a human adult. It inevitably causes us to ask just what is adult social activity. Language, a key feature of social interaction (as well as more generally being central to the transmission of knowledge of the culture), provides us with the principal means of understanding each other. A prerequisite of social interaction is that we realize that others have minds different from our own in terms of knowledge, attitudes and abilities, among many other things, together with knowing that there is sufficient overlap between different minds to make communication possible. Communication itself is also predicated on the assumption that other people's minds are different from our own (perhaps they know more or less than us). Otherwise there is no point in communication since everything we could know would already be in our minds. The only change possible would be to restructure the contents of our own minds. Children, then, come to realize that other people have minds (though, of course, they will not use the word 'mind' as such) and we will see that social interaction and conversation in early infancy are responsible for this.

Something else follows. By becoming aware of the distinctiveness of others, one inevitably develops a conception of oneself. Coming to the idea of 'self', therefore, is part of the realization that the environment is social in nature.

Children's social psychological development is a vast subject — ranging from how social skills, perceptions and knowledge develop, to the social aspects of any developmental process one cares to consider, such as education, toilet training, and delinquency. Selectivity is necessary in order to paint a coherent picture. By concentrating on the way in which the processes involved in conversation originate and develop in childhood a dauntingly large prospect remains, but one which is just about manageable and, more importantly, central to our knowledge of social psychology.

Characteristics of adult interaction

What is it in adult social behaviour that we are trying to explain? Goffman (1971) draws attention to the routine acts adults carry out, such as apologizing, greeting, or taking leave of each other. He concentrates on small-scale social exchanges (the micro-social order) with their rules, rituals and cognitions which enable us to act meaningfully in everyday social encounters (see Chapter 3). Apologies, greetings and partings are subject to social conventions of how, where, by whom and when they are performed but also to the evaluations and assessment of the participants (or *actors*). They are occasions when it is possible to offend people, to be unduly obsequious, to commit social gaffes, to lose face, and to enhance the other person's impression of us. How we greet and part from each other depends on the length of the parting and expectations of how long we will be parted. An example, typical of Goffman, is how we greet the guest of honour at a going-away party. We cannot simply return shortly after elaborate farewells to retrieve the umbrella we left behind. It is necessary to 'save face'. Complex rules and expectations are involved in such occasions. For Goffman, these are of an essentially 'moral' nature (see also Shotter, 1984). The term 'moral' is used in the sense of defining what is bad, deviant and embarrassing and what is good, appropriate and acceptable.

How do children acquire such subtle competence? What produces this capacity to move around in the everyday 'moral' world of actions and interactions, mutual understandings, rules and rituals? How do children learn to understand what other people say and do, let alone anticipate how their own words and actions will be understood and reacted to? And what of conversation itself? Children relate and talk to other people quite apart from understanding the broad rules which structure interactions. If technicalities like developing vocabulary and syntax are taken for granted, learning to converse is closely related to Goffman's concerns.

The philosopher, Paul Grice (1975), has suggested that the ability to engage in conversations (and presumably many other types of meaningful interaction) depends upon people sharing a set of ground-rules that define normal practices in conversation. These are encapsulated in his *co-operative principle*, which he expresses as follows:

Make your conversational contribution such as is required, at the stage at which it occurs, by the accepted purpose or direction of the talk exchange in which you are engaged (Grice, 1975, p. 45).

There are 'maxims' spelling out in detail what the principle entails. These are:

1. The maxim of *quality* (truthfulness). Contributions should be true and one should not say things one believes to be false or for which one lacks adequate evidence.
2. The maxim of *quantity* (informativeness). Contributions should be as informative as the purposes of the current exchange require and should not be more informative than is required.
3. The maxim of *relation* (relevance). Contributions should be relevant to the issue.
4. The maxim of *manner* (intelligibility). Contributions should avoid obscurity, ambiguity, over-lengthiness and disorderliness and one should be perspicuous.

So, people talk and interact with each other against a background set of conversational norms which sometimes are broken. Indeed, when norms are flouted (or perhaps apparently so) they reveal most for social psychological analysis. Take the following familiar exchange:

A: Are you going to the party tonight?
B: I've got an essay to write.

On the face of it, B's response does not answer A's question, and flouts the maxim of relevance. But connections are made and gaps filled to *make* it relevant. B's response is initially *assumed* to be relevant as a first step in the inferential process. It is an inference that having to write an essay constitutes an impediment to B's chances of attending the party, despite the strictly literal possibility that the essay is not due to be completed for five months. Similar effort helps ensure that conversations fit in with the other maxims. We normally treat *anything* a speaker says as directly or indirectly embodying the co-operative principle. So, if a friend recommends a restaurant we would be surprised and annoyed if he or she knowingly failed to tell us that it had closed down: in this case, the maxim of quantity requires a fuller disclosure of information.

Children have to acquire more than the tools of language, words and grammar, in order to converse as adults do. Subtle inferences about the other person's state of mind have to be made in order for us to know whether to agree or disagree, inform or request, or attempt to persuade them. Account has to be taken of what the other person already knows or believes; what he or she needs to be informed of; and the inferences which have to be made about a speaker's likely purpose and meaning. How old are children when they can do these things? How are they learned?

Discovering that other people have minds

Until quite recently, many psychologists were convinced that children, even as old as five or six years, are incapable of the inferences and calculations of other people's thoughts essential in adult interaction and conversation. Freud's conception of the normal infant mind sees it as 'autistic', that is, self-centred, pleasure-seeking, ignorant of the world beyond its own direct experience, unaware of itself as a being, and blind to the mentality of other persons in the early months of life. The full socialization of the mind requires the formation of the *superego* (the internalized set of rules and moral strictures formed through identification with the child's parents). A child's mind then becomes an inner struggle – a largely unconscious conflict between the primal motives of self-gratification and the internalized superego's standards of acceptable thought and conduct.

Partly in response to Freud's ideas, Jean Piaget (1926; 1932) suggested that children up to the age of about seven years remain locked within a self-centred view of the world which he called cognitive *egocentrism*. This can be seen as mid-way between Freudian infantile autism and the fully socialized awareness that adults possess. Despite being able to talk, infants fail to realize that other people may perceive and know different things from themselves. This means that the child does not understand itself properly as a thinking being since it has not realized that its own thoughts, perceptions, knowledge and memories are dependent on its own particular experience and perspective. Only when children realize that other people can have systematically different experiences and perspectives (that is, 'decentre') from their own, are they able to take a perspective on their own thoughts and, one might say, know *about* their own minds.

Piaget (1926) presents examples of children's talk which apparently reveal their inability to take the perspectives of other people. Without any proper grounds, they talk about things as if the listener already knows about them. In a typical study, the experimenter tells a story to a child, who then retells the story to another child who has been out of the room. In the retelling, significant details are omitted, which would allow the hearer to understand what is being described. To use the pronouns 'he' or 'she' requires that the hearer understands who 'he' or 'she' is. It is almost as if the child were retelling the story to the original story-teller who already knows all the details. On the face of things, it is

A: If I grow up my voice will change, and when you grow up your voice will change. My mom told me. Did your mommy tell you?

B: No, your mommy's wrong. My voice, I don't want it to change. Oh well.

A: Oh well, we'll stay little, right?

B: What?

A: We'll stay little.

B: No, I don't want to. I want my voice to change. I don't care if it changes.

A: I care.

Finally, we can invoke *studies of infancy and early language*. In infancy, before children have acquired even the rudiments of spoken language, they cannot properly be described as 'egocentric'. Research supports, if anything, the opposite conclusion:

> by the end of the first year, at least, the child is able to enter into a number of complex role relationships in which, through communication, the child's knowledge of the physical world can be brought together with knowledge of the social world ... From the start, children are predisposed to share with others their experience of the world – before language is even part of the repertory. Language is a refined continuation of a strong biological tendency that is there from the start (Bruner and Sherwood, 1981, pp. 46–7).

The sort of evidence and theory that support this conclusion form the basis of the developments described in the next section.

Communication and cognition in infancy

The following is a transcript, taken from Edwards (1978, pp. 451–2), of social interaction between 'Mark', aged 17½ months, and his mother. The boy had not yet spoken his first recognizable word. On the right-hand side are notes describing some of the action and physical context that was simultaneous with the speech transcribed alongside.

> *Mark pulls his toy telephone out of a box of toys, brings it to his mother, offers it to her, looking at her face. His mother reaches out and accepts it.*

Mother: Oh great. We can have a telephone conversation. Who are you going to ring up Mark?

curious that the idea of egocentricism ever became accepted. (
learn to talk well enough to go to school and to understand and
with an experimenter's demands but, despite this, they are pres
be so inept at communication as to be unaware of its mc
requirement.

The notion of childhood egocentrism, even in early infancy
but been abandoned in the light of research and theorizing
appears that Piaget's methods underestimated young childrei
municative abilities. Evidence against egocentrism comes fron
lines of research. The first of these was *experimental studie*
suggest that Piaget's subjects did not understand what was rec
them; that their performance was hampered by irrelevant dif
such as excessive burdens upon memory; or that children are u
put difficult concepts into words. Various improvements to
methodology have shown that children as young as three or fc
are capable of a sensitivity to the listener's informational neec
previously had been obscured (see, for example, Maratsos,
which an adult listener wore a blindfold, to make it clear to t
that the objects being talked about could not be seen).

The second line of research to provide evidence against egoc
was *studies of children's conversation*. Research shows that e
the beginnings of language learning, children develop commu
and pragmatic skills that are founded upon a recognition
people's perspectives. One might be tempted to think that t
ability to ask questions (an ability that young children displ
exasperating extent), demonstrates their non-egocentrism. /
why ask questions unless you are assuming that the othe
something that you do not? Unfortunately, things are not so s
the study of conversational discourse, as the last sentence
question, shows: there are lots of pragmatic purposes for usi
tion' forms in speech, other than for seeking information. For
questions are often used as a polite way of making requests ('w
mind shutting the door behind you?'). In school, teachers cc
ask questions of their pupils, without any implication
teachers themselves are ignorant of the answers, though they
assumes, often seeking to discover the extent to which the
knowledge compares with their own (Edwards and Merce
Nevertheless, everyday observation and experience of young
confirms that much of their questioning is of the more
information-seeking kind. Moreover, the same sort of na
observation confirms a wide range of non-egocentric conver
young children, such as the following extract (from Garvey an
1973, p. 565), in which two pre-school boys engage in argur
disagreement:

		Mark, lifting the receiver to his ear, looking into his mother's eyes.

Mother: Hello, Mark.

Mark: Eh. Eh.

Mark talks into mouthpiece.

Mother: Hello, how are you today? Hello Mark.

Mark: Huhhh.

Mother: How are you?

Mark replaces receiver.

Mother: That's very rude. You've hung up.

Mark lifts receiver to his ear again.

Mother: Hello. Have you had your dinner?

Mark: Uh uhhh.

Mark talking into mouthpiece in 'eye contact' with mother.

Mother: Was it good? Was it a good dinner?

Mark: Uh uhuh uhhh.

Mother: It was?

Mark: Uh uhhh.

Even this one transcript tells us much about what Mark understands, what he can do, and how his mother interacts with him. To begin with, he knows his way around the small familiar world of his home: where and how to find his toys, for example. Mark seems previously to have developed with his mother a routine interaction involving the toy. Note the detail. It is Mark who initiates the interaction by holding out the telephone for his mother to reach out and grasp – he acts toward her as to someone whose co-operation is expected. She is not an object upon which he places the telephone as if on a table. He differentiates between people and things, and can, to some extent at least, communicate his intents and wishes to another person. His mother reads his intentions and offers him appropriate words – this is the routine activity called 'having a telephone conversation'. She invites and encodes the next step: 'who are you going to ring up Mark?', as he is already in the act of lifing the receiver to his ear.

Throughout the interaction the mother gives a rich interpretation of Mark's intentions, talking to him as if he understands and intends much more than dispassionate observers might assume. But this is perhaps the whole point of the transaction. By over-interpreting what Mark understands and intends, she guides him forward by providing him with, first, a culturally defined context for his actions; second, appropriate language to describe his actions; and third, recognizable structures or ways of understanding interaction and intention. Close monitoring of the direction of his actions allows her to create a route leading to a recognizably co-operative and communicating person. His action of replacing the receiver, for example, was not interpreted merely as physical action. His mother sees it as culturally meaningful (the same action by a chimpanzee might have been treated differently). She offers him the language for interpreting his action as a cultural symbol: 'That's very rude. You've hung up.' (For an extended treatment of this sort of thing, see Lock, 1978; 1979; Bruner, 1983.) It is only very rude to hang up abruptly because we have developed culturally accepted ways of interacting on the telephone.

In Bruner's terms, infants and mothers develop a series of routine interactions called *formats*, consisting of mutually shared expectations about what each is likely to do next, and how each other is likely to respond. Formats describe the communicative routines involved in normal upbringing such as feeding, nappy changing, chastisement, and to more obviously linguistic routines such as pointing at and naming things. Once the other person's reactions become expected or predictable, they can be made to happen by signalling. We can see how the process unfolds in the development of *requesting*.

The ability to request other people to do things for you is one of the first linguistic functions to make its appearance. These 'services' include to give or fetch things, and to make particular things happen. The developmental sequence seems to be something like this. At first, babies and infants cry, make noises, look around, and reach for and grasp things. Older members of the family interpret the behaviour of even newborn babies as being more intentional than that – as trying to communicate recognizable and sensible meanings ('Oh look, she wants her dinner'). They respond to infants in regular ways, such that infants come to *expect* those responses. Having established that people in the social world react to their actions in predictable ways, the ground is established for the child to repeat these actions *in order to make* those responses happen again. By this point, actions have become gestures which signal to other people to do things. On top of this parents introduce language, but the activities to which this language refers are already understood by the child. Language puts into words the child's existing understanding. Parents tell children in language what they are doing already, what they are intending to do, what they are listening to, and so forth. There is more than enough surplus information in communications for the child to grasp what the mother's *words* mean in terms of what the child is doing.

It is often argued that language is the vital distinguishing feature of human beings. But we do not become human only when we learn to speak. Pre-linguistic children are not like non-human animals. For example, the filmed evidence of the various attempts to teach language to apes (see Sebeok and Umiker-Sebeok, 1980, for comprehensive discussion of these studies) demonstrates how difficult it is compared with the ease with which children master language. The trainers resort to the most deliberate and systematic efforts to gain the animals' co-operation in learning language, physically moving their heads and hands into position, and offering constant rewards and inducements. Most of the time the apes just want to play and tumble, groom and hug, and tickle. Apes are intensely social animals but, unlike human infants, show little interest in sharing a joint orientation towards the world with others and in gaining and communicating a shared perception of it. They are not, apparently, 'predisposed to share with others their experience of the world' (Bruner and Sherwood, 1981, p. 47).

Bruner's account of these early developments owes much to Lev Vygotsky, the Soviet psychologist, whose ideas, formulated around the 1920s, have increased in influence (see especially Vygotsky, 1987; Wertsch, 1985). Vygotsky suggests that language-governed mental processes (such as reasoning and voluntary remembering) derive developmentally from social communications. Inevitably, then, the human mind is at heart socio-cultural. The care-giver opens up a framework before the child, onto which its actions and intentions can be culturally coded and meaningfully organized. Vygotsky conceived this socially-created framework as a space – 'the zone of proximal development'.

The notion that young children are intrinsically communicative, rather than egocentric, gains further support from studies of the language and make-believe play of the pre-school years. Before three years of age they use appropriately words that describe their own and other people's mental states, such as *know, believe, think, remember, wonder, pretend, dream* (see Shatz, Wellman and Silber, 1983). They can cite 'identifying information such as "she's my friend" or "that's my aunt", instead of just a proper name, in an account to a person who cannot be assumed to know the person referred to' (Ervin-Tripp and Mitchell-Kernan, 1977, p. 10). They engage in elaborate role-playing, adopting the behaviours and verbal style of the role in question. They argue with each other, and by the time they go to school, use indirect hints in place of straightforward requests in order to get people to do things for them (see Ervin-Tripp, 1977).

By the age of four, children are able to predict the behavioural consequences of someone having a mistaken belief (Wimmer and Perner, 1983). Without recognizing the distinct mind of the other, the child would assume that the other would share the child's own correct knowledge. Typical of such studies is one in which a child watches as someone hides a piece of chocolate in a box and then walks out of the room. Another person appears and removes the chocolate and places it into a basket. The first person then returns and the child is asked where this original hider will look for the chocolate. Younger children nominate the basket, but the four-year-olds switch from the basket (where they know the chocolate to be), to the box (where they realize the hider must assume it to be). Further questions establish that it is not simply that the younger children do not remember the sequence of actions, neither are they unaware that people have perceptions and thoughts of their own. Leslie (1987) suggests that not until four years does a child understand that people not only *have* mental states, discernibly different from the child's own, but also that people's mental states account for what they do. Children clearly learn to discern and differentiate mental states, as well as ways of explaining people's mental states and how to take these into account.

Argumentation and thought

While it seems fruitless to label childhood thought as egocentric, changes do occur in how children conceive of the minds of others. In this respect, it could be that Piaget's theory has something to offer. If the critical process in such change is in social communication (the clashing of perspectives that children inevitably meet in conversation), then, by arguing about perspectives and wishes, children will increasingly construe their own perspectives as different from those of others. The important development is not just coming to act on the basis of such differences, but becoming *consciously aware of mind itself*. This means viewing one's own and other people's minds as objects in need of examination and conceptualization. Thought then becomes subject to scrutiny, open to argument, requiring justification.

Since the social world is essentially *moral*, built on subtle ground-rules of social action and mutual interpretation, the process of becoming aware of moral issues has to be incorporated into our discussion. Piaget (1932) revealed limitations of infant thought in their understanding of and attitude towards moral rules. At four or five years, children are largely ignorant of the rules governing playground games, and inconsistent when applying them. They can play together, while at the same time falsely believing that the others share the same understanding of the rules. They think the rules of games and those for more general moral conduct, such as lying, stealing and breaking things, are fixed and cannot be changed. The origins of the rules are seen as residing in some external authority. By seven or eight years this 'heteronomous' view has changed; rules are seen as being open to disagreement and revision by mutual consent ('autonomous').

A key factor in these changes in understanding morality is argumentation. In play with other children the different perspectives of the participants clash in open dispute. Without teachers, parents, or other authority figures being present to arbitrate, there is no external reason why one side should win over the other. Arguing children have to sort out for themselves what the rules really are, ought to be, or shall be. Notice how once again participants must scrutinize their own 'minds' and those of others. In this early research, Piaget presents a rhetorical, rather than logical, basis for the development of mind.

Lawrence Kohlberg (1968) refined Piaget's work on moral development. In Kohlberg's account, moral development is a series of argumentative stages. Children and adults are given a set of stories to consider, each of which poses a moral dilemma of some sort (for example, of the general type 'If you had the opportunity, would you have assassinated the mass-murderer Hitler?'). According to how people argue for one side or the other, they are classified as having achieved one of a series of stages of moral development, ranging from simple principles of conformity and avoidance of punishment, through the need for maintaining the social fabric of law and order, notions of a mutually defined 'social contract', to an adherence to 'universal ethical principles' (see Lickona, 1976). The essence of this is clear; social life is governed by our understanding of rules, and these in turn are the outcome of argument and deliberation. Mental life is, as Vygotsky argued, shaped by and derived from social activity and discourse.

The social use of language

So far we have seen that the social origins of language and mind are interdependent. The social uses of language (pragmatics) mean that social relationships, moral orders and the development of the 'self' have to be involved in describing language and cognitive change. Neisser's (1988) systematic account of what we mean by 'self' distinguishes five different 'selves', each with its own principles of organization, development and pathology. They are:

1. *Ecological self*: corresponding to our perception of ourselves in a here-and-now physical setting, engaged in perception and action.
2. *Interpersonal self*: also in the here-and-now, engaged in direct interaction with another person.
3. *Extended self*: the projection of our personal identities and life

histories, backwards through remembering, and fowards through anticipation.

4. *Private self*: the discovery of the inner world, the realization that our thoughts and experiences are unique, particular, specifying us as unique individuals *vis-à-vis* other people.

5. *Conceptual self*: corresponding to what is conventionally called the 'self-concept', and includes the way we consciously reflect upon, categorize and theorize about ourselves.

Neisser's 'extended self' is particularly important to social psychological understanding. It is 'the self as it was in the past and as we expect it to be in the future, known primarily on the basis of memory' (Neisser, 1988, p. 46). This notion of a continuing life history also appears in the notion of *scripts* (Schank and Abelson, 1977). Scripts are mental representations of routine social activities, such as knowing what to do in a restaurant. There is a standard script, with variations for different sorts of eating place – sit down, waiter provides menu, order meal, pay. This is general (semantic) knowledge in which specific episodes are not involved. Memories of specific meals in restaurants tend to focus upon the exceptions to the rule – the unexpected things that happen beyond the conventional scripted scene, like the time in Majorca when the waiter brought us a paella which was frozen in the middle. The 'formats' structuring interactions between parents and children discussed earlier, are further examples of 'scripted' activities at the level of action and gesture at least. They demonstrate that infants develop expectations and intentions about what will happen next in communications. By the age of three years, this sort of knowledge has been raised to the level of conscious reflection and can be formulated in words. If asked what happens when you make biscuits, three-year-olds can answer:

Well, you bake them and eat them.

By four and a half years, they can articulate a more elaborate version:

My mommy puts chocolate chips inside the cookies. Then ya put 'em in the oven; then we take them out, put them on the table and eat them (Nelson and Gruendel, 1986, p. 27).

By this age, children are clearly aware of themselves as participants in a world of regular events and routines, each with its expected activities and roles to be played. As adults this may strike us as a totally banal point, but even this shows that scripts are so vital that they are routine. Early remembering is more than merely sorting out mental representations of the routines of social life. It provides a sense of unique personal identity, a personal and family history, emotional significances for experiences, and defines why some things matter and are more important than others. These are elaborations, in a sense, of the elementary recognition of the distinctiveness of minds.

So, if the nature of 'mind' is such that it can see the 'self' and action as being extended (or continuous) through time and space, the important question has to be how this realization comes about. Once again this lies partially in the interactions between the child and significant others in its life. Interaction does not explain everything, however, and it is likely that infants will develop at least a rudimentary sense of their 'extended self' without such conversations. Interactions, though, may help produce a more elaborated conception of the 'extended self'. Not only this, but if the conception of the 'extended self' develops through interaction with significant others, it can only do so because adults concern themselves with the past history of the child and the family.

For example, Edwards and Middleton (1988) examined conversations between parents and children about their family snapshots. These discussions reveal how parents and children begin to share a framework which determines that some events become significant, interesting and memorable. Children are helped to talk about past experience as meaningful, and thereby how to 'remember'. The following conversation between Paul (aged 4 years) and his mother (Edwards and Middleton, 1988, pp. 7–8) shows these processes at work. The child was initially preoccupied with looking at the photographs through a magnifying glass. Diagonal slashes indicate pauses.

Mother: It must have been a sunny day in that photograph/ mustn't it?

Paul: Yeh// Oh let's see/ see/ that/ comes/bigger.

Mother: Mm. (. . .) Where were you then?/ Can you remember?

Paul: There/ and there's Rebecca look at/ her ugh! (*laughs*).

Mother: She's pulling a funny face/ isn't she?

Paul: Yeh/ she thinks it/ it's so mum/ let's see/ let's see what the boy/ done/ let's see if there's any/ agh/ it's so big/ do you like/

Mother: You didn't like that bouncing castle did you?/ Do you remember?

Paul: Yeh.

Mother: It kept falling over/ you couldn't keep your balance.

Paul: No// (*laughs quietly*).

Mother: Do you like them now?

Paul: Yeh.

Mother: (*doubting tone*): DO you?

Paul does not seem particularly keen to 'reconstruct memories of past experiences', preferring the delights of the magnifying glass. His mother, in marked contrast, can see the photographs as a mediating between the present and the past. They stimulate memories of a distinctive sort – those involving the activities, preoccupations and reactions of Paul and his sister, Rebecca. Repeatedly the mother tries to focus Paul's attention on salient features of the pictures about which she introduces other memories not contained in the photographs themselves. The criteria for what is memorable are her notions of what Paul himself would be interested in – his dislike of and misfortune with the bouncing castle. She also demonstrates that information can be inferred from the pictures: 'It *must have been* a sunny day . . . '. What exactly Paul is learning cannot be known from the conversation alone. However, the impression is inescapable of a *lesson* in progress on how to define and talk about a memorable past. The mother is opening up a 'zone of proximal development' for memorization as she is providing the pathways along which to go to achieve a social memory.

Perhaps even more illuminating is the following conversation (Edwards and Middleton, 1988, p. 23) involving Michael (5¾ years) and his sister, Katie (3½ years). Michael and Katie are notable for the sibling rivalry they demonstrate, and in this Michael is particularly vociferous. This rivalry becomes involved in the construction of accounts of past experience.

Mother: Who's that? (*Pointing to a partially hidden figure*).
Michael: It's me.
Mother: Well who's that/ there? (*Pointing to another partially obscured figure, with protruding hand*).
Michael: My hand.
Mother: All right/ if that's you/ that can't be your hand.
Michael: It must be Katie because this is my hand.
Mother: It's not. That's you (*pointing to first figure*)/ that's your jogging bottom.
Michael: Ah.
Mother: (*Pointing to second figure*) That's Katie.
Michael: Ah/ I had the idea of putting my hands out.
Mother: Did you?
Michael: Yes/ and she shouldn't have done it when it was my idea.
Mother: Why not?
Michael: Because it was MY idea.

Both Michael and his mother are fully engaged in using the picture to construct memories. Again, the mother uses inference in this – Michael could not be two people at once, and his true identity was proven by the 'jogging bottoms'. For Michael, of course, physical identity in the picture was only part of establishing a more important *social* and *moral* identity; the figure with the protruding hand *should* have been him, and not his sister. *He* had thought of putting hands out like that so copying his idea was wrong. Obviously there is more to collective memory than this. Children's memorization and other understanding of the world are closely bound up as well with their emotions, morality and social relationships. Each of these is the subject of conversation, including explanation and argument.

As we have seen, largely in interaction and discussion do children become aware of their own distinct identities, aware of the nature of their own thought and perceptions, and of how these relate to and differ from those of other people. It is the beginning of a life-long process:

> The extended self becomes increasingly important as we grow older. Most adults develop a more or less standard life-narrative that effectively defines the self in terms of a particular series of remembered experiences. These accounts are continually being extended (and occasionally revised!), creating a narrative structure much like that of more formal autobiographies (Neisser, 1988, p. 49).

Indeed, by the time of old age, the extended self may take over as the central focus of life and reminiscence of life's successes provide a basis for continued self-worth.

Concluding comments

We have seen in this chapter how several aspects of the development of children from infancy into adulthood need the input of social inter-action in the form of conversation to be fully developed. Once this is accepted then it extends our understanding of the mature adult since there is nothing intrinsically child-like in the processes of conversation. Children's conversations may be different in some respects from those of adults, but there is nothing in this chapter which could not be applied to adult conversation and much in it which is specifically about the conversations of adults with their children.

One thing warrants particular comment: the remarkable way in which a totally misleading view of the nature of infant thought, egocentrism, dominated developmental psychology for so long despite the fact that its disproof is evident in the act of conversation itself. Perhaps the influence the concept of egocentrism had is one of the best illustrations of the need always to examine ideas, to criticize and reassess. Ideas need to be challenged and should not readily be accepted as some doctrine or orthodoxy. It is further evidence also of the constraining influence that methodology can have on ideas since, despite the fact that in appearance Piaget's methods are simple and close to real life, they had to be replaced by more systematic experimentation, as well as observations of more natural conversations, in order for their inadequacies to be revealed. Even more remarkable than any of this is the revelations that parents (deprived, perhaps, of Piagetian theorizing) act on the assumption that even the youngest of babies has an essentially communicative nature. That is, they talk and interact with them at quite sophisticated levels compared to what would be required if egocentrism truly described childhood thought. Many psychologists spent a lot of time studying infants and still misunderstanding them. (Perhaps egocentrism was more characteristic of psychologists' thought than that of the babies!)

Also noteworthy is the *type* of evidence cited in this chapter. As well as drawing on a variety of experimental studies, the chapter also makes use of extracts of conversational data. Studies of conversation are generally as thorough and systematic as those that use experimental manipulations and statistical procedures. But it is striking how even a single snatch of conversation can help to clarify and illustrate theoretical ideas, as well as forming an appropriate basis for evaluating theories of mental and social processes and their development. The choice of conversational data is a good example of choosing a method for its usefulness and appropriateness, especially where some sensitivity to the naturalness of people's everyday social activity is needed. In some of the other chapters, where appropriate, we shall place a heavier reliance upon experimental and statistical approaches.

Finally, the issue of continuity and change is easily addressed by this chapter since it deals with both the way in which cognitions change and the way in which they come to fit in with those of other people. Thus change *and* stability are both assured.

3

ROLES, RULES AND GROUPS

Social life is played on a multitude of stages. Each of us belongs to different groups within which we play chosen and allotted roles. Despite the individuality of people, we tend to share expectations about how we should act, say, in the role of parents, members of a family, or responsible colleagues. Taking part in the social world brings us inevitably face-to-face with its formal and informal rules. The terms *roles, rules* and *groups* are in common usage and appear in ordinary conversation to explain someone's behaviour:

No, she was never really part of our group, not one of us you might say.

Well, I said to him, 'if you expect me to play the role of skivvy, you've got another think coming'.

Of course, it just wasn't cricket. If he wouldn't play by the rules I told him, I said, 'You'll have to go'.

These examples are quite revealing. Notice the references to be-longingness (to groups), to feelings of right and wrong, and to what is reasonable and proper. More than this, the statements indicate that when we ordinarily speak of any one of these things (roles, rules and groups) the others are tacitly invoked. Hence, to be part of a group is to take a particular part in its activities, but in a way which is consistent with its overall outlook. Being a group member is not only turning up and doing one's bit at the appropriate time, playing one's part means doing things in a way which in some way enhances the group. A child who sets the breakfast table with 'good grace' when requested is an example. The child's action reveals not just the role of a child and the existence of rules concerning task sharing in the home. As Newcomb

(1963) once put it, the style of behaviour demonstrates that the people concerned share expectations *about* each other, *with* each other.

This chapter discusses how roles and rules operate in the group context. Specifically, it shows the ways in which the concepts of 'roles', 'rules', and 'groups' help us to understand how people live together. There is a real difference between taking roles and rules to be the 'stuff' of social life, as if they were the atoms and molecules of interaction, and seeing them as concepts helping to explain important aspects of people's behaviour. This will become clearer later. For now it is enough to realize that social change where rigid rules and roles apply would not be possible.

Older ideas: roles and norms

Roles

'Role' is used by social scientists to describe the functions of a particular social position. In the traditional family there are the roles of mother and father, of 'eldest child' and 'youngest child'. The role of mother includes, loosely put, the things that 'a typical mother' does. She might be expected to cook the meals, to look after the children's needs, and know where clean shirts are when her husband needs one. However, she might do none of these things and still be a mother. The idea of roles involves making gross generalizations about those people called 'mothers' or any other roles held. We may know no mothers precisely fitting the stereotype. Clearly the concept of role needs to cope with differences between people to be useful. In part, role theory allows for this by distinguishing a role from both the position in a specific group or organization with which it is associated, and the individual who is incumbent in that social position. 'Mothering' can be considered as a set of behaviours and sentiments which can be carried out and expressed by anyone, not just the child-bearer. We are used to thinking of the woman of the household as the 'wife and mother', but the role can equally be held by the male of the household. It may need a challenge or a change to the occupancy of a role before the essence of the role itself becomes apparent.

Social psychologists have no agreed definition, but there is a broad consensus that roles are sets of behaviours tied together by shared understandings of the function of a position. Thus roles express differences between members of a group, so that what is done as part of a role is understood by the group as role behaviour. This is what underlies the earlier statement that people share expectations of each other about each other.

Roles do not exist in isolation but are connected with other roles. The role of mother crucially depends upon the role of child. This may be why some children find it hard to grow up; not because they cannot adapt to new roles in relation to people outside the family, but because their parents need to cast their offspring continually in the role of 'child' in order to remain parents. Perhaps this is a little too slick to be persuasive but it highlights that expectations which people have of each other organize and direct relationships in ways which often keep them tied together.

Roles are not always easily identified with positions, or at least not positions such as teacher, chairperson, or other aspects of formal group structures. The position of eldest and youngest children of the family may or may not be clear-cut in any given household. In some cultures (as in earlier times in European history), the first-born had both privileges and obligations thrust upon it. By comparison, the youngest child might attract the special attention of the parents or even older siblings. The Biblical story of Joseph, his envious brothers, and little Benjamin, illustrates the dangers which strong valuations of these roles can bring. However, in present-day Western society it is virtually impossible to find any consensus on how first- and last-born positions reflect different roles. Distinctions may occur in some families, but they are made by the particular families concerned. Society no longer lays much store by birth order, so the role of first-born has ceased to be formal. As society alters, so the ways in which roles interweave with the warp and weft of rights, duties and morals change as well.

The work of R. F. Bales (1958) provides a further example of the difference between formal and informal roles. He studied how groups organize themselves to solve problems. In certain types of temporary grouping there emerged largely distinct 'task-leaders' and 'socio-emotional leaders'. Task leaders were people who took charge of the working of the group (how it should solve the problem) while socio-emotional leaders were individuals who became the focus of sentiments (feelings) between group members and helped sort out the interpersonal aspects of the group. This does not mean that each kind of leader was restricted to just one form of behaviour: those who focused upon the task were also able to participate in the socio-emotional interplay between members and vice-versa. Bales's work shows that people may have to operate in several more or less formal roles simultaneously. This is what makes it impossible to study roles and rules separately, and why it is vital to understand roles in the context of groups where the social action happens. It is no use describing these things in a vacuum, or as generalities which somehow apply to everyone no matter who they are or what their social standing.

Norms

Not only are there specific behaviours attached to particular roles, but there are shared expectations which embrace all of the individuals involved. These shared expectations, or 'norms' provide a set of guidelines or standards against which the group members may judge their behaviour. Norms are invoked to account for what it is that allows people to act together in mutual awareness of the group's activities and structure.

This was demonstrated by Muzafer Sherif in the 1930s. People were shown a tiny spot of light in a darkened room and made judgements about how much the light moved. Essentially this is an optical illusion as in reality no movement takes place. Having set a personal standard alone, an individual's judgement shifts when subsequently he watches the light in the company of another person who expresses a different view on the amount of movement. That is, a norm is established. More important still, the shared standard, established jointly, continues to operate when each makes judgements alone some time later. What emerges is a common frame of reference which then guides the actions of each person even when away from the group. It is notable that replacing one member at a time by a newcomer, once a judgemental norm has been established, does not destroy the norm, although it may be weakened. The norm refers to the group and not merely to the amalgamation of individuals who represent it at any one time. (This is evidence that the group has a dynamic of its own and is not merely the sum of its participants.)

It could be objected that Sherif's experiments reflect the oddity of the situation – people do not usually make judgements about trivial optical illusions but about important matters. Keep this in mind, not because it undermines Sherif's conclusions, but because it highlights an interesting issue in the theory of norms. This is the difference between norms of which we are fully aware and those which operate without our full understanding of what is guiding our behaviour. However, we shall return to this when we have discussed rules of conduct in relationships.

More modern ideas: rules

What is a rule?

Norm theory emphasized people sharing frames of reference, or more directly, the same way of looking at things. Norms described how interrelating people are tied together in their actions, and by implication, constrained. Probably because sociologists were also concerned with norms (though from the standpoint of formal positions within institutions) and the psychology of the time was firmly behaviouristic, it was inevitable that norms were generally regarded as causal determinants of features of social life. Only when the idea of rule-following was clarified within the context of a newer social psychology, emphasizing individual choice in actions, did the constraining function of norms begin to be given less emphasis. Remember that the concept of norms had covered two functions within social conduct: the sharing of joint frames of reference by group members; and the prescriptions for actions within the group. The latter function gave rise to studies of how action in the group context was subject to guidelines which were enforced by the group members as a form of social control. For example, the ostracism of fellow workers who refuse to strike can be seen as a punishment for failing to fulfil the requirements of a norm of solidarity. More recently, emphasis on seeing shared expectations as constraints has been replaced by their conceptualization as guidelines or rules for action. So the modern view is that social life is guided (but not determined) by rules which individuals use to fashion their conduct. While this may seem a heavy-handed way of saying that behaviour is rule-guided, this is not so, because it emphasizes that rules do not act, people do. Rules are not laws in the sense of being things which determine what shall be done. The essential aspect of a rule is that it offers the possibility of doing one thing *or* another. Rules can be broken and they can also be changed, either in the course of conduct or by the agreement of those who utilize them. Breaking social rules may precipitate sanctions in the form of punishments or admonishments. Indeed, at times rules may be more important for their role in making social life *appear* orderly than for actual influences on action (Wieder, 1974). What interests social psychologists about rules is not just their pattern (who does what to whom and when), but how rules come to be perceived as rules, and how they are then employed to expand and curtail the scope of actions in the group.

How are rules made?

To understand the establishment of rules requires that we distinguish between those rules which individuals help to make, and those to which they are always subject. This is not unlike the distinction between groups which people help form from the beginning and those already established prior to their joining, which have a pre-existing normative structure into which the new member must enter. In the experience of individuals, this difference is important. Groups in which people are founder members have a psychological history which they can recover (founders remember how things developed and their involvement in bringing them about). It is not the point that founder members have *accurate* knowledge of what went before, but that they have in their common experience the knowledge of how things *might have been different* (and what was discussed at the time decisions were taken). Such direct knowledge is unavailable to people joining an already established group for whom there is an air of inevitability in the way the group functions. They may not like it; they may try to change it, but their appeals cannot be to experience and past action which helped form the rules in the first place. This mix of rules 'made by us' and 'what must be done' is universal, giving society a reality which is experientially both subjective and objective.

Rules, then, are made by people, though not necessarily by the people who are subject to them. This is true both historically (we are born into a culture which has been long in the making), and in terms of contemporary events. In social groupings often the responsibility for rule-making is not shared evenly. In groups consisting of individuals occupying different statuses this may be understood from the beginning. Different roles will mesh with the rules of the group in distinct ways. It may be a rule that children do not speak with their mouths full at the dinner table, yet parents may sometimes do just this when telling a child how to behave at the table! The frequent failure of rules to be specified as specific actions in fixed settings is the root of many children's pleas that things are not 'fair'. Status and power differences ensure that a single, undifferentiated rule to be applied to all, may not necessarily emerge.

An example of research on this is the study of Strodtbeck, James and Hawkins (1958) in which mock juries heard recorded evidence. The jurors had to deliberate upon this, as in a real trial, and to return a verdict. The groups consisted of men and women from different occupational levels. It was found that people of higher social status tended to be more often chosen to be the jury foreman; rated by the other jurors as having participated more in discussions of the evidence; and chosen as people whom the others would like to be judged by if they were themselves on trial. The conclusion was that persons of higher-status occupations have a greater influence upon the group's way of functioning, in part because they are perceived, at the outset, as being more capable. Norm-setters (or rule-makers) in groups tend to be of higher status, leaving those of lower status to follow the guidelines set.

This is interesting, but not an absolute finding. We might expect status effects to change during the course of group discussion. Having engaged in their deliberations, jurors might be expected to alter their choices of whom they would like to be judged by. As a consequence the initial social status differences might well become less extreme. Rather than being 'locked into' their roles, as lower-status individuals gain experience of their contributions in relation to the others, they might challenge or modify the course of events which they had previously only accepted. We are more likely to be acceptors of the rules laid down by others where we feel that they have a greater capability than ourselves, or that the task is one about which we know little. Both of these criteria apply to those rules which, embodied in the legal system, appear to have been arrived at by experts with knowledge that we do not share.

Formal rules which are clearly stated and can be used to account for actions are special compared to the informal rules which govern much of everyday conduct. For example, the rules attaching to ceremonies in public life specify co-ordinated roles which together constitute the enactment of that episode. Getting married demonstrates this since appropriate things must be said and done by people occupying specified roles designated for that ceremony. Provided the things are as they should be (that is, co-ordinated by the formal rules of the marriage ceremony), the couple emerge married in law and 'in the sight of God'. In an influential book which examines social life as a complex of role-rule episodes, Harré and Secord (1972) emphasize that this outcome depends upon the correct enactment of the ceremony, not upon the detail of how each act occurs or on private motivation. The bride may be marrying the man she feels she *ought* to marry; the bridegroom may have designs on his future wife's inheritance, and the vicar may dislike them both intensely – but all to no effect, as married they will be. This may seem at odds with the earlier suggestion that norms are more than the categorization of particular behaviours. Norms, it was said, involve joint understandings between people about people. How can we account for this apparent contradiction? Are rules and norms really different in this respect?

Social life demands that we are both public figures and private individuals. The norms of public life which govern our actions are grounded in the positions which we occupy. There are expectations of doctors, of bus conductors and of teachers. When meeting briefly in public roles our business is not with the finer points of the other's behaviour or with their inner feelings. Our business is to do that which we are there to do. How different this is from our relationship with friends and family. Here the rules of conduct are not so easily specified, and there is little formal ceremonial. In our private lives, it is not just 'what is done when' that matters, but how it is done in relation to the group norms. The example of the child who sets the table with 'good grace' reveals what is meant by norms being derived from an interdependence of action and sentiment. This interdependence goes well beyond the idea that rules simply control behaviour, as in the written rules governing moves in a game of chess. In reality, playing many games involves this interdependence since 'playing the game' relates to the manner as well as to the procedure of game-playing.

Although this distinction between what can be called 'formal' and 'informal' roles is an important one, it does not follow that our lives are rigidly compartmentalized. We do not at one moment obey the rules of public episodes (such as doing our job, buying a loaf of bread) and at the next immerse ourselves in the expectations we share with friends and family. Common experience is that we have to work with and within these two kinds of rules simultaneously. The loaf of bread may be bought from a nice person or an ill-mannered lout, a friendly or a supercilious individual. These blunt descriptions show that, irrespective of circumstances, we continue to expect to be treated with a little humanity, a recognition of ourselves as individuals in dealings with each other.

A key feature of norms and rules is the extent to which they can be specified by the people who use them. This does not mean that they will necessarily be clear as there are some rules and norms which people have not articulated. It may take someone to act in an unexpected or a disturbing fashion before we try to work out what has been done wrong, by whom and to whom. Often the rule or norm will not be enforced through collective discussion on the workings of the group. Life is ongoing, and while psychologists may wish to take it apart to see how it works, many people find this uncomfortable and unnecessary. The group communicates its norms through action – the enacted demonstration of how the members want to conduct their affairs.

To give an example, Homans (1951) describes how people who did not adhere to the output rate in a factory were subject to the process of 'binging'. This entailed being struck on the arm by the others in a fashion which symbolized their view of the worker's deviance from the norm. It may be seen as a coded message, but why send it in code? Why not sit the man down and show him the required output figures? One reason is that the workers' work-rate norms were different from the official rates laid down by the management. This difference was central to the 'unofficial' culture of the group, and dependent, in part, on its being kept quiet. It is an example of the mix of formal and informal rules, in which the communication about the rule cannot be a simple matter of what a person should do 'privately' and what they should do 'publicly'.

Rules are made both from 'above' and from 'below'. It is not just a matter of our being simultaneously subject to formal and informal expectations. We also act with regard to rules which we can articulate and norms which, like those of Sherif's subjects, have become shared frames of reference without our necessarily realizing their existence.

When rules are broken

Whether we refer to norms or to rules, our arguments are based upon the assumption that these guidelines can be broken. This might occur unintentionally or else premeditatedly. The reactions of others depend on the nature of any problems so created and the individual's way of excusing or apologizing for the error. For example, if Mary publicly mentions something about Jane which the others feel should not have been said, the group may let Mary 'save face' by allowing her to excuse the remark as a 'slip' or the result of an understandable lack of knowledge. Goffman (1955) has described many kinds of mistake making-good routines which people employ as a group in order to repair crises in the flow of interaction. During these routines, the group members work together, so to speak, to remind each other of the rules which they tacitly work by and to admonish gently the person who has stepped out of line. This effectively restores everyone's allegiance to the group.

More problematic, however, would be if one of the guests at a party is seen pocketing one of the host's silver spoons. It is possible to imagine a routine similar to that described above in which other party guests remind the miscreant (with a joke) about the sanctity of private property and the obligations of being a good guest, finally reaffirming their friendship in another drink. However, this scenario is unconvincing because of the seriousness of the offence. Simply saying that there are more serious and less serious rules guiding social actions, and that breaking the former will lead to major consequences, the latter merely resulting in a moment's collective embarrassment, is not good enough. It completely ignores the way in which the decisions are made about the scale of the offence which has taken place and how the offending person should be treated in future.

Rules are not simply 'there' but are invoked when there is a need to make judgements which affect the group members' futures. To take the spoon-stealing episode, it is quite possible for the individual concerned to make a number of claims about why it was taken (for example, in preparation for a magic trick he was to perform; as a joke to play on the host; or due to a momentary 'loss of memory'). Research has shown that whether individuals who fail the group are seen as blameworthy depends on their capacity to fulfil their role. Where a person is seen as lacking the necessary skill to act appropriately he is less likely to be sanctioned. Nevertheless, such a person is still likely to suffer a loss of status in the group.

Pursuing the spoon example, whether the other guests would be convinced by the miscreant's explanation or not includes other processes in rule-invocation. The nature of the action and the circumstances in which it took place will be involved in examining the various accounts of the events which the guests exchange and deliberate upon. Rules are not applied mechanically, but are often teased out after some out-of-order behaviour occurs. It might be objected that a rule must have been invoked in order that the spoon removal is seen as stealing in the first place. Perhaps it would be better to say that unusual actions which breach several norms simultaneously cause the norms to enter into consciousness – the spoon is where it should not be and we are at a party with the problem of dealing with an embarrassing, potentially damaging, situation. At this point the task of deciding what has 'really' happened and what 'ought' to follow emerges and is executed in discussions among those present.

What follows depends upon the status of the group members. We have already seen that norm formation in a mock jury group is not equally spread across the members if they are of different status. In the informal ethos of a party, it is likely that the examination of rules and the establishment of 'facts' will be subject to similar differentiations. What if the accused is an important guest? A neighbour? The host's brother? The need for the group members to embrace and to deal with this problem has to be set against the possibility that it could damage them in the 'public eye'. As a result the episode may either be reduced in significance, or, alternatively, the police called in. Both lines of action have important consequences for an understanding of how norms and rules operate in everyday life. For the minimization of the offence means that the rules have had to be 'bent' so that the expectations of the group members may become weakened and the group's unity also reduced. If the offence is maximized (the culprit may be expelled from the group, with reputation tarnished) the moral standing of the members, in their own eyes, may be raised. The affirmation of the strictness of a rule may produce a change in the group's normative expectations in general. Equally important, whatever the outcome, is that the parts played by various guests in the 'defence' or 'prosecution' of the accused have consequences for their standing in the group in future. All this shows that principles are not merely worked out in the course of being applied, but the application process depends on the group structure while having consequences for this very structure in future. Roles, rules and group structure are inseparable in our social existence.

Much of the above has been discussed by sociologists in terms of Lemert's (1972) concepts of 'primary' and 'secondary' deviance. For rule-breaking may or may not result in the perpetrator's being labelled socially as 'deviant'. Where such labelling occurs those concerned may be identified as a distinct group, or take on the norm-breaking as a sign of their particular interests. An example of this is vegetarians. For these, non-compliance with dietary norms does not produce exclusion from their primary groups, but the establishment of a dietary order with peculiar (in its true sense) behaviours and justifications for its rules which are at odds with those of the meat-eating majority.

There is a measure of toleration of acts which defy rules, particularly those seen as being externally imposed and where the breach appears to be innocuous. Few people, apparently, are outraged by tax-avoiders. There were even some who saw the 'Great Train Robbery' of the 1960s as a 'daring' escapade. These include, probably, the same people who would express outrage at the thought of the theft of their own property. Norms and rules *are* a function of our membership of social groupings together with the accounts we give to justify them. In a complex and changing world, we continually reappraise both actions and norms. This does not mean that we change our standards every day, but we may have to find different reasons for why we want the rules of daily life to stay the same.

Implicit in the idea that rule-breaking is acceptable is the notion that certain classes of extraordinary action are deemed as the province of extraordinary people. The person renowned for making preposterous remarks, which in others would be seen as gauche or rude, may be given a licence by the group to operate 'on the fringes' of norms by playing the role of jester. Indeed, historically the position of jester was defined as a role which, if carried out by any other member of court, would result in severe penalties. In modern society, where the presentation of oneself as a personality (as someone who has cultivated skills and gathered special experiences) is paramount, there is often a real benefit to be gained from working at the fringe of social norms. One may well be seen as a creative or otherwise exceptional person as a consequence. Such audacity can be at times readily marketable, as can be seen from a glance at the titles in any bookshop. While most of us consider ourselves to be norm-abiding citizens, the reading matter available suggests that, in our fantasy lives at least, we relish not only the breaking of social rules but the complexities which flow from the moral tangles precipitated by this. There is an appeal in being 'licensed to kill' despite the normative constraints against killing.

When rules break down

Social norms act as guides and standards for social conduct. In abiding by them we take for granted that the world is a relatively stable place. As ways of anticipating events, norms provide a structure for our social existence. It can be disconcerting if the rules are altered during 'a game'. Asch's (1952) well-known experiments on conformity (see Chapter 4) are illustrative of this. Striking accounts have been given of real-life occasions on which people have suffered a severe disruption of the rules which they understood to guide their existence. They provide insight into how people cope when this happens, and what they do to re-establish some semblance of 'normality' to their lives.

It is worth reminding ourselves that norms, in part, enable a group's members to define themselves as a collectivity. People not only belong to a group but they *know* that they belong. Furthermore, they also know how they play their particular roles within it. We can say that group membership provides both certain freedoms and constraints on action, while enabling the members to identify with the group and to know themselves as 'their selves' in a social context because of it. Social norms are not just a matter of rules which steer people around society, making sure that they say and do the correct things as appropriate. The idea of sharing expectations about each other with each other inevitably includes the proposition that we share beliefs about ourselves with others as part of this grand conception.

In 1938 thousands of American radio listeners heard of an invasion of Martians. Some left their homes, fleeing with their families to escape the oncoming aliens. In fact, they had been listening to a very realistic dramatization of H. G. Wells's story *The War of the Worlds*. A study of their beliefs and reactions by Cantril *et al.* (1940) revealed that the panic was caused by a number of factors. Many failed to check what they had heard because it fitted in with their beliefs about what could happen to the world, because they were told about it by other people whom they trusted and because they believed their whole way of life was at stake. In this situation the rules of everyday behaviour were overthrown; some rushed into the streets and sought help from strangers, others asked neighbours if they could hide in their cellar. This did not mean that they were free of all norms, if by this is meant that their behaviour had become in some way detached from social influence. To the contrary, in such panic situations people are more likely to seize on frames of reference which accord with the frightening experience shared by others. Rather like Sherif's experiment with its apparently moving point of light, individuals work our a shared referent in order to make their social world meaningful. What is fascinating about the 'invasion from Mars', then, is that the relinquishment of everyday norms left people prey to the formation of *ad hoc* rules of conduct once they took to the streets. Divested of the constraints of social life, we may also abandon the freedoms of action and thought which social roles provide.

In the example of the panic, people abandoned rules in order to save themselves, but in other circumstances, people may do precisely the opposite under pressure. During the Second World War, concentration camp inmates were taken from the Jewish civilian population of many European countries. Among them, in one such camp, was the psychologist Bruno Bettelheim (1958) who recorded the reactions and behaviours of the prisoners over time. He noted that the aim of the Nazis was to break down the roles, personal identities, and even the common humanity of the internees. In effect, people who had until recently been ordinary, middle-class, law-abiding citizens found that the very authority which they accepted was turned against them. Where they lacked a political frame of reference to interpret what was happening to them they were most at risk of psychological collapse; many committed suicide. Extraordinarily, as time went by some of the survivors began to copy the actions of their guards and tormentors. Bettelheim explained this as a need by those inmates to establish some identity, some scrap of self-value, and this was achieved by their identifying with their criminal torturers! In the midst of being abandoned by society, having all rights and semblance of respect stolen from them, these inmates nevertheless sought a role in the execution of rituals which, to the observer, appear bizarre or even macabre. For those who could not survive 'in their minds', such seemingly abject rule-following created a residue of freedom in a world where normal life had vanished.

The two cases cited above are polar opposites and yet both provide evidence that, while we often think of norms as residing within distinct groupings, there are occasions when certain rules of conduct may be seen as either irrelevant or declared inappropriate by particular groups. Just as rules are articulated through discussion in specific applications, so norms are dissolved and reconstructed in the large settings of ideological struggles and conflicts between interest groups in society. The roles played and the rules followed and justified are not immune from these sea changes in social life.

Concluding comments

The comparison between social life and games is often drawn when psychologists speak of rule-following. This metaphor of the game has not been used in this chapter because it lends itself too readily to the idea that rules are preformed and are somewhere 'out there' beyond the players. The intention has been to show a different, if a somewhat more complicated, picture of norms as things which are altered as they are applied in the course of social interaction. This different picture also promotes the role of norms in social change. A norm is invoked in order to mark a behavioural difference that makes a difference. Rules do not just tell us what to do. In the language of some current authors, they are not 'scripts' which individuals carry onto the social stage. They are often much more elusive and yet important than that. The co-ordination of roles depends upon shared norms, although the employment and the articulation of these will vary with the different roles taken by group members. The standards individuals in the group share about each other with each other are norms, but these are not necessarily equally or wholly shared. It is into the 'gaps', as it were, between specific behaviour and expectation (and between the under-standing of one person and another) that deliberation and discussion of what 'should, ought or must' occur take place. And it is here, when one listens to what people say about these matters, that one senses the stretching of rules and the fitting of social roles.

The distinction between norms and rules seems difficult to maintain in the light of this discussion. Once seen as negotiable and changeable the norms are less easy to identify as different from rules. Of course, given that conceptions of roles have changed in this way, it is not surprising that some have chosen to introduce the term 'rules' to highlight a different emphasis not present in the original rigid view of roles. Rules refer to a slightly narrower concept than roles which have substantive aspects other than the rules which govern behaviour in a particular role (such as the specific tasks and duties performed as part of the role). However, this is a matter of the scope of the two concepts, which overlap in significant ways in terms of social psychological explanation.

4

SOCIAL INFLUENCE

The idea that we are substantially influenced by other members of our society is an important one. The explanations may sometimes be expressed in terms of the requirements of 'a herding instinct' but, as we will see, this would appear to do great injustice to the complexity of the social processes. Understanding how we are influenced by others became a major theme of social psychology, particularly after the Second World War, and it has to be contrasted with other views which tend to suggest that society is relatively fixed and unchanging. The concern with social influence has been a particular feature of North American social psychology. Perhaps it is the relatively root-less background of this society which encouraged this interest in how to change people. Much of previous thinking was dominated by the views of society reflected in European psychology, entrenched in a more traditional culture. William James, the American psychologist, writing in 1890, provides a good example of the earlier view that society is relatively unchanging. He wrote of the 'enormous fly-wheel of society', as if the sheer weight of society provided all the momentum to keep it going, mechanically and unchangingly, on course:

Already at the age of twenty-five you see the professional man-nerism settling down on the young commercial traveller, on the young doctor, on the young minister, on the young counsellor-at-law. You see the little lines of cleavage running through the character, the tricks of thought, the prejudices, the ways of the 'shop', in a word, from which the man can by-and-by no more escape than his coat-sleeves can suddenly fall into a new set of folds. On the whole, it is best he should not escape. It is well for the world that in most of us by the age of thirty, the character has set like plaster and will never soften again (James, 1950, p. 121).

This picture of a rigidly unchanging society is the antipathy of the modern perspective. We now believe that our thoughts and behaviour are influenced by an interaction of internal (personal) and external (societal) forces. North American psychology had its theoretical origins in this new, rootless society – unlike its European counterpart which was steeped in rigid class structures, evolution and genetics. The belief grew that people were amenable to social pressure to change and to be manipulated. Two main factors accounted for this. First, politically anxieties about the instability of the mass of the population were further fuelled by the ever increasing availability of the media and their use in various forms of propaganda – advertising being a prime example of this. There were even reports of 'brainwashing' of soldiers. Second, society was changing rapidly and a psychology which emphasized the resistance of people to change could scarcely cope. Gradually a view of people developed, encouraged by the preoccupations of psychologists, that they were, in a sense, weak and bobbed along in the tide of social pressure changing their behaviours, attitudes and beliefs and following a line of least resistance. Certainly much North American psychology has looked at optimum strategies of changing people. There is a lot of popular appeal in this since if we look around any society overall we find people doing very much the same sorts of thing. In a sentence, people within a society tend to be a lot more like each other than they are like others outside that society. The temptation is to assume that we are all weak and unwilling victims of the forces of conformity in society. In social psychology a whole area of research and theory on 'social influence' developed which conventionally looks at interpersonal influences on our behaviour rather than, say, the more diffuse forces of class structure or culture. Sometimes it appears to be naively assumed that if people are seen to be doing the same things as other people psychological pressure has been put on them by the others which they are powerless to resist. It is important to realize that this may not necessarily be the case.

What is conformity?

The assumption seems to be that when individuals adopt the behaviours of those around them, they are under the influence of, or are being manipulated by, others almost against their will. Just as likely, exactly the opposite may be happening. The person who conforms on something they have no strong feelings about may be saving themselves effort by adopting the strategies others have probably given much thought to. Also, or alternatively, they may be ingratiating themselves to others through the flattery of imitation. This can be done extremely effectively by complying with others' orders, conforming to their behaviour, or functioning within the confines of the role they have adopted. The act of allowing oneself to be 'influenced' by others should not be assumed to be necessarily a negative thing. The question in these circumstances is perhaps who is manipulating whom. Obeying others can be a royal road to promotion in certain organizations and essential in some relationships (such as in the traditional view of the roles of men and women within marriage). Being ruggedly individualistic may be the essence of 'Westerns', spy films, and other heroic social images, but it is a mistake to assume that it is the secret of contentment and happiness. Likewise, one must be wary of seeing 'conformers' as weak, social cripples.

In many instances it is situations rather than people which determine apparently conforming behaviour. Entering a church, for instance, inspires a very different behavioural response from entering a football stadium. While ultimately socialization has determined how we feel we should behave in different circumstances, this is a somewhat removed and different explanation of our behaviour than would be an assessment of the situation in terms of group pressures to change and conform. Just because we all tend to behave similarly when entering a library does not mean that there is any particular great and threatening social pressure on us at that time.

Although much of modern social psychology might imply otherwise, what we do is not necessarily determined solely by our own wishes, desires, or cognitions about the world. Often we act under the, sometimes covert and subtle, suggestion of other people. Although much of this chapter is devoted to the ideas of the dominant American social psychology of the 1950s, 1960s and later, in no way is it an unqualified celebration of the achievements of this genre. Particularly, there is no intention to reproduce the usual textbook view that there is a powerful social stimulus which produces a conforming response in people. We have already begun to dismantle that oversimplistic notion.

'Conformity' without attempts at influence

One major determinant of behaviour, of which we tend to be unaware, is what social psycholgists have termed 'the demand characteristics of situations'. The demand characteristics of the library encourage us to be quiet and studious. In the environment of the doctor's surgery we tend to feel confident and hopeful that our problems are going to be sorted out. The traditional, row-by-row, formal classroom is laid out to allow the teacher to pontificate and control any feedback from students to the moments when the teacher wants it.

The impact on our behaviour of the situation in which we find ourselves has, in the main, been the subject of study and theorizing only indirectly. Perhaps the most dramatic illustration of the impact of the demand characteristics comes from the study by Orne and Scheibe (1964) which sought to explain a particular set of dramatic research findings. A whole series of experiments had been carried out by other researchers on what was known as 'sensory deprivation'. These concerned the effects of cutting down as much physical stimulation to the individual as possible. In the studies, usually using university students, people might have worn translucent goggles over their eyes, cardboard gauntlets over their forearms and been immersed in a tank of water at body temperature, or otherwise restricted in the exposure to sensations. Invariably, many subjects in these studies displayed symptoms of disorientation which in some cases went as far as an apparent deterioration in mental and emotional behaviour, verging on the psychotic (Solomon *et al.*, 1961). Orne argued that sensory deprivation as such was not responsible for these changes but that the procedures employed in the studies imposed demand characteristics which pressured subjects to behave as they did. In some studies 'panic buttons' were present in case the experiment got too much for the individual and served as a signal to 'get me out' of the apparatus, others had subjects sign a frightening disclaimer form which absolved the experimenters and institutions from any terrible consequences of the experiment for the subject. It has to be left to the imagination to speculate the rumours on campus when the volunteer subjects were being solicited! To support the alternative interpretation, Orne described an experiment in which either the fear-inducing features were present, or, in the control condition, were absent. Anxiety was heightened by using a hospital location, experimenters wearing white coats, and a tray of things to be used in an emergency. Obviously the study could not prove that sensory deprivation did not have an effect (as appropriate controls for the control group were absent, so to speak), but it did show that the anxiety-arousing features of the procedures produced many of the apparent effects of sensory deprivation in their own right – demand characteristic effects and the effects of the intended experimental treatments were confounded. In other words, people basically appear to respond to what the situation tells them that they are expected to do! Other research suggests that rebellion against such pressures may be as much of a possible outcome as conformity to pressures – it all depends on a complex equation of precise procedures, personality, experience and probably other factors.

Although we saw in Chapter 3 that roles have many different aspects, the manner in which we act out the roles we play in society has a lot in common with this idea of demand characteristics. By this is meant that when we carry out many of our social roles we are simply adopting what we see as the demands of the role rather than somehow being forced and cajoled into adopting a particular set of role-appropriate behaviours. This does not mean that social pressure is never applied but merely that it is not inevitable. The manner in which we execute roles is a result of a mixture of situational and interpersonal factors, and is often a compromise between personal desires and the expectations of others. In the home, for instance, although we may have to act the role of husband or wife, how we play that part depends on characteristics of ourselves and our relations with others. Increasing demands of the workplace force women (and less obviously the increasing demands of the home on men) to adapt to the dual expectations of the home and the workplace. One researcher found that in order for a woman to resolve the problem of the role conflict between being a paid worker and a mother, structural role-redefinition appears to be the most time-effective way of managing family–career role conflict since it involves reducing the woman's workload to a manageable level (Kaitz, 1985). Indeed, for dual-career couples, time management to relieve the overload of responsibilities on the partners is necessary to minimize the problems of multiple-role occupancy (Kater, 1985).

While in some cases there is direct social pressure on how we execute our roles (for example, the pressure brought by some husbands on their wives to perform their wifely roles in a particular way, for example to cook all the meals), there is a degree of independent influence exerted by the incumbents of the role themselves. A dramatic example of the manner in which the role can affect behaviour comes from Zimbardo's 'Stanford Prison Experiment' (Haney *et al.*, 1981). There was a pool of middle-class, emotionally stable university students from which was selected a number to act the role of 'prisoner' and a number to act the role of 'guards'. They were strangers when the research began. For a two-week period 'prisoners' were divested of their personal possessions and clothed in uniform smocks. The 'guards', working on rota, wore uniforms and 'worked' for eight hours a day. The effect of the two roles on the participants in the study was dramatic. The 'prisoners' became obedient, and cowed – they even judged their 'guards' to be physically bigger than they were in reality. The 'guards', on the other hand, became assertive, utterly dominating and demanding, demeaned the 'prisoners', and were totally supportive of each others' actions, regardless of their extremity. No one told the participants to behave in the ways they did but within the role their patterns of behaviour became radically different according to whichever group they had been allocated to.

It is not realistic to try to explain the findings described in this section as being in any sense the result of any directly operating attempts to influence individuals on the part of others. Although the situational factors result in behavioural similarities among people, it is hardly appropriate to describe them as, in any way, weak and overcome by social pressure. One reason for this statement is that it is essential to remember that part of the equation comes from internal motivations and thoughts. It is far too easy, especially looking at many psychology texts, to get carried away with the belief that we have no say in what is happening to us.

The classic 'conformity' studies

The 'classic' demonstration of conformity in social psychology came from the experiments by Solomon Asch which, as we shall see, involved the effects of a 'mistaken' group consensus about a very simple judgemental task. The experiments themselves, however, do not define what conformity is, they merely show it taking place in unusual situations. Indeed the best thing to do, for now, is to assume that there is not a single 'thing' which may be defined as conformity and that it is merely a blanket term for a range of different processes. Much of the behaviour which we loosely call 'conformity' is things like eating with a knife and fork rather than our fingers and driving on the correct side of the road. It would be almost impossible for us to function within society if the great majority of us did not operate within a comprehensive network of norms. Similarly, it would be difficult for us to cope with our everyday lives if we had to make decisions about each and every one of our actions. We would be preoccupied wondering whether to wear a tie, whether to use our left or right hand for a fork, and what to way when we are introduced to people. We would consequently not have the energy and time left to get involved in the more complex aspects of life such as balancing the family budget, flying to the moon, or studying social psychology. Operating within norms is not the same as conforming in the sense that conformity implies we have to change in some way from one point of view to another. Norms sometimes are arbitrary and we do not care which of the options is adopted but whichever it is helps to make co-existence possible. Conforming involves a conflict between the behaviour adopted and one's previous desires or beliefs – a clash between the social and individual.

Asch (1952) placed his research subjects in a group of seven to nine other people who were in reality all confederates of the experimenter. The group was then, shown successively, two cards. The first contained a single standard line, and the second card had three comparison lines – one of which matched the standard line in length. Each member of the group had to say in turn, openly, which of the three comparison lines was identical to the standard line. From time to time, the confederates picked out one of the comparison lines which did not match the standard line as being the same as the standard line! The experimental subject could either go along with the group or say what their eyes had seen. Asch found that in approximately one-third of cases his subjects, in these circumstances, opted for the same comparison line as the majority (though a quarter never conformed). One common reason for this appears to be that they wanted the social approval of other members of the group. Some subjects reported that they did not wish to feel inferior to the rest of the group. Nearly all of them said that they felt disturbed or puzzled and that they felt that if they went against the group they would be considered peculiar. In short, people went along with the group or did not go along with the group, but always with the expense of a good deal of psychological energy. Films of the experiment reveal subjects to be nervous, anxious, withdrawn, and all manner of other responses.

The circumstances in which conformity takes place have subsequently been researched in great detail. Asch found that if even one other non-conforming group member was introduced the effect of conformity was drastically reduced. There appears to be little conformity when the group consists of one or two others but much more when there are three others. The impact of increasing the number of conforming individuals over and above this is negligible (Asch, 1956). While many subjects do conform, far from everyone does. Indeed, Harris (1985) argues that the popular view of these conformity studies is incorrect. Although some individuals did tend to yield to the majority position, even when that position was clearly incorrect, most subjects remained largely independent in their decisions. They are really unconformity studies, if anything!

Furthermore, Perrin and Spencer (1981) claim that the Asch studies do not show a universal effect, but rather reflect a particular historic and cultural state of the United States at the time of the 1950s. Nicholson *et al.* (1985), found no differences between British and American students in conformity rates in the Asch paradigm. They did, however, find markedly lower rates of conformity than Asch had done 30 years earlier. There is, none the less, a small minority of students who conform to group pressure.

In another replication of the Asch studies, Perrin and Spencer (1981) used 53 subjects, 17 male undergraduates, 20 people on probation, and 16 unemployed West Indians. Compliance rates for the 17 students were found to be just once in 396 attempts to influence them! Levels of compliance similar to Asch's were found among those on probation where both the confederates and the experimenters were probation officers, and by the West Indian subjects where the experimenter was white. They drew the conclusion that the Asch conformity effect is substantial only when the personal costs of not yielding to the majority are high. Notice also that these are circumstances in which social structure in the form of social status differences is heightened.

The classic obedience studies

Stanley Milgram (1974) carried out a series of studies which have been among the most widely known experiments in social psychology. He was interested in how far people would be willing to go under social pressure. His special area of interest was obedience. One can only speak of obedience if there is differentiation of social power. That is to say that obedience implies social structures. In his work he capitalized on the status difference between the experimenter and his subjects.

Milgram investigated the impact of authority on behaviour. Initially he solicited people at a university campus to take part in a study. The task of the subject was to 'teach' another person to learn certain things. Whenever a 'learner' made an error, the subject was instructed to administer an electric shock to the 'learner'. The subject was told to increase the amount of shock given each time a mistake was made. The levels were clearly marked on the apparatus and included labels indicating how dangerous each of the levels of shock were. The 'learner' was a collaborator of the experimenter and received no real shocks during the course of the experiment. He did, however, play-act being shocked. Milgram (1974) reports that, as prearranged, the learner started making mistakes and the shock levels began to rise. With each increase in voltage the learner's reactions became more and more dramatic ranging from grunts at 75 volts to an agonized scream at 225 volts, and after 330 volts the learner fell silent as if either unconscious or dead! Whenever the subject was reluctant to continue shocking the learner, the experimenter calmly directed that more shock should be given – even using phrases like 'the experiment requires that you must continue'.

Milgram found that over three-fifths of the subjects, under this pressure, continued to shock the 'learner' right up to the maximum shock levels – in spite of the fact that many subjects were concerned about the 'learner' (even pleading with the experimenter in vain to go and check that the learner was alright). In subsequent experiments, Milgram found that obedience was reduced by having the subject and learner in the same room, by having other subjects present who defied the experimenter, and running the experiment in a seedy city-centre office well away from the prestigious and imposing university setting.

Clearly, authority can push people to almost unpredictable limits – certainly experts canvassed in advance believed that people would not go anywhere near the lengths to which they were forced in the experiment.

'Shocking' demonstrations such as these need to be interpreted with some caution when we begin to make generalizations about real life. Epstein *et al.* (1973) suggested after completing a survey of 300 students, that the whole aura of an experiment creates in the subject certain obligatory preconceptions among which, typically, is that of being co-operative. As Milgram used willing volunteers, it is probable that they, too, wished to be co-operative. Epstein *et al.* (1973) also found that the students had expectations of experimenters including that they should behave in a professional manner – which inevitably means that we 'hand' over responsibility to the professional for what we do. After all, we do not insist on being awake during surgery so we can tell the doctor how to carry out the operation.

There is a vast literature which seeks to explain what is happening in these experiments of Milgram's as well as much debate over the ethics of what he did to his subjects. At this point, perhaps the most important thing to remember is that there was nothing automatic and routine in the way both Asch's and Milgram's subjects responded. Quite the reverse, in fact. Social influence results in a wide variety of subjective experiences and behaviour patterns. How can we make sense of them?

Why do we conform?

Up to this point we have tended to imply that conformity is merely the adoption of the 'ways' of the majority around one. Although we have cautioned against imposing any value judgements on the terms 'conformers' and 'non-conformers', this still leaves us at a rather unsophisticated level of analysis, and, for example, might push us in to using concepts too loosely. We might, for example, want to say that members of any minority group (teddy-boys, mods, rockers, punks, and so on) exhibit the *traits* of non-conformity because they do not follow the ways of the majority of the population. This is clearly erroneous in that they may equally be seen as conformers in the context of their particular youth sub-culture. Are they merely 'conforming to non-conformity' (Jahoda, 1959, p. 101)?

Considerations such as these should encourage attempts to analyse varieties of conformity and non-conformity. One of the simplest and at the same time most illuminating attempts at this came in the work of Marie Jahoda. Essentially all that she does is point out that there are three spheres of experience to be considered in 'conformity situations'.

Table 4.1   Types of conformity and independence

	Initial investment high on issue		Initial investment low on issue	
	Public and private agree	Public and private differ	Public and private agree	Public and private differ
Adopts group position	Independent consent	Compliance	Conformity	Expedient conformity
Does not adopt group position	Independent	Undermined	Compulsive resistance	Expedient resistance

These correspond to the individual's degree of emotional and intellectual investment in the 'issue' in question, the degree to which the individual adopts the position of the group, and whether in the individual's private experience there is a difference between what he does publicly and his inner feelings. To simplify matters, Jahoda dichotomizes each of these three factors for illustrative purposes which allows her to consider eight possible types of conformity and independence formed from the three dichotomized factors as shown in Table 4.1.

This reveals an awful lot about social influence situations. It also moves us considerably towards a relatively value-free scheme for understanding conformity and non-conformity. Notice how conformity is defined by Jahoda's scheme not simply in terms of overt behaviour matching that of the social pressure, but also partially in terms of internal psychological states. Notice also how the scheme gives some dignity to individuals by not implying that following the group's behaviour is necessarily sheep-like. There are four types of people who do not 'go along with the crowd': the genuinely independent person who believes strongly in something and is not affected internally or overtly by the group pressure; the apparently independent person who covertly is shaken (undermined) by the group pressure, but not manifestly so; the person who does not care much about the issue, but both refuses to go along with others overtly and will not give internally; and finally, the person who does not care much about the issue and covertly accepts what the group wishes, but for other motives does not wish to be seen to be going along with the group.

Those who go along with the crowd also fall into four types: independent consent where the individual feels strongly about the issue but decides that the group is correct and indicates agreement; compliance in which the individual decides that they should go along with the group on an issue which they feel strongly about while retaining their original convictions; conformity, in which there is no strong conviction but no reason to reject the group consensus; and finally, expedient conformity in which, despite no particularly strong feelings and the fact that the individual does go along with the group, the individual actually does not truly accept the consensus.

No doubt we could find more subtle ways of looking at individual responses to group influence, but for now the above sounds many warning bells about sloppy thinking. It also brings us to an examination of the different reasons and motivations why people behave differently in social influence situations.

Perhaps it is worth mentioning that others have differentiated among types of what we 'sloppily' term 'conformity'. Crutchfield (1955) also points out that some people conform due to reasons of expediency while others do so because they have genuine doubts concerning their own judgement and tend to carry longer-term influences from the experience. 'Non-conformists', according to Crutchfield, fall into two types: those who are hostile to the group and deliberately go against any group consensus; and those who are independently-minded and quite simply stick to their own views when these conflict with those of the group. Notice how these research-based observations match well with the categories formed from Jahoda's theoretical examination of social influence.

The idea that there are vulnerable people has been examined in various ways. Clearly some people are more influenced by the group in some circumstances than other individuals would be. It is going too far to speak of a 'vulnerable personality', but certainly, under some circumstances, people with certain characteristics are more likely to respond to the pressure than others. Tisak (1986), for instance, reported how, in the 6–11-year age range, children considered their parents to have changing levels of authority over aspects of their life. They felt that, as they got older, things concerning only themselves should be under their own jurisdiction and not that of their parents. This highlights the importance of the perceived legitimacy of the authority of the person giving commands. This is fundamental to whether they are obeyed and it needs to be allowed for when considering individual responsiveness to influence attempts. An early study by Crutchfield (1955) assessed people from very varied backgrounds on a series of different tasks in order to see who tended to be influenced by the remainder of the group irrespective of the issue to hand. Those less likely to adopt the pattern of the group were those of above average intelligence; those with a high degree of originality; those with psychological strength in terms of ability to cope with stress; those with a high degree of self-confidence; and those with so-called 'optimal' social attitudes and behaviours (including tolerance, responsibility, dominance, and freedom from disturbed and dependent relations with other people). There are many other factors which relate to people who go along with social influence. It has been shown, for instance, that people with self-esteem are more easily conditioned and more prone to imitating (Rosenbaum and de Charms, 1960). Less competent people are more prone to imitate models (Lanzetta and Kanareff, 1959).

More recently, children have been shown to differ in their willingness to copy the misbehaviour of their peers in school. In a series of studies conducted in the school environment, some children's reactions to misbehaving models were far more easily influenced than others'. It was noted (Kniveton, 1986), that children from large families – defined as four or more siblings – imitated the misbehaving peer more than those from smaller families. Birth order, as such, was not an influential variable. However, Howitt and Cumberbatch (1975) found that first-born children tended to imitate mass media figures more than those with older siblings, perhaps because they lacked more appropriate real-life models. Kniveton (1987) noted that working-class children imitated more than middle-class ones, but that this was not accounted for by intelligence differences.

There is an important theoretical issue in the topic of 'vulnerability' to social influence which may explain the following 'odd' sex differences. Crutchfield (1955) noted that, on average, females were more conforming than males. This sex difference in response to social pressure has not been found consistently in research so there is no conclusion to be drawn that females are more passive and compliant than males. Sistrunk and McDavid (1971) explained the lack of consistency in the findings by demonstrating how willingness to yield to the influence of others is inversely related to the individual's interest and familiarity with the subject matter under consideration. They wrote a questionnaire with items of primary interest to one or other sex. Next to each question was an indication of how the majority had answered. Items about which males had little interest or familiarity produced more male than female conformity and vice versa. This relationship between conformity and interest or familiarity is fascinating and goes some way towards explaining why high levels of conformity are found in psychological experiments where participants are rarely interested in the subject matter of the influence attempt. It may also explain why a clear personality profile of the conforming individual has not emerged.

It is worth pointing out that the 'traditional' methods of studying social influence in social psychology, as exemplified by the work of Solomon Asch and Stanley Milgram, tend to encourage the view that people are 'receivers' of social influence rather than 'participants'. This is despite the fact Asch and Milgram are among the most sensitive researchers as they try to establish the 'meaning' of the experience for their subjects. The trouble is, of course, that the subject is relatively powerless in the experiments as they are constrained by the situation which is unfamiliar and gives them few opportunities to 'initiate' anything. The usual social world has a much more dynamic quality which allows other factors to come into play. So again, as implied by Jahoda's scheme, in explaining why any one individual does or does not comply with social pressure we may wish to examine motivation in the context of that situation. Psychologists have identified some important aspects of this.

One reason for complying with others is to ingratiate oneself with them. Christie and Geis (1970) looked to the writings of Machiavelli and read of his view that interpersonal behaviour is totally selfish. Devising a psychological measuring scale based on aspects of Machiavelli's writings, it became possible to separate people who scored high on manipulative interactions with other people (highly Machiavellian) and those not so inclined. They found that when they had something to gain from doing so, Machiavellians were far more likely to cheat than others. Lying relates closely to conformity as one tries, by lying, to provide the answer one believes the other party requires.

The relationships between those involved in the social influence process are a key to its fuller understanding. Parents can be excellent at using guilt as a means of making their children comply with their wishes ('After all I've done for you, the least you could do in return is . . .') If one feels guilty because the relationship is in some way 'one-sided' one may wish to help right the balance by complying with the wishes of the other person. Influence, then, is not merely saying what one wants or one thinks, it is often involved with *techniques* for getting what one wants. Fern *et al.* (1986) found that trying to influence another by the use of 'door in the face' techniques worked less well than what might be termed the 'foot in the door'. In the former strategy, the initial request is relatively very large and a majority of people refuse to comply. This is followed by a small request, the actual target behaviour required. To some extent this uses guilt at having refused the first request as a lever for compliance with the second. The 'foot in the door' technique is commonly adopted by door-to-door sales people and works on the assumption that once a customer has acquiesced to a small request, perhaps having bought an inexpensive item, they will, at a later stage, be more willing to purchase a larger one. Freedman and Fraser (1966) demonstrated this technique in a study in which they first asked housewives if they would mind answering a few questions about soaps used in the home. A few days later they asked the same housewives if the research team could do an inventory of the whole household. A second group of housewives were merely approached with the second of these requests. Just over 50 per cent of the housewives who had complied with the first and smaller request agreed to the second but of the other group less than a quarter agreed to have the complete survey done.

All of this says, one way or another, that we need to take great care when we consider the social psychological studies of conformity, obedience and other social influence attempts. A too rudimentary reading of the literature (and this is encouraged by many textbooks) reduces social influence to the net product of a system of forces or pressures. Unfortunately, there is no way in which social forces can be measured in the precise way that this implies. The active participation, the manipulation, and many other things people do in society have a role to play in the social influence process.

Disobedience and non-conformity

Marie Jahoda's classificatory scheme (Table 4.1) alerts us to the range of situations which we could justifiably describe as disobedience and non-conformity. Like conformity, the failure to conform to social pressure is not a single entity but may take several broad forms which represent totally different social psychological processes. While there is a ready, but doomed, tendency to seek the 'conforming' personality, much less research has been devoted to trying to identify what those least likely to conform have in common. One must not fall into the trap of believing them to be simply at the opposite end of some continuum from conformers. The reasons why people fail to conform can relate closely to the circumstances of the situation, or to characteristics of the individual as they interact with the situation.

London (1970) interviewed a group of people who could be described as resisting intense social pressure. These were the German citizens who, during the Second World War, has risked their lives to rescue Jews. They clearly went against the dominant mores and norms that Hitler had sought to impose on Germany. London found three major factors of a personal or situational nature which typified non-conformers: they were high risk-takers who enjoyed taking a chance; they had a strong identification with one of their parents who tended to be highly moralistic; and they were not strongly identified with the mainstream of German society. There are many extreme examples of non-conformers. One might argue that some psychiatrically ill people are non-conformers. Diagnosing someone as being mentally ill is a haphazard affair at the best of times. Many people are initially seen as being 'sick' because, according to their friends or relatives, they fail to conform in some aspect of their lives. Thereafter, the professional practitioner takes over, but according to some (Draguns and Phillips, 1971) the evidence of actual 'illness' is more likely to occur in the minds of the diagnostician than in the actual behaviour of the patient. Diagnoses can be, at best, subjective, and at worst, positively harmful.

There are circumstances which encourage individuals to be non-conforming. Psychological reactance theory (Brehm, 1966) suggests that we each have behavioural freedoms which are important to us. Any threat to restrict these free choices of action results in a reaction by an individual whereby they strive to re-establish that freedom of choice. This can result in deliberate non-conforming behaviours, as is illustrated in a study by Brehm and Sensenig (1966). Here the experimental scenario was that the subjects were asked to select one from two pictures of a person they would prefer to work with. They were also told that there was another subject in a nearby room performing the same task as themselves. They were given a self-descriptive statement supposedly written by this other subject (who, in the nature of social psychology experiments of this period, did not exist) and were told they would receive regular information about the other person's choices. People in the control group received a note supposedly from this other person which simply read 'I prefer . . . ' and indicated the person chosen. The people in the experimental group received a rather different note which read 'I think we should both do . . . ' and again referred to one of the photographs. Essentially those in the experimental group were being deprived of their freedom of choice – someone was telling them what to do. In the control group, where there was thus no pressure from the other, most of the subjects actually went along with that other's choice. In the freedom-deprived experimental group, however, very few conformed to the views of the 'bogus' other person. Studies of this type show that, while in many circumstances we are willing to conform, if the element of choice is removed then there is a distinct possibility that we may react against the influence of others.

Reacting against the wishes or orders of others, being a non-conformer and going against the views and wishes of the group to which one belongs is not something done lightly. Society, groups and other individuals often do not like non-conformers for two main reasons. First, the non-conformer is publicly rejecting the views and/or behaviours of the group – we rarely like being told by others that they think we are wrong. Second, because he does not fit into the mould the other group members cannot predict how the non-conformer will behave. This, in turn, leads to uncertainty on the part of the others who, not knowing how the non-conformer will react, become ill at ease and anxious in their presence. Generally speaking we do not like states of uncertainty. When another's behaviour is unpredictable then we have to take steps to reduce our own discomfort and the anxiety caused: if the non-conformer does not become predictable we will decide to exercise sanctions against them.

One conclusion which can be drawn from the diversity of research which relates to the various aspects of social influence is that our behaviour is affected in many and varied ways by the social situations we find ourselves in and by the people we interact with. Reaction against pressure to conform is as human a reaction as conformity.

Leadership

Once we recognize the importance of social stratification in our consideration of group processes (as Milgram did) then it becomes important to highlight the key features of the group structure which have a bearing on the way in which the social influence process operates. One of the most interesting examples of influence over others occurs in leadership in group interactions where one member acts and the rest of the group agree to be led. The idea of dominance hierarchies has a long history. Although animals quickly establish a pecking order within a species or group, this is a very different thing to the leadership displayed in human societies. Russell and Russell (1957) point out that with animals competitive–dominant–submissive behaviour is displayed which is not at all the same as human leadership. With animals one takes precedence over the other in any aspect of their lives when there is competition.

Leadership in humans is far more complex. Rauch and Behling (1984) explain human leadership as 'the process of influencing the activities of an organized group towards goal achievement'. Bryman (1986, p. 2) stresses that there are two main circumstances in which leadership occurs:

> one form of leadership . . . is that which emerges from situations in which there is no formal leadership. The second way in which the leader/non-leader distinction is likely to occur is in the context of formally designated roles. The people are appointed to positions in which the exercise of leadership is a prime requirement . . .

It appears that the former has been neglected by researchers in favour of the latter as a result of a persuasive preoccupation with leadership effectiveness. Effectiveness includes group productivity and the satisfaction, involvement and contentment of the subordinates. The essence of this picture of leadership centres around the exercise of influence and this largely within an organizational environment. It is this latter aspect which offers the clue as to the distinction between other types of social facilitation and leadership. Some approaches to the subject (for example, French and Snyder, 1959; Homans, 1961) have regarded it as synonymous with the study of other general aspects of the facilitating effects of other people. They have seen it in terms of power, authority, rewards and costs. This is typical of earlier studies of informal leadership. The typical scenario was that in a non-structured group situation an individual would naturally emerge as the leader.

One early interest was in whether there were any personality traits typically to be found in those who emerge as leaders. The logic of this 'trait' approach is that someone who displays leadership qualities in one situation will also display them in another. Psychologists have always been reluctant to give up in this search to link personality characteristics with various aspects of behaviour. This was probably encouraged by early achievements in the area of intelligence where a high degree of consistency across situations occurs. Leadership, like all other aspects of social influence mentioned in this chapter, is a totally different sort of concept as it is meaningless without interaction with others. Interaction is responsible for the inconsistency across situations for where leadership occurs depends not only on the actions of one individual but on the reactions of others. Initially this line of research seemed to be quite promising, with about 12 characteristics consistently differentiating leaders from non-leaders. Borgatta *et al.* (1954) identified a group of men who scored highly on a number of 'leadership traits' and a larger number of others who did not fall into this category. This was achieved by observing and recording interactions in three-man groups composed of enlisted members of the US Air Force. Leadership was determined on the basis of total activity rates, sociometric and leadership ratings of co-participants, and individual intelligence quotients. The groups were then reformed, each person being combined with two new ones, a further three times. Again, ratings of leadership were taken and by the last session over half of the original 'leaders' were still at the 'top' on the leadership scores. Groups containing one of the 'leaders' were more productive in terms of the number of suggestions generated and the members were more satisfied with their membership. The results, however, were mixed in that, although there was some support for the idea of traits, usually reviewers of this literature have been extremely lukewarm about the idea. Bass (1981, p. 65) concluded that: 'The qualities, characteristics and skills required in a leader are determined to a large extent by the demands of the situation in which he is to function as a leader' Notwithstanding this, he did find 23 investigations that reported leaders to be brighter than their followers and only five reported no differences in intelligence between leaders and followers. None reported leaders to be less intelligent than their fellow group members. Mann (1959) reported that in 28 studies the overwhelming majority reported higher intelligence among leaders than followers. The bad news, however, for those who want simple predictors of complex social processes, is that the typical correlation between intelligence and leadership was quite low.

To come to conclusions as to the importance of traits is not easy because of the ambiguity of the research. Some traits have emerged but they have not been too conclusive. It has been shown that some people identified as having 'leadership abilities' do function as leaders in a variety of situations, but many others do not. This confusion can be resolved by looking at the practicality of leadership. If informal groups are considered then the leader who emerges is the one who can help the group achieve its goals. In most circumstances the person most able to do this would be the one who possessed most of the 'leadership'-type traits identified by researchers – relatively high intelligence, activeness, adaptability, self-confidence, among others.

More recently, the study of leadership has moved away from this approach and has looked more at the formal leadership which tends to occur in an organizational context. The emphasis here shifts away from personal authority and tends to adopt Gibb's (1969, p. 270) assertion that leadership involves 'influencing the actions of others in a shared approach to common or compatible goals'. Or, taking the words of Bryman (1986, p. 30) 'leadership is not simply a matter of effecting changes in other people's behaviour, but more to do with enhancing their voluntary compliance'.

The latter neatly links leadership with many of the other themes of this chapter. It reduces the emphasis on the influence of leaders themselves and replaces it with the view that leadership involves interaction, for if the 'leader' does not appear to be responsive to the people in the group, the legitimacy of his position as 'leader' may be considerably undermined. As we saw with other social influence processes, then, it is as inadequate to view leadership as a one-way process as it is to assume that conformity is a one-way force. The person who conforms at one time in one situation could in another situation be the leader influencing others. Additionally, the leader of a group may comply with the requirements of the group to maintain the status quo or to instigate change. As was argued earlier, the idea that some people are born conformers and others born followers is neither substantial nor particularly relevant. Within a short period of time the follower may turn into the leader, and the leader may at one and the same time both be the leader of the group and also conform to the group's expectations.

The studies of leadership traits proved unfruitful exactly in the same way as many other attempts to link a fixed, immutable, personality with behaviour have been. There is no more a leader type than there is a conforming, vulnerable type.

In the 1940s, leadership research began to concentrate on the different styles of leaders. The most famous early studies (the 'Iowa Childhood Studies') were concerned with creating different leadership climates to see what the effect was on groups of children. One well-known study (Lippitt and White, 1943) looked at the effects of three different types of leader on the group:

1. Authoritarian leaders determined all policy, dictated the techniques and activities of the group, and remained aloof from active group participation.
2. With the democratic leadership, all policies were discussed by the group and the leaders tried to be regular group members in spirit.
3. In the laissez-faire condition, the researchers admitted the leaders did not really act as leaders at all.

It is worth noting that this study had a number of limitations which restrict the application of the findings. First, the leaders, who were adults, were imposed on the groups of children. Second, the groups were not organized to strive towards any particular goal. Third, the leader's behaviour was rigidly prescribed by the experimenters so that they could not act in a manner which they considered best fitted the group's needs even within their allocated styles. Bearing these in mind, there was a tendency for the most work to be completed by the authoritarian groups and the least by the laissez-faire groups. The motivation to work tended to be greatest, however, in the democratic groups. Members of these groups were also happier and more self-reliant than those in the autocratic groups.

The nature of the task involved is very important. After all, most of us would be more likely to follow a mine-disposal expert through a minefield than an army cook. Fiedler (1969; 1972), using a scale based on the leaders' feelings towards their least preferred co worker (LPC), produced a categorization of leaders which has some resemblance to the authoritarian–democratic dimension. Leaders with a low opinion of their LPC, tended to be controlling, active and structuring, less tolerant of irrelevant comments, and produced less pleasant relationships within the group. Those with a higher opinion of their LPC were permissive, passive, relaxed, and less directive. It was found that with a structured task, leaders with a low opinion of their LPC were more effective when they were strong and assertive, but not so when they were of lower status than the rest of the group. Leadership style, then, simply cannot be examined in isolation, but must be viewed as both a causal and reactive aspect of an interaction between leader, task and subordinate.

The two-way nature of group performance and leadership style was demonstrated very convincingly by Barrow (1976), who found that subordinate performance affected leader behaviour. Barrow varied the experimental procedures such that some subordinates were good performers while others were poor performers. The complexity of the task was also varied. Poor subordinate performance tended to result in a more punitive, autocratic style with greater emphasis on production, but little consideration. Good performance on the part of subordinates had the opposite effects.

Concluding comments

A lot of ground has been covered in this chapter, with good reason. The most important thing that needs to be drawn from all of this is that the hackneyed description that people behave 'like sheep' has no part in the social psychology of social influence. It is unsound both empirically and theoretically. It is akin to describing people in terms of being either leaders or followers, which again is a pale version of the truth. In a way, if we concentrate on the idea of social change for a moment, we can perhaps begin to see why. Social change is a meaningless concept to apply if society is controlled by rigid and immutable power structures. Since social change does occur, we need to modify the picture in some way in order that the mechanisms of change can be incorporated into our understanding of the world. This does not seem to be very realistic if we assume that social influence and leadership are immutable one-way processes. Hopefully, what we have shown in this chapter is that the social influence process is a much more dynamic and interactive exchange than traditional social psychology emphasizes. By doing so, we will have shown that social psychological explanations once more are not only useful but essential to social behaviour and experience.

It is not possible fully to understand social phenomena in terms of the personality predispositions of the individual participants in a social situation. This is very clearly established in the case of leadership but applies equally in the case of other social influence processes. Perhaps there is more truth in the phrase 'it takes two to tango' than in the view that there is a trait of leadership potential or that the world divides into the socially weak and the socially powerful in a simple all-or-nothing manner. Unfortunately, much of social psychology has tended to work to the common-sense, but inadequate, model and many students are left almost believing that there is a single thing called 'conformity'.

In the area of social influence, there is clear evidence that an effective social psychology analysis has to respect the human potential of the individual participant to achieve anything near a full understanding of the situation. In this chapter we have looked at the reasons for this, including Jahoda's synthesis of the observable and the internal in classifying 'conformity' behaviour. This is important because it means that we cannot judge behaviour to be conforming without reference to a number of aspects of the situation. It has been stressed, furthermore, that what appears in lay terms to be conformity, in reality may be nothing of the sort. This is because of the virtually inbuilt requirement that for conformity to occur the individual has to move from believing or doing one thing to believing or doing something quite different. Many of the ways, however, in which people are highly similar do not involve this change in stance but merely the adoption of society's ways of doing things during socialization. This is not the same at all as being changed. Even in areas like this the adoption of clothing fashions, the idea of slavishly following the dictates of others, seems to be often less than adequate. After all, people may follow fashion because they *want* to, not because they are *forced* to. This is an important distinction when we try to apply the social psychology of social influence to everyday situations.

Briefly, the main points to remember are:

1. Social influence is an interactive process involving the needs and motives of those influenced as much as those doing the 'influencing'.
2. 'Conformity' refers to many distinct social processes which need to be examined in detail.
3. It is not useful to consider conformity and leadership as being personality traits of those who occupy these roles. In some situations they may be, but generally it requires a careful social psychological analysis of particular situations to understand how conformity takes place and how leaders and followers emerge.

5

INTERPERSONAL ATTRACTION

Those with whom we enjoy close relationships are paramount in most of our lives. They are the people with whom we are emotionally involved and with whom we usually want to spend time. We usually turn to them for comfort and help when life has dealt us a blow, and when we are down, upset or distressed. Our happiness is as much determined by these relationships as anything else. People who feel that something is wrong with their current close relationships tend to feel more psychological distress in the form of anxiety, depression and lower self-worth (Cramer, 1985; 1988). Remarkably, they are even likely to die younger than those finding fulfilment in their nearest and dearest. One would expect that social psychology could explain what leads to attraction and satisfaction in relationships which may, in its turn, help us to lead more fulfilling lives. This is a rather tall order, however. One has only to think of the vast range of different sorts of relationship which appear 'to work'. Even ignoring the divorce statistics which show currently that about a third of marriages will end in divorce, a majority of marriages last in spite of all the pressures and stresses they face.

Just what is it about close personal relationships which makes them both so important and emotionally supportive? They serve several functions which may explain why we struggle to maintain them despite the pain that they can cause:

1. *Security*. Knowing we can turn to someone on whom we can rely makes us more confident about exploring unknown situations. It helps to remember that there are people who care for us. People whose lives are under threat tend to think about their loved ones in order to help sustain themselves.

2. *Self-worth*. The knowledge that others value us almost no matter what, makes it easier to accept ourselves.
3. *Expressing feelings*. When we are upset, we find it comforting to discuss and express our feelings. There is more than a grain of truth in the phrase 'a trouble shared is a trouble halved'.
4. *Social comparison*. Comparing our views on a problem with those of people who care for us may help us to decide on what action to take. Having talked matters over may energize us to tackle the problem in an optimal manner.
5. *Advice elicitation*. Close others, with whom we are willing to share a little of ourselves, may provide inspiration as well as practical help.
6. *Sense of well-being*. Being with our favourite people may create a sense of feeling good or well-being. Having a good time may make us feel good about ourselves and distract our minds from pondering on difficulties.

All of this says what we get out of relationships but nothing about the people we like and why. After all, many of the people we loath and detest nevertheless have their own close personal relationships but not with us. Clearly there is an infinite variety of patterns of interpersonal attraction and it is obviously not dependent on absolute criteria of attractiveness which are held by everyone. Social psychology, as we shall see, has developed theoretical notions which help explain the individuality of interpersonal attraction while at the same time couching this individuality in universal theories.

It must be borne in mind that the interpersonal attraction has two basic dimensions. The first is *how much we like someone*, while the second is *how much we want to be with that person*. The former is an evaluative emotional component and the latter is an intentional behavioural one. This distinction is important since it rejects simplistic notions such as that people can be rated on a single dimension of good or bad. In everyday conversation we tend to express specific things we like or dislike about other people rather than overall, all-or-nothing, assessments of attractiveness. Wanting to be with someone may be as important a piece of information about the relationship as loving or liking them. In general the two aspects go together, though sometimes we seek the company of people that we fundamentally dislike. For example, we may want to be with someone because they are an interesting conversationalist, though we may find them most unpleasant in other respects.

It is useful to distinguish three types of 'interpersonal' relationship which differ in the degree to which we are aware of other people and expect to interact with them.

1. Awareness of the other person but *no expectation of interaction* (for example, seeing someone on television, or watching people strolling in the park).
2. Awareness of the other person and *expecting to meet them* (for example, looking at the details of an applicant on the short-list for a job or details of a would-be computer-date). This type of situation is more complicated than the first in that it may involve predictions of how we expect the other person will react to us.
3. Awareness of the other person together with *actually meeting them* face to face, particularly for the first time (for example, meeting the computer-date in a restaurant for a first date).

These three types of situation may represent the typical sequences or steps gone through when relationships are initiated. Suppose we enter a party or disco full of strangers. Our immediate reaction is probably to quickly survey those present in the hope of finding possible people to approach. Guessing (perhaps from their appearance) that one person will be friendly, we go over and talk to them. The pace of these approaches will vary from person to person, some getting no further than gazing around the room, too shy to even look someone in the eye, whereas others barely stop to think before initiating a conversation. These three essential steps in initiating a relationship help us break down a very complex process into the elements which make it easier to describe and comprehend. While identical underlying processes may operate in all three situations, they are not always immediately obvious in complex ones. Fewer constraints exist in the 'admiration from afar' situation. We may be more interested to understand why a couple are deeply in love with each other than why an adolescent has a mild crush on someone who does not even know they exist. However, sometimes the 'crush' may be the trigger to the first date and 'living happily ever after'.

In view of the complexity of interactive situations, it is not surprising that social psychologists have tended to study interpersonal *attraction* rather than close, interacting, relationships. There are at last three important aspects of interpersonal attraction which social psychologists need to explain:

1. The greater attraction to some people or to some characteristics than to others.
2. The intensity of interpersonal attraction, interpersonal avoidance, and rejection. What is the relationship between attraction and rejection? How do we account for the differences in the intensity of these experiences?
3. Changes in our feelings including the object of our feelings, their strength or intensity, and their direction.

An adequate theory of interpersonal attraction must address all of these. Furthermore, it ought to be stated in a way which allows it to be disproved. Simply put, concepts like 'apple' only have meaning if we can distinguish apples from non-apples, including pears, Kiwi fruit and bananas. If everything can be called an 'apple', then the word 'apple' has little value and mother's home-made apple pie might taste suspiciously of blackcurrant ice-cream. Similarly, if there is no situation for which a particular theory does not provide an explanation, then the theory cannot, in principle, be falsified. It would explain everything and nothing at the same time. More instructive and efficient is to think of situations or experiments capable of disproving an idea. Unfortunately, there is a human tendency to want to confirm rather than destroy our pet theories. When considering theories of interpersonal attraction, we should seek situations in which they may be wrong. It is also worth noting situations not satisfactorily explained by our theories. After all, theories should explain everyone's everyday experience, not some remote ritual on a far-away continent.

Theories of interpersonal attraction

Transactional analysis and interpersonal games

Unlike any of the purely social psychological theories which follow, the transactional analysis approach to interpersonal relationships has been adopted as a therapy seeking to improve our relationships with others. Groups using transactional analysis are common when trying to deal with 'sick' aspects of relationships. Notice the use of the word 'sick' which Eric Berne (1964), the major figure in transactional analysis, suggests is typical of social psychiatric approaches to promoting mental health rather than the detached, more neutral and uncommitted position usually found in pure social psychology and sociology.

A central assumption is that each of us have three distinct selves or ego states:

1. Ego states which resemble those of a *parent*. In these, the arguments, language, postures and attitudes are like those of a parent authority figure.
2. Ego states which resemble those of an *adult*. In these objective appraisals of situations are formed and individuals form judgements which are not unduly based on prejudices.
3. Ego states which resemble those of a *child*. These essentially represent the mode of relating in childhood.

Each of these is present in all of us to varying extents and at different times. It is less abnormal to demonstrate all three than to be invariably, say, in a parental ego state. All three are necessary for a healthy mental life. However, it is possible that, for example, the child ego state takes over in inappropriate circumstances and causes problems in relationships.

Since two people may each be operating in any one of these three *states* at one time, various patterns of interaction are possible: child–child, adult–adult, parent–parent, child–adult, adult–child, parent–child, child–parent, parent–adult, and adult–parent. Furthermore, this is complicated if one of the pair wishes to adopt a particular *pattern* and the other chooses to use a different one. So, for example, if one of the pair wishes for a playful child–child exchange while the other wishes for an adult–adult exchange this is clearly going to result in a strained relationship (a *crossed transaction*). A *complementary transaction* would be when the two individuals operate at levels appropriate to each other – this may be adult–adult, or adult–child. If one is upset and wishes to be cuddled like a child by the other acting in a parent state then this is complementary. However, if the partner chooses to act as an adult and fails to understand the problem realistically this is a crossed transaction since the child-like needs are not met.

Another 'layer' to the exchange is added by an individual operating at two different levels at the same time – that is, there is a 'hidden' significance to what is being said. Take the following example based on Berne (1964):

Salesman: This one is better but you can't afford it.
Customer: That's the one I'll take.

On the face of it the salesman's comment is an adult, unprejudiced comment but underneath it really aims to bring the irresponsible child out of the customer so they impulsively buy despite being short of cash. It is not intended to encourage the adult response 'can I have a discount?'. As it is likely that the salesman is aware of what he is doing the exchange may be seen as a *manoeuvre*.

Unconscious exchanges such as these are essentially *games*. Berne identifies many such games. An example of a game is 'first degree "Rapo" ' or kiss-off. At a party Julie makes it very clear to Jack that she is available. She tells him she is alone and that her marriage is all but over. She does a little pouting and stands very, very close. However, her objective is not to 'get' Jack but the pleasure she gets from being pursued by a man. As soon as he commits himself by perhaps asking for a date she drops him flat – she has by then got all that she ever wanted from him. Superficially this may at first appear as an adult–adult interaction; it is only later that the child-seeking attention reveals itself.

Criticisms of transactional analysis

1. It fails to meet the criteria relating to a testable theory. There do not seem to be any circumstances which disprove the theory since it is based on subjective interpretations which can be very idiosyncratic to the people involved. We can easily find hidden significances in interactions which are not necessarily really there.
2. On the positive side, it does recognize features of human social nature which are often ignored by social psychologists. For example, people are seen as active manipulators of situations rather than rigid initiators and responders. Furthermore, the content of the inter-action is a primary concern as is its meaning. These emphases are missing from the more formal theories following.

Attraction towards others: the reinforcement-affect model

There is an old adage which suggests that birds of a feather flock together, the implication being that people seek out the company of people similar to themselves. Social psychological research, from 1906 onwards, has shown that friends and married couples tend to be rather similar in terms of their attitudes, opinions and values compared with the same people but randomly paired together by the experimenter. There are even hints in the literature that happily-married couples are more similar than unhappily-married couples or divorced couples. Why should attitudes be similar in close relationships? Does it mean that we are attracted to those who share our ideas, or that we change to be like the people we like, or do the people we like help us change our ideas?

Byrne (Byrne, 1971; Clore and Byrne, 1974) emphasizes that we are actually attracted to those with whom we agree (though this is not to deny the other possibilities). The underlying idea is that we are attracted to those who 'reinforce' us in some way. Although there are many different potential sources of reward in interpersonal relations, Byrne suggests that we like those who share our views of the world because they confirm our position and do not undermine our cosy perspective. People who see the world in a very different way from us may be tolerated within reason but they tend to make us feel uncomfortable and anxious. Much of Byrne's work depends for theoretical justification on Festinger's (1954) ideas about social comparison processes. This theory argues that we have a need to evaluate ourselves in relation to the relevant characteristics of others. By comparing ourselves with others (in terms of attitudes, values, income, morality, and so on), we are able to develop socially accurate impressions of ourselves and our environment which help our psychological survival in a hostile and threatening world. We rely on others substantially to provide our understanding of the world and ourselves. In both the social and the physical worlds it is essential to find out whether the beliefs that we hold are correct. So if in a foreign country we wish to know which foods are safe to eat and which may be risky we can, broadly speaking, do one of two things. Either we can rush around eating everything and note which make us violently ill (for example, eat seafood in June and July) or make decisions based on the collective or individual knowledge of the local people (who may tell us not to eat shellfish unless there is an 'r' in the month). Since it is often easier and safer to find out from what others think, frequently we test our ideas against social rather than physical reality. If we believe that New York is a dangerous place and feel that we would rather not go there, how much better that our friends agree with us than that we go to New York to find out by being clubbed to death on the streets.

Naturally, for many aspects of our social world, there is no single, universal attitude, value or belief which is shared by everyone. Some people think capital punishment is wrong, whereas others believe that it would cure a lot of ills in society. Our attitudes, beliefs and values tell us a lot about who we are and how to relate to the world. It is not easy to know for certain that they are right or wrong, so how much more psychologically comforting it is if we find that those who surround us actually agree with us. They are satisfying in that they do nothing to shake our confidence in the world that we have personally created for ourselves.

The trouble with investigating Byrne's hypothesis (that we like people who share our attitudes and opinions) is that we cannot simply look at attitude similarity and interpersonal attraction as they exist in groups of people in the real world. If holding the same attitude and being attracted to particular people do correlate in these circumstances, this could just as well be because of attitude changes resulting from attraction as because of attraction being the result of attitude similarity. Furthermore, they may be similar in other respects (such as age or social class) which determine both greater attitude similarity and attraction. (People of the same age or social class tend to have more similar attitudes and are more likely to be friends in any case.)

To prove that interpersonal attraction is the *result* of attitudes being alike (and not vice versa), it is necessary to vary attitude similarity experimentally. Byrne (1971) did so in a study which asked people their opinions on a variety of topics ranging from belief in God to enjoyment of Westerns. The experiment was explained as being concerned with accuracy in forming impressions of people about whom we have very little information. Subjects saw the replies of complete strangers on attitude questionnaires in which the strangers had indicated their opinions. They were told to form an impression of the strangers from this and then asked to indicate how much they liked them and would enjoy working with them. The experimenter varied the 'strangers'' view on the questionnaire to be similar or dissimilar to those of the subject. Despite its artificiality, the advantage of the procedure is the ease with which causal links between similarity and liking could be investigated. Byrne, his colleagues, and others carried out numerous studies using this experimental procedure (which he called the 'attraction paradigm').

The extent to which the stranger was liked was not primarily dependent on the simple total of the number of attitudes held in common, but much more on the ratio of shared to non-shared attitudes. A stranger sharing the same attitudes on two out of two issues on the questionnaire was more liked than one who shared attitudes on four out of eight topics since the first stranger shows 100 per cent agreement whereas the second stranger only 50 per cent. Interpersonal attraction also relates to the importance of the topics on which the attitudes are shared. The more important the topic was to the subject, the greater the effect of similarity on liking. Even more crucial, though, was the stranger's attitudes towards the experimental subject. If the stranger thought well of the subject this had a greater effect on liking that stranger than other attitudes. So interpersonal attraction is not simply a function of the proportion of attitudes held in common but also their importance. The general relationship between attitude similarity and interpersonal attraction has been found in various groups of people – students, schoolchildren, women clerical workers, hospitalized alcoholics, and schizophrenic patients. Furthermore, similar results have been obtained internationally including not just Western countries such as Canada and the United States, but 'Third World' countries such as Mexico and India.

While so far we have concentrated on the rewards coming from attitude similarity between people, the reinforcement-affect model is much wider than this. It includes any positive or negative reinforcements found in relationships. In other words, characteristics in relationships such as physical attractiveness or personality may also provide the rewards which lead to attraction. Stated in its broadest terms, the reinforcement-affect model of interpersonal attraction is based on the following four assumptions:

1. Aspects of the environment are evaluated as being either good or bad. This has obvious survival value in that it alerts us to what is harmful and beneficial in our environment (physical or social).
2. Beneficial events create good feelings, while harmful effects make us feel bad.

3. Events which make us feel good are liked and those which make us feel bad are disliked.

4. Events which have no effect on our mood, if they are regularly associated with positive events, will eventually make us feel good on their own. Those previously 'neutral' events (which are regularly associated with negative events) eventually produce bad feelings on their own. These associations are learned through a process of classical conditioning. So people associated with events making us feel good are liked while those associated with events causing bad feelings are disliked.

Obviously it takes a very careful analysis to understand what the rewarding properties of any event will be for any particular individual.

Criticisms of the reinforcement-affect model
Earlier three criteria were suggested for judging the adequacy of any theory of interpersonal attraction. The reinforcement-affect model deals with all of them.

1. The direction and intensity of feeling depends on the proportion and importance of the positive and negative events which are associated with people.

2. The person one is most attracted to depends on who is most consistently associated with the greatest proportion of positive and important events.

3. Any significant changes in reinforcements will bring about corresponding changes in feelings.

This, however, does not mean that the theory provides a complete account of interpersonal attraction. Two issues are not addressed or accounted for sufficiently. The first of these is *interaction and attraction*. Because of the methods he employs Byrne presents a very static view of interpersonal attraction. His methodology had people aware of another person but not expecting to meet them. This is the simplest interpersonal attraction situation – 'attraction from afar'. The theory does nothing to deal with interacting individuals between which interchanges of information occur which allow them to uncover their partner's attitudes. Of course, once interaction has been initiated there may be no effect of attitude similarity on attraction since other features take over as determinants of attraction.

The second problem is *the looseness of the concept of reinforcement*. Reinforcement and association with pleasant and unpleasant events are such general concepts that they are of little practical value in predicting people's feelings. The question is what sorts of event experienced in what sorts of conditions produce reinforcement. Without firm ideas one is left being able to explain what has happened in the past (Jim is attracted to John because John reminds Jim of his father – an association with a reinforcement) but unable to predict with any precision whether Jim will be attracted to Fred who he has just met. Consequently, it is difficult to find examples of current relationships which cannot be explained by the theory. For example, we might explain the case of a woman who loves a man who abuses her and is generally unkind on the basis that he must have redeeming features which give her pleasure. How else could she love him? However, without knowing precisely what things are reinforcing to the woman, it is sloppy to assume that they must be present though it is very easy to imagine that they must be. After all, she may believe that she has to love a man to have sex with him and it is this sentiment she is expressing in her 'love' rather than any intrinsic reinforcement in the relationship.

Interacting couples: interdependence theory

Attraction is only a small aspect of relationships and not always necessary in interaction between people. However, we tend to assume that it is necessary in friendships and the next step after attraction is to try and explain the nature of the interrelationship that may emerge. This is obviously a major task since interaction between couples incorporates most social psychological processes and so it is necessary to concentrate on particular aspects. Inevitably, a single theory concerned with the development of relationships over a period of time cannot be very specific and may well appear to be extremely abstract. One way of theorizing about interrelating couples is to conceive of the process in terms of the rewards each partner receives from the relationship. It is reasonable to presume that if these rewards are insufficient then this might result in the break-up of the relationship. Obviously rewards stated in these general terms can only deal with the merest skeleton of the relationship, the complexity of which should not be forgotten merely for the convenience of theory. The following letter from the 'problems' page of a teenage girls' magazine (*My Guy*, no. 491, 7 November 1987) illustrates this very well:

> I am writing to ask you for advice. I am sixteen and there is a lad that I like a lot. The problem is that when he comes to my house, which is every night, he kisses and cuddles me. He is very kind and gentle with me. I think he likes me but he has never asked me out. What should I do? Should I make the first move or should I let him make it?

Clearly the initial stage of interpersonal attraction has taken place, and equally obviously some relationship is developing between the two. Nevertheless, the girl is not happy – so bothered that she seeks advice.

However, at a distance the nature of her unhappiness is a little bizarre. She has this boy who is making sexual advances to her, she admits she likes him, she thinks that he likes her, but still she is not happy with this. What he is failing to do is ask her out which, for her, is an essential step without which the relationship cannot develop. Why it is so important we can only conjecture about (perhaps she thinks that dating is essential to courtship or maybe she wants to show off to her friends that she can attract a boy) but it is nevertheless a major stumbling block. Predicting precisely what is going to be rewarding for a particular person at a particular time in a relationship is not easy – we can say with more certainty that some things will be rewarding and not others and what these are will vary from person to person, time to time, and culture to culture. What is important is that some aspects will be rewarding and others not. Consequently, we have to generate rather all-embracing theories of interpersonal relationships.

Thibaut and Kelley's (1959) interdependence theory differs from Byrne's reinforcement-affect model in being concerned with the development of relationships between two or more interrelating people. To keep everything simple it is necessary to concentrate on the simplest case of the developing *two-person* relationship.

Imagine two young people, Pam and Pete, at a party. Their eyes meet across the crowded room. What do they do? Is it love at first sight? do both smile meaningfully? Do they both look away in embarrassment? Does one smile while the other looks away? According to interdependence theory, both should try and maximize their *outcomes* achieved in the situation. 'Outcome' is a technical term and refers to the net result of the rewards received in the situation minus the costs incurred. That is, the pleasant things less the unpleasant things. Costs include the effort, the anxiety and the embarrassment involved in doing something, and the rewards forgone in choosing a particular course of action.

It is useful to represent what might happen by means of 'an interaction–outcome matrix'. This simply records the gains and losses for each party in an interaction between two people. People differ in terms of the magnitude of rewards and costs to be gained so the matrix would differ according to the circumstances and the actors. Again for simplicity's sake, assume that Pam and Pete are only able to do one of two things – to smile or to ignore the other. In the matrix, the columns refer to the two alternative courses of action available to Pete, whereas the rows refer to the two alternative courses of action for Pam. Because Pete and Pam probably have different gains or losses, it is necessary to enter different values for the two of them. So the outcomes for Pete are the numbers found in the top half of each cell, those in the lower half are outcomes for Pam. In Figure 5.1 the magnitude of the number indicates the size of the outcome, the positive sign means a rewarding outcome,

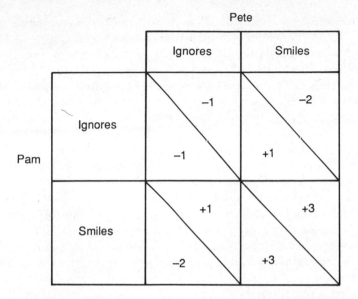

Figure 5.1   An Example of an Interaction–Outcome Matrix

and the negative sign an unpleasant one. This gives four possible combinations of ignoring and smiling: both ignore each other, both smile at the other, Pam smiles but Pete ignores her, and Pete smiles but Pam ignores him.

Figure 5.1 tells us that both Pete and Pam feel slightly unhappy if they ignore each other but feel happiest if they both smile. Where only one smiles the outcome for the smiler tends to be slightly unhappy whereas that for the other tends to be slightly happy. Since, according to the theory, people try to maximize outcomes in any situation, Pete and Pam may both feel safer ignoring the other rather than risk being hurt. Whatever happens at this stage affects subsequent events. If both ignore each other then the chance of future interaction is reduced since this signals disinterest. If they both smile, future interaction is more likely since this in itself is rewarding and indicates further rewards to come. (Of course, there are other aspects of the situation which may influence which actions are followed – Pam may be less inclined to risk being slightly hurt if Pete is not her type or if she is with her jealous husband, for example).

Assuming that both smile and approach each other, things may not proceed smoothly. Pete may say something about her dress which annoys Pam. To retrieve the situation, Pete would have to try to make Pam feel good. Clearly, what Pete does has an effect on Pam and vice versa. In other words, their behaviours are interdependent.

Interdependence theory draws a distinction between being *attracted to* and being *dependent on* another person. *Attraction* is defined somewhat technically as the difference between the current outcome (net rewards) of a relationship and past outcomes. As long as the current outcome is greater than past outcomes, attraction occurs. Otherwise dissatisfaction will result and the other person becomes less attractive. *Dependency*, though similar, is crucially different. It is the difference between the outcome of our current relationship and the outcomes possible from other relationships. Unable to obtain a better outcome from other relationships, we are dependent on our current relationship for pleasure. However, if able to do better elsewhere, we cease to be dependent on our current relationship. Previous experiences of relationships will affect our judgements. A previous pleasant outcome raises expectations so that greater rewards are necessary to produce the same satisfaction. (Perhaps the failure of many widowed people to establish a new close relationship comes from the high expectations developed out of a satisfactory marriage.)

This leads us to suggest that there are categories of relationship to be defined by different types of past experience. Althought Thibaut and Kelley do not do this, they can be thought of as four successive stages in the development of relationships:

- STAGE 1: *Attraction without dependency*. The outcome of our present relationship is positive but less than we could obtain elsewhere. Typical of this would be a first date with someone we have just met.
- STAGE 2: *Attraction with dependency*. Our present outcome is greater than both our previous relationships and other available ones. This is typical of a couple newly in love, having only eyes for each other.
- STAGE 3: *Dependency without attraction*. Here no better alternative can be seen. In this situation, our present outcome is less than we have received in the past but greater than we can expect elsewhere. This is typical of when a relationship goes stale.
- STAGE 4: *Neither attraction nor dependency*. At this stage, the outcome of the present relationship is less than those of past and alternative ones. This is typical of when deciding to end a present relationship and 'entering the market' for a new one. Another divorce statistic hits the dust!

Note that in all of this, attraction is not assumed to be based on some absolute level of net rewards, but on outcomes relative to past ones. In other words, if the present relationship's outcome is negative but less so than previous ones, then the result is attraction towards the partner. Similarly, if the current outcome is less positive than those of previous relationships, the result is lack of attraction towards the partner. How satisfying the present relationships is depends on previous ones.

Criticisms of interdependence theory

1. There is no objective way of calculating the rewards and costs associated with any course of action, so it is difficult to estimate what the outcomes should be. After all, many people involved in a relationship may be very undecided about its true value to them.

2. In theory at least, the task of weighing up the value of relationships seems enormously complicated. So many different things need to be taken into account. It is difficult to recognize the process of consciously calculating the outcome of all of the minutiae of a relationship. But if outcomes are not consciously calculated then how are we to investigate what people's 'outcomes' are? Thibaut and Kelly suggest that the process is really simpler than it appears since people have limited options for appropriate behaviour in any particular situation. This seems to imply that what happens in most social situations is fairly consistent – bound by rules rather than calculations of gains and losses. (Perhaps the tendency to seek a divorce as a consequence of marital infidelity demonstrates such rule-following rather than outcome assessment.) Interaction–outcome matrices may be most useful for analysing unfamiliar situations such as meeting someone for the first time or when a major decision has to be made.

3. Although conceptually it is easy to differentiate present from past outcomes, just what constitutes a present outcome or a past outcome is unclear in practice. What separates the two? Do we compare our present relationship with someone as it is now with the moment we first met them? Do we compare our current relationship with the way it was ten minutes ago? Furthermore, what is it about the past relationships that are remembered? Do we remember good or the bad things according to whether the present situation is pleasing or not? The enormous complexity of this hinders applying the theory precisely to any relationships.

4. Finally, how do satisfactory outcomes produce attraction? This is not as simple as would appear. For example, a person may be doing all of the 'right' things in initiating an interaction – looking interested, smiling, standing close, and so on. However, the person they are interacting with may, in spite of feeling good, decide that they are a flirt and seek out others to interact with. Unless we can state more clearly how outcomes are determined, the theory does not provide a more adequate account of interpersonal attraction than did reinforcement-affect theory.

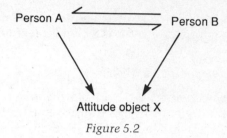

Figure 5.2

Thinking in relationships: interpersonal balance theory

Interpersonal balance theory (Newcomb, 1961) concentrates on the way relationships are perceived, and, as such, it is a cognitive theory as it concerns thinking processes. The basic proposition of the theory is that people like to see the world in a consistent (balanced) way. Inconsistency in our cognitions motivates us to create a state of balance by changing either our thoughts or behaviour. Imagine a woman who loves a man who beats her appallingly. If she believes that he loves her, then the fact that he is violent towards her is inconsistent with his loving her. Something would have to happen to remove the inconsistency, the theory argues. She could do many things – perhaps it is most comfortable for her to decide that he is the product of a violent father and he cannot help being violent. In this way the abuse has no bearing on his love for her.

It is not intended to give the impression that people cannot cope with inconsistency (there is plenty of evidence that they can). Newcomb wrote when the belief in cognitive consistency as an overriding motive was strong among social psychologists. However, it is worthwhile pointing out some of the circumstances which might encourage the restoration of cognitive balance. The basic circumstances dealt with by the theory can be expressed schematically as shown in Figure 5.2. Person A has a relationship with person B (which can be evaluated as positive or negative overall) and vice versa. Both have attitudes towards the attitude object X which can be evaluated as positive or negative overall. Essentially the idea is the familiar one that attitude similarity produces attraction. But, of course, things are not quite that simple. There is greater effort to achieve balance in the following circumstances: the stronger our attraction is to the other person; the more important the attitude is to us; and to the extent to which the object of the attitude has the same consequences for both parties (if the consequences favour one person then the results of holding that attitude are unequal – if a couple both like to dominate and they have plenty of children, employees, and pets to boss, then both of them can dominate as much as they like and the situation remains balanced, but if there is

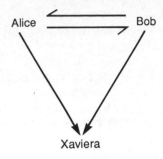

Figure 5.3

no one to dominate but the other, then the situation would be unbalanced since only one of them could achieve that need).

Imagine a couple, Alice and Bob, and the exotically named Xaviera who is known by both of them and is the object of their attitudes. The basic structure is shown in Figure 5.3. For Alice there are three features of the situation which have to be considered: how attracted she is to Bob; her attitude to Xaviera; and what she thinks Bob's attitude to Xaviera is. If Alice likes both Bob and Xaviera a state of balance exists *if* she believes that Bob likes Xaviera too. However, imagine that Alice thinks that Bob does not like Xaviera – this would be imbalanced, (or what Newcomb prefers to call a 'state of intrapersonal or psychological strain'). To reduce imbalance something has to change. Alice could do one of several things:

1. Adopt Bob's attitude – that is, decide that she does not really like Xaviera.
2. Reappraise Bob's attitude – that is, decide that she has got him all wrong and that really he does like her.
3. Change the importance of his attitude – that is, decide that she so seldom sees Xaviera that it does not matter if Bob likes Xaviera or not.
4. Change the relevance of his attitude – that is, Bob does not mind her having her own friends and never interferes.
5. Change her attitude to Bob – that is, decide that he is a bit boring and his views do not matter.

Obviously there are many variants of these five strain-reducing strategies.

This is so far to consider Alice's point of view alone. Incorporating Bob's viewpoint makes things more complicated (we are ignoring the final complication in all of this in that since Xaviera is also a person, not an inanimate or abstract attitude object, she will also have attitudes). Taking both Bob and Alice together, there is a total of three *pairs* of related attitudes: how attracted Alice and Bob are to each other; what Alice and Bob's individual attitudes to Xaviera are; and what Alice and Bob think each other's attitudes to Xaviera are. Imbalance exists when there is a discrepancy within one or more of these pairs of attitudes. Imbalance motivates efforts to reduce discrepancies. These might involve changes in attitude towards Xaviera, each other, the importance of sharing attitudes about Xaviera, or the importance of Xaviera. If a discrepancy exists between what one of them *thinks* the other believes and what the other *actually* believes, then this may eventually become obvious and balance therefore restored. So, if Alice thinks that Bob dislikes Xaviera when he in fact likes her, Alice may well come to realize this and balance is achieved.

Clearly Newcomb believes that interpersonal attraction and attitude similarity are interdependent. The greater the attraction to someone, the more likely are our attitudes to move in line with theirs. Similarly there is stronger attraction to someone who expresses the same attitudes as ourselves, particularly if these attitudes are important to us. (A rabid feminist will hardly be keen on a mouse-like housewife.) Some of these ideas were tested on two groups of male students, initially strangers to each other, who were put together in a house and studied over a four-month period. In line with his predictions concerning balance and strain, Newcomb found that the more attracted a student was to another student, the more the student *perceived* that person as having the same attitudes towards the others in the house as himself. Furthermore, the more closely two men *actually* agreed about the attractiveness of the others, the more strongly they would be attracted to each other. Additionally, the more that the students got to know each other over the course of time, the stronger was the relationship between agreeing with each other and liking each other – in the first few weeks of acquaintance, there was little relationship but later on there was a strong relationship between agreement and mutual attraction when the friendships had become consolidated.

Criticisms of balance theory

1. It does not explain why we have positive and negative attitudes in the first place. Why are we attracted to some things or people, but not to others?
2. Since balance can be restored in many different ways, it is difficult to predict precisely what will happen in any given situation.
3. The appropriate level of analysis of attitudes is not defined. Imagine the last chocolate in a box being shared by two lovers. Newcomb suggests that in this kind of situation strain might exist because

only one of the two people could have the last sweet. However, whether or not this is so depends on the exact nature of the two people's attitudes to chocolates and the situation. If one person only likes nut chocolates while the other likes any kind, should the chocolate happen to be a strawberry one, then no strain exists. Alternatively, if one of them believes that it is better to give than to receive while the other one is selfish, again there is no strain. In other words, we may have to refer to more specific attitudes or to other attitudes to determine whether or not there will be a strain in a particular situation.

4. Similarly, by reducing human interaction to positive and negative signs, substantial issues to do with the content of interaction are lost. For example, if Alice likes Bob and she also likes Xaviera, if she found Bob and Xaviera in bed together this should be a balanced situation since Bob has demonstrated his liking for Xaviera. Something suggests that this interpretation is a little wide of the mark! In many cases Alice would immediately dislike Xaviera, and either Bob as well or insist that he stops liking Xaviera. Human conduct is governed by rules over and above simple mathematical equations. (One can detect a hint of Heider (see Chapter 7) in Newcomb's work.)

5. The theory presents a fairly passive view of people in relationships which does not accord with reality. Yet another way of reducing strain which the theory does not consider is to attempt to alter the other person's point of view through argument, discussion, threats, rows, nagging or any other method we know people use to attempt to change situations. This suggests a more active model of imbalanced situations – but, of course, one which does not reside in the minds of individuals which the cognitive approach tends to encourage.

Concluding comments

In this chapter we have discussed some major theories of interpersonal relations. Clore and Byrne's (1974) reinforcement-affect model, Thibaut and Kelley's interdependence theory, and Newcomb's balance theory, together with Berne's theory of transactional analysis. The reinforcement-affect model postulates that interpersonal attraction is a function of the proportion and importance of positive reinforcements that are associated with someone. Interdependence theory, on the other hand, states that it results from perceiving the outcome from the present interaction with someone as exceeding that received in the past. Balance theory argues that it depends on the perceived similarity, importance and relevance of an attitude that is held in common. It has been suggested that none of these theories as presently formulated provides a complete and satisfactory explanation of interpersonal liking. Perhaps this is not surprising given the complexity and the difficulty of the task. None the less, each of these theories has suggested a partial solution to the problem.

However, the theories tend to demonstrate a shared concern with abstracting social relationships down to quasi-mathematics – whether this is degrees of attitude similarity, the signs of attitudes towards others, or the values given to outcomes of interpersonal interactions. This contrasts markedly with the way in which other disciplines have dealt with relationships (for example, sociology) where the content of the interaction and the nature of the people taking part are given more careful consideration. Transactional analysis, as we saw, provides in many ways the fullest picture, despite its limitations.

6

CONFLICT AND CO-OPERATION:
Constructive and destructive forces in social behaviour

A central issue in the social psychological definition of human nature involves the destructive and constructive stresses in social life. Human societies attempt to regulate and control many things which threaten the community. Violence at the extreme level profoundly affects the security of the social order. This does not mean that violence is simply barred since cultures handle violence in a number of secure ways. Ritualistic violence is common: violence as a public spectacle is frequent, as exemplified by gladiators, boxers and wrestlers; and violence has always been a common theme of plays, literature and mass media. While states as well as criminal sub-cultures have used violence as a means of internal social control, by and large, ideologically communities find violence between individuals abhorrent and deviant. At the same time, there are factors which seem to bind society together, to unite people, and to promote considerate and caring interaction. Among these are the many kinds of co-operative act which give cohesion to society.

Violence and co-operation cannot be simply dismissed as diametrically opposed aspects of human nature. We need to understand why and how they occur. Clearly these are issues which bear strongly on the social psychological conceptualization of human nature. Furthermore, one must be wary about assuming that violence in itself is necessarily maladaptive or that co-operation is necessarily good. This may seem odd and unacceptable but in the context of discussion of stability and change in society it makes more sense. In part aggression is bad in that we have been encouraged to view it as a leftover from our animal origins, and as such, it is a manifestation of the failure of socialization processes.

But it goes without saying that, in many cultures, aggression is used to bring about social change. This may be in the overthrow of a government, or the forcible eviction of a shopkeeper holding up 'progress' in a redevelopment area. Violence also prevents change. All of these things happen in cultures which we describe as 'advanced'. Co-operative social bonds may similarly work to prevent change – the Luddites who broke up machinery to slow down the pace of modernization did so in part through motives of co-operation. It is a narrowly biological or psychological conception of aggression which obscures how violence and aggression, no matter how much they might be regretted, are integral rather than peripheral.

Aggression and violence

One of the achievements of social psychology has been in extending explanations of aggression and violence away from merely being reflections of the inner state of individuals. Theories of aggression have moved outwards towards the level of interactions between groups and cultures. By and large, however, everyday explanations have remained grounded in individuals and individual responsibility.

Powerful phrases are common in day-to-day language which reflect the belief that in some way aggression and violence are built into our nature. 'The mark of Cain' and 'War is in our genes' are good examples. More mundanely we hear 'It's a dog-eat-dog world', 'It's the law of the jungle', 'We're just animals really', 'The killer instinct', and even read headlines like 'Animals attack defenceless pensioner'. Such words are not simply empty, unthinking phrases, they are explanatory tools for the mass of ordinary people in our culture. Their inadequacy ultimately determines how ineffective we are in understanding the role and functions of violence and aggression in society. We panic over what is to be done about violence and shelter in the belief that we are dealing with the inexplicable. Our common-sense explanations are clearly not good enough as we are frequently brought to despair by violence which is thereby beyond all explanation and understanding.

Urban riots have shocked our Western cultures in recent years. People find it extremely difficult even to conceive of such events as being anything other than irrational. Reading of a child tortured by its parents and finally murdered, we feel unable to understand other than in terms of the psychopathology of the murderers. We find violence easiest to deal with if we compartmentalize it as being one of the baser instincts of man. Not surprisingly, we have sometimes even found it preferable to ignore violence or hide it. A very significant example of this is that society has only gradually and very recently acknowledged the extent of violence within the family. Indeed the family is the most dangerous place to be. There is almost a paradox in that we believe violence and aggression to be part of our make-up, but are shocked when we discover its extent even in the most 'refined' strata of society.

Perhaps it is easy to see why violence and aggression are the object of generalized and unanalytic concern. After all, the control of aggression is an important objective of early socialization. Toddlers are punished for grabbing the cat's tail, for spitting at siblings, and for biting and scratching. We are punished as adolescents for verbal aggression towards our parents. Berkowitz (Berkowitz and Rawlings, 1963) has written of 'aggression anxiety', the discomfort and distress we feel about even the prospect of being aggressive.

The social psychologist cannot afford to leap at simple solutions of the sort just described. Unfortunately, such simplistic solutions concerning human violence and aggression abound and are often linked with recommendations for social policy which are most kindly seen as untaxing. While most people can blame television, lack of discipline in the home or school, the lack of good old-fashioned policing, and alcohol for much of the violence in society, the social psychologist needs to avoid scapegoating easy targets and over-simplifying complex social issues.

Explanations of human aggression range throughout most of the spectrum of social psychological approaches to explaining human activity. Not all of them by any means are the work of social psychologists and there has been a good deal of influence from disciplines on the periphery of social psychology. As such, explanations of aggression can be seen as an object lesson in social psychological theorizing.

Biological explanations of aggression

Ethology

The biological approach to human aggression is fundamental and its popularity in the public mind is evidence of the appeal of instant single-dimensional explanations of very complex social phenomena such as violent crime, warfare, and urban unrest and rioting. In the 1960s there emerged the ethological view of human nature. Perhaps the most popular approach of all has been the work of Desmond Morris, in books like *The Naked Ape* (1966). But there have been others, especially those of Richard Ardrey (1966) and Konrad Lorenz (1963). The underlying model is very familiar. It is that one can take studies of animal behaviour in its natural context, decide on the underlying determinants of this behaviour, and then generalize to human societies and individual human behaviour. This, then, is the ethological approach.

Considerable enthusiasm may be aroused for ethology as a scientific approach to understanding the ways in which the animals interact and live in natural environments (as opposed to, for instance, the way in which psychologists have studied the behaviour of rats in artificial environments such as mazes since time immemorial). However, intellectually it is a giant step from this to saying that animal ethology has a lot to offer our understanding of human beings. A simple, but telling, exercise is to reverse the argument and ask why we do not abandon ethology and generalize from studies of humans in their natural environment to explain how animal communities are structured and operate. What would one say about the social organization of ospreys, chimpanzees or field mice on the basis of an intimate observation of the human being in its environment? One would be reluctant to say much, arguing that human society is too complex to allow any generalization to simpler animals. It is almost like trying to explain how a slide rule or log tables work on the basis of knowing how computers work. In addition, one would be disinclined even to generalize from lion communities to alligator communities. Unfortunately, there seems to have been no reluctance to generalize speculatively from a variety of animal to human beings.

Perhaps the most compelling concept to come from ethology and be applied to people is that of territorality. This is the idea that some animals need a certain amount of physical space within which to operate. If this space is breached by others of the same species (especially males) the animal will act aggressively in an attempt to exclude them. Given that war is often the result of the invasion of territory and that the inner-city areas where physical space is at a premium seem to be especially violent, superficially there is great appeal in assuming that humans are territorial. Certainly Richard Ardrey (1966) advocated it strongly. There are two big problems with such an assumption: first, the fact that territorality is by no means universal in the animal kingdom, and the related issue of whether it is universal in the primates which are biologically and ecologically closest to early human beings, such as chimpanzees and gorillas (Crook, 1968); and second, whether there is any justification for assuming that territorality is more powerful than cultural forces which may act against it. There is a simple parallel in this second problem: by and large human beings are biologically contructed for at least a partially carnivorous diet, but for large sections of humankind major cultural forces associated with religion determine a vegetarian existence.

It so happens that this idea of territorality is also easily confused with the ideas of a personal physical or psychological space which restricts closeness in human beings. By not maintaining a distinction between the two it becomes easier to slip into the ethologists' assumptions. Personal space is easily demonstrated by the discomfort produced if one gets into a virtually empty railway carriage and insists on sitting next to the only other passenger. The idea of personal space is clearly a social psychological concept as it deals with relationships between our individual psychologies and other people in our social environment. It has two dimensions. The first is the purely physical one which involves issues such as the distances people keep between themselves during their interaction, whether touching is permitted, and similar 'proxemic' patterns. The other dimension is the psychological one which would include how much psychological intimacy is permitted between people – how much of their private thoughts, feelings, and fears they are willing to reveal to others.

Territorality seems to have only a superficial resemblance to the latter and dubious resemblance to the former. It is largely determined by basic biological needs and preserves a domain for feeding, for example. There is no suggestion that the robin or any other territorial animal is keeping secret doubts and fears to itself. The physical dimension of personal space similarly cannot be equated with territorality. Personal space varies tremendously from sex to sex, culture to culture, and situation to situation. What might be acceptable personal space to an Italian might seem oppressively intimate for the more reserved English.

It might be argued at this point that there are other reasons why the idea of territoriality should not be lightly dismissed. A disproportionate amount of violence seems to occur in the crowded inner-city areas and it is common knowledge in many big cities that there are areas to avoid. Overcrowding, then, seems to be related to crime and violence. This can be interpreted to mean that crowding is bad for people. Measures of population density per household or per room in inner-city areas have worried some and concern has been expressed about delinquency rates among inhabitants of high-rise blocks of flats. However, it does not follow from this that crowding is the direct or indirect cause of violent and criminal behaviour. Indeed, evidence suggests that we are carelessly using lay explanations of dubious validity if we make a connection.

Factually, there is no relationship between population density (and similar measures of crowding) and a whole range of measures of social pathology (including crime and suicide) – that is, *if* one makes allowances for factors associated with living in crowded inner-city areas which are known to be associated with social pathologies. Studies of urban change show that inner-city areas are not particularly attractive to people and so are cheaper. Because of their cheapness the poor are more likely to live in them. Given that poverty is (statistically) associated with crime and overcrowding, it is not surprising to find that the relationship between social pathology and population density disappears when income is allowed for.

One only has to take the example of immigrants from Bangladesh in London who are forced to live in the most overcrowded conditions but are part of one of the least violent and least criminal sectors of society in order further to appreciate the inadequacy of the ethological approach. This example clearly constitutes a major blow against the argument that we have an inbuilt territorial instinct which society interferes with at its peril.

Eyebrows might be raised at this point because, as they could rightly claim, research has shown some quite dramatic changes in animals placed in very overcrowded conditions. The glands of the sex organs tend to get smaller (less productive) and a lot more of the hormone adrenalin is produced. There is also an increase in fighting among the animals. Is this not evidence that crowding is a bad thing? Unfortunately, it is not as simple as that. It appears that crowding as such is not an important feature of the situation because it does not matter how much space per animal there is but how many animals there are in total. So two animals in a small cage seem less affected than 20 animals in a cage ten times the size. The increased production of adrenalin may then simply be an adaptive response to allow the animal to cope with its vast range of social, physical and sexual contacts within the cage. The increase in fighting and aggression can then be similarly conceived as the consequence of the sheer number of different contacts. The change in the sexual organs is a normal consequence of increases in adrenalin levels.

Similar irritability might be expected in human beings in similar demanding conditions but this is not evidence of a territorial instinct in operation. Many animals seem more than happy to snuggle up as part of a group to sleep. (See Stockdale, 1978, for an overview of the literature on crowding.)

Ethologists have made other suggestions about the relationship between our animal nature and violence. Those of Lorenz (1963), in particular, gained some attention. Among other things, he pointed out that human beings are just about the only species which extensively brings about the deaths of members of that species. Fighting, in other species, tends to have a much more ritualistic nature and to be much more strictly controlled. What tends to happen is that signals are sent from one fighting animal to the other which switch off the aggression of the dominant animal usually before the injuries get too serious.

Much of the aggression between humans takes place at a distance (using guns, rockets, intercontinental ballistic weapons, and the like). This distance means that the biological mechanisms which would switch off aggression (the indications of pain and deference, for example) are absent; the implication is that human aggression (in the form of warfare in particular) is out of hand and destructive in a way in which animal aggression is not among members of the same species.

This sort of argument in itself does much to invalidate the ethological perspective. For instance, it suggests that human aggression is radically different from animal aggression. Animals kill virtually only for food, human beings for a multitude of reasons. The point about the impersonal and distanced nature of warfare indicates that the explanations of warfare have nothing to do with built-in and perhaps instinctive mechanisms. Our understanding has to move elsewhere. This does not imply that human beings owe nothing to their animal ancestry, but only that their animal nature is a distinctively human one (as a rat's animal nature is distinctively rat-like). Mechanisms proposed on the basis of more or less adequate ethological data do not seem particularly pertinent to our understanding of human beings.

Aggressive instincts

Psychologists, and not just ethologists, have seen aggression as instinctive. Freud (1930) proposed *thanatos* as a sort of destructive instinct and William McDougall (1908) proposed a whole series of different instincts, including pugnacity, with corresponding emotions, as the basis of a system of social psychology. Unfortunately, the use of instincts as an explanation of the complex social behaviour of human beings achieves very little. For example, there is little which seems standard in human aggression, which can take so many different forms. Instincts are clearly at the roots of the aggression of some animals (such as sticklebacks) but human beings are clearly far more complex and it is difficult to relate human activity directly to instincts. Sex is a good example in that in many animal species it is clearly controlled by innate mechanisms and takes a very specific and typical form. By contrast, human sexual activity takes a wide variety of forms which seem to be aberrations rather than direct expressions of innate mechanisms. Human being sometimes live in institutions (monasteries, nunneries) which suppress rather than express sexuality and aspects of human sexuality seen unrelated to what would be biologically sound (for example, sexual attraction to children incapable of reproduction).

One could describe the biological approach as an 'animal metaphor' for human aggression. That is, we are violent because we are *like* animals. Being animal is the opposite of being civilized. So the idea is that in some way, from time to time, the animal in us breaks through and disturbs our civilized ways. What we have seen so far seems to imply that we have a poor understanding of animal aggression if we equate it with human violence.

Psychological theories of aggression

Frustration-aggression

There is a second metaphor in ideas about violence: that is to suggest that human beings are like young children in relation to violence. In a sense, when we resort to violence we are operating at the level of the unsocialized, immature, infant which becomes frustrated and aggressive when it cannot get its way. Dollard *et al.* (1939) formalized this as an explanation of general human aggression in their 'frustration-aggression' hypothesis. Essentially this says that if an individual is frustrated, if he is prevented from achieving a goal, this frustration leads to aggression. Superficially this has a lot of appeal in that it seems to deal effectively with many everyday situations. For example, if the family car blows a gasket on the way to the coast, the driver may become very annoyed and irritable until the car is repaired; or when one sister gets angry and abusive because the other will not lend her a dress to go to a party in. One could argue that in both of these circumstances there is a goal which cannot be reached (getting to the coast or looking one's best for the party) which leads to frustration which leads to aggression.

But this may be wrong. Remember that it requires that the aggression is the result of the frustration of a goal and not the result of any other factors which lead more directly to anger or annoyance. Often the driver feels disappointed rather than frustration at being unable to reach the coast and behaves 'like a raging bull' because of stress due to the breakdown (for example, worry about the likely cost, being responsible for getting everyone home, being constantly asked how long the repair will take). The sister may be angry, not because she is frustrated in her goal by the refusal to lend the dress, but because she has lent her clothes many times but finds that the favour is not reciprocated. Here it would be the failure to meet with the norm of reciprocity of exchange of favours which would be responsible for the aggression. The intermediary state of frustration is not necessarily required even to explain aggression in these circumstances.

Dollard *et al.* (1939, p. 1) also made the assumption that 'the occurrence of aggressive behaviour always presupposes the existence of frustration'. This is patently unsound as it implies, for example, that a soldier kills because of frustration. Although this requirement was quickly abandoned by other psychologists, one is left with the difficulty of deciding which kind of aggression is caused by frustration and which is caused through other means. In other words, the frustration-aggression hypothesis is powerful only to the extent that all aggression is the result of frustration; it becomes disproportionately less useful when there are many causes of aggression and one has to choose between explanations.

Typical of the evidence cited in support of the frustration-aggression hypothesis was that it seemed to explain data on the relationship between the number of lynchings in the American South and the price of cotton (Hovland and Sears, 1940), the lower price of cotton being taken to mean that people were more frustrated in their economic goals. But there was no direct evidence that the whites were in some way frustrated in trying to achieve their economic goals and that this frustration led to aggression. After all, there is no evidence that mass unemployment in Britain and other countries in the 1980s produced similar responses purely and simply of itself. However, one should be aware that part of racist ideologies and belief structures is the (historically and factually inaccurate) notion that black people take work that white people need. When economic situations are bad this racist idea is used as part of the discourse and propaganda against blacks. But this applies equally to those in work (who by implication are not particularly frustrated in their economic goals) as to those out of work (who might well be frustrated in their economic goals). Racism was and is part of the way of life for sections of white people in the American South and one might prefer to find explanations of the lynchings in terms of white racism rather than in terms of frustration.

This is in no way to suggest that there are circumstances in which frustration of goal attainment leads to aggression, merely to point out the relatively lean understanding of violence in society which comes from the hypothesis. Later work which attempted to establish that it is the perceived intent to frustrate or harm the individual which leads to the aggression does little to retain much faith in the power of the frustration-aggression hypothesis since it comes as no surprise to find that we are more inclined to retaliate if someone intends to harm us than if they do something perhaps for 'our own good'. We do not bite the doctor giving us an injection whereas a dog, not knowing the intent, might well try to bite the vet injecting it.

Comments on biological and psychological theories

It is perhaps the parallels between the animal metaphor and the infant metaphor of human aggression which reveal most about earlier attempts to explain aggression. Neither approach considers it central that aggression and violence are built into advanced cultures and complex societies through social forces. Each assumes that violence and aggression are the vestiges of our animal origins and our pre-socialized childhood bursting through. What seems to be missing is the recognition that violence is something other than a hiccup in a well-ordered and civilized society. It seems essential to recognize that violence is endemic and rooted in society.

There is a similar tendency to try to explain violence on the basis of some psychological abnormality (for example, the mistaken belief that mentally ill people are more dangerous than others) or a genetic abnormality (for example, that violent men tend to have an extra male chromosome). Neither of these arguments is true but each had or has gained a fairly high level of public acceptance. They are misleading beliefs because their effect is to marginalize violence, to move it away from the mainstream of social life.

If violence is shown to be part of the mainstream of social life then it becomes necessary to re-examine our explanations of aggression and violence. Family violence research has a lot to contribute to this. For example, Gelles's 1976 survey in the United States (Gelles, 1979) found that about 70 per cent of parents had slapped or spanked their children, about 20 per cent had hit their children with something, and about 4 per cent of parents had beaten up their children in any one year. It was also found that violence had once occurred in more than one in four marriages and in any one year in about one in six marriages. Whatever the motives for violence, there is no argument that these are everyday manifestations of acts which in other contexts fill us with horror. That they are commonplace is as important to explain as the fact that they exist at all. It must be noted that violence is frequently an attempt at social control, as is clearly the case where a parent disciplines a child. Others would add that violence between spouses is just another form of using violence to exercise presumed social (sexual) power.

Violence is also extensively perpetrated by the state, in such forms as war, state torture, violence in crowd control and school discipline. While one may wish to argue that some sorts of violence are justifiable and legitimate, it should not be forgotten that arguments about legitimacy are themselves socially and contextually bound. For example, although most of us would now agree that wife-beating is unacceptable, historically it has been accepted in Western society as legitimate and even incorporated as a right into the legal system.

The animal metaphor, and to a lesser extent, the infant metaphor, tend to imply that aggression is a form of psychological energy which has to be got rid of if it is not to escape in undesired ways. Anger boils up inside us (or so the cliché goes) and will escape in unacceptable ways if not released in a controlled manner. Society has to regulate the release of this energy. Based on this model, 'common-sense' recommendations about the use of sport to dissipate this energy have been put forward regularly during this century. The psychological theory which is closest to this is that of catharsis. There are several versions of this. The one which suggests that we feel less aggressive after being allowed to aggress against the source of our aggressive feelings is not in doubt (though the idea that this is the result of inhibition of aggressive feelings rather than their discharge is equally viable). What is very unlikely is that witnessing aggression against another person other than the one which angers you has the same effect. This is particularly so when the aggression is viewed on television and takes place between third parties (Howitt, 1982).

Equally important is the extent to which the animal and infant metaphors encourage us to think of the aggression and violence as things that one individual does to another. This discourages thinking in terms of how a social situation results in aggression and violence. One can point to the example of the violent sexual attacks that men perpetrate on women, such as when a lone female walking down the street at night is subjected to sexual violence. One could say that such an attack is the result of one man's individual psychological problems – but this is to neglect the common social belief that a woman out at night is either 'no good' and deserves what she gets or is 'asking for it'. The man himself is not responsible for the creation of such stereotypes – no more than there is anything in a woman's individual psychology which determines that she is expected not to be out alone at night. It would be odious to blame her for being attacked (that is, being a violence-eliciting stimulus) and strange to hold his particular psychological quirks to blame for attacking in themselves.

By virtually the same token, the two metaphors also fail to explain how violence carries over from one generation to the next and how change occurs in the acceptability of aggression and violence over time. By assuming the innateness and internality of aggression, it becomes very difficult to explain change over history. One requires mechanisms which are responsive to change to explain change.

Simple social theories of aggression

Imitation and modelling of aggression

The work of Albert Bandura (1962) was perhaps the breakthrough from the individually based metaphors of aggression to a more social type of explanation. Bandura's starting point was the behaviouristic psychology which dominated psychology during the first half of the twentieth century. This had as one of its corner-stones what is generically known as *learning theory*. Although there were many varieties of learning theory (perhaps the most famous and current being that of Skinner (1974)), most tended to assume that learning resulted from rewarding, in some way, a sequence of attempts at the behaviour which was to be learned, the idea being that if a behaviour led to a good consequence (reward) the associations between the environmental stimulus and the behavioural responses would be strengthened (reinforced).

Bandura showed that behaviour did not have to be constantly repeated and rewarded before it was learnt. He demonstrated that children were capable of learning as the consequence of just one exposure to a particular sort of behaviour. Quite simply, children could learn by imitation (or by *modelling*, as it was also known) without frequent repetition. Furthermore, there was no necessity for the child to have overtly rehearsed the learning in advance of putting it into practice. This perhaps came as no surprise to anyone at all other than psychologists whose thinking was blinkered by the dominance of behaviouristic learning theory. What Bandura did was let children see adults acting aggressively towards an inflatable plastic clown. The children were later studied in a situation where they were free to play with the doll. Children who saw the adult acting aggressively towards the doll tended to reproduce those aggressive words and actions when playing with it.

Bandura's studies have been frequently criticized for their artificiality. This is deserved if one instantly jumps from the research to the conclusion that the children invariably reproduce any behaviour that they see modelled. The reproduction of the aggression against the doll is not too difficult to understand because the doll was designed to be aggressed against – its nose squeaked if hit and the base of the doll was weighted so that the doll rolled back upright if it were knocked over. However, most of us have observed others doing things which we have not reproduced ourselves although we could if motivated to do so. That we can learn by imitation is not in doubt; why we only sometimes do the things we have learnt is the problem to solve. Social learning theory (which is largely based on Bandura's idea that much is learnt socially through similar processes to any other learning) attempts to do that, among other things.

Perhaps the most important thing about social learning theory's achievements from our point of view is that it is unnecessary to assume that parents are actively or intentionally training their offspring in the use of aggression in order for aggression to be learned. Indeed, the parent may be actively punishing aggression or rewarding non-aggressive behaviour while at the same time the child is learning through modelling. The parent may be punishing aggression with a slap, that is, by himself committing an act of violence.

There is a real sense in which the basic concept of social learning theory is somewhat trivial – after all, to demonstrate that aggression can be learnt is hardly a powerful explanation of aggression and certainly does very little to explain the circumstances in which aggression will take place. For example, if a social psychologist claimed that violence in inner-city riots came about by a process of imitation few would fail to be unimpressed. All sorts of objections would be raised. For example, how did the first collective violence come about and why do only some people become involved? There has been work within the social learning framework which tries to increase our understanding of the circumstances in which the learning takes place and what is learnt is put into action. Unhappily, in the sense that this introduces far greater complexity than the simple idea of modelling warrants, the theory cannot effectively cope with the ramifications of the individual and the culture without abandoning its behaviourist foundations and origins. Inevitably the theory has been forced to introduce more and more social and cognitive concepts. Once this stage is reached then there is little advantage in maintaining the pretence of a purely behaviourist approach to learning.

The cuing of aggression and generalized arousal

Similar intellectual roots underlie certain other 'external explanations' of aggression. Berkowitz, like Bandura, was interested in the way in which external factors might lead to aggression. However, he concentrated much more on the factors in the environment which trigger off aggression than on how the aggressive behaviour patterns arc learnt in the first place. Unfortunately, this led to a lot of apparently rather silly research. Among the research, for example, was that in which the name of an individual against which aggression was possible was made similar to that of someone that the subjects had already seen aggressed against. It would appear that such name similarity acted as a cue to aggression since aggression was greatest when the names were similar!

There is a strand in the experimental social psychologist's conceptualization of aggression which gives an important role to physiological arousal – this is to be found in Zillman (1971) and Tannenbaum and Zillman (1975), for example, as well as to a lesser extent in Berkowitz's formulations. If we were to apply a metaphor to this scheme of things we might come up with a phrase such as the 'thinking physiologist'. The argument, simply put, is that violence typically takes place in circumstances in which the individual is in some generalized state of emotional or physiological arousal. This arousal need not necessarily be one which might correspond directly to the physiological pattern which we call 'anger' (for example, the pattern identified by Ax (1953) as anger in which levels of adrenalin and noradrenalin hormones are high). Indeed, it may be physiological arousal caused by sexual stimulation or practically any other event. It is argued that this generalized physiological arousal increases the individual's rcsponsiveness to any sort of stimulation. This makes a lot of sense in terms of our day-to-day experience that feeling 'high' or 'on top of the world' makes us more aware and responsive to the environment.

What Berkowitz says is that cues to aggressiveness (presence of weapons, seeing a violent film, for example) result in a greater likelihood that violence will take place. (In point of fact this arousal is not a necessary condition but it is a facilitating condition.) We have to characterize the individual as 'thinking' as there is at least some evidence that the level of physiological arousal is important in determining the person's response. Too much arousal seems to encourage the person to inhibit rather than exhibit aggression. It seems that strong emotion produces guilt feelings about feeling aggressive which overcome aggression (Berkowitz, 1982).

This sort of theory has enormous difficulties – particularly the problem of what cues arouse aggression. It is not easy to imagine anything which could not serve as a cue to aggression in some circumstances. So, for example, the sight of a bride walking down the aisle produces all sorts of emotions. By and large for most people these would be positive, but for a jealous ex-boyfriend this sight may be an aggression-eliciting cue. So, the aggression is not inherent in the cue but in psycho-social history of the individual actors in the scene. The issue then becomes one of understanding the cognitive basis of the aggression and it is doubtful whether knowledge of the cue in itself provides us with any understanding of the ex-boyfriend's behaviour.

Comments on simple social theories of aggression

Despite their relatively simple underpinnings, in many ways the work of Bandura and Berkowitz has to be seen as a remarkable advance on other theories such as the biological and the frustration-aggression theory. This is so for several reasons. The first is that the closely coupled link between biological drives and aggression is broken. In social learning theory, for example, there may well be many different learned response to, say, a verbal insult which might include withdrawal, conciliation, or ignoral as well as verbal retaliation or even physical violence. This is because the assumption is that no direct biological mechanisms determine response.

Following on from this, the theories are optimistic about the potential of society to avoid aggression. The biologically based theories which we have discussed are essentially pessimistic because it is assumed that in the absence of opportunities to discharge aggression, a reservoir of aggression energy builds up which has to be discharged in some way. 'Safety valves' for aggression to be discharged in harmless ways are needed. The older theories assume the inevitability of violence, while the more recent theories provide for the possibility that society might change quite simply because what is learnt may well change. How the content of what is learnt becomes transformed is clearly complex but at least we are not dependent on rigid social engineering (as in the provision of physical games) but can call on all elements of human learning processes to achieve change. Although social learning theory may have been heavily dependent on behaviourist learning theory in its conceptualization, fortunately it has been at least willing to assume that cognitive principles are involved and that human learning is not simply mechanical.

Having outlined some of the social psychological theories of aggression, it will be useful to examine the concept of aggression in a little more detail. So far it has been neglected in order that more important basics could be covered.

Conceptualizing aggression

At this point it would appear that the word 'aggression' seems to have been used in a variety of senses. No attempt has been made to define it so far, and with good reason. The most important aspect of this is that the different theories themselves are not particularly specific about what is meant by 'aggression' mainly because they do not need to be for the most part. In this section some definitions are offered, but it should be noted how theory-dependent they tend to be.

According to Selg (1975, p. 10),

Aggression is any series of actions whose goal response is injury to another organism or its substitute.

This definition has its problems – particularly that it would exclude a good many acts because their goals are not primarily to injure another person. For example, if a security man is shot during an armed robbery we do not claim that this is not aggression simply because the main aim of the robbery was to steal a lot of money.

Schott (1975, p. 154) says that

The predicate 'aggression' can be attached to an action if, from the agent's point of view, its direct purpose (as distinct from the final object) is to cause damage or injury (in the widest possible sense).

This clearly avoids the problem of overall goal in that it classifies slapping a child while teaching it mathematics as aggressive because the intent was to cause the child discomfort. However, it leaves aside problems such as deciding what a direct purpose is – so, for example, if a parent slaps a three-year-old who is pulling the parent's hair very hard the purpose of the slap may be to make the child let go rather than to hurt the child.

For Bandura (1973, p. 8),

> Aggression is ... injurious and destructive behaviour that is socially defined as aggressive on the basis of a variety of factors, some of which reside in the evaluator rather than in the performer.

Again many issues are dodged – for example, if aggression is socially defined how is consensus to be reached in order to decide that an act is aggressive? For example, if either the aggressor or the victim does not consider the act to be aggressive, are we forced to accept this?

These definitional problems notwithstanding, by and large, the issue of definition has produced few problems for research into aggression. This is largely because much of the empirical work since the 1960s adopted a particular method of measuring aggression (the apparent delivery of a noxious electric shock much as in the Milgram experiments described in Chapter 4). Very little attention has been devoted to investigating the wide variety of types of aggression. (It is typical of social psychology in general that a particular paradigm for doing research is adopted and substitutes for a vast range of different 'real life' situations – conformity, attitude change, decision-making, and other topics clearly demonstrate the influence of paradigms on social psychology.)

Although others have conceptualized different sorts of aggression (for example, hostile aggression, instrumental aggression, and impulsive aggression), typical theories have tended not to make distinctions. Indeed, it could be said that they almost perversely assume that aggression is a unitary thing. So the ethologists see great parallels between territorial aggression and warfare, the frustration-aggression theorists might regard inner-city violence as the consequence of frustrations caused by lack of economic opportunities, and the social learning theorists might claim aggression learnt in one set of circumstances will be reproduced in radically different circumstances, for example. But there is something entirely unsatisfactory in this tendency to act as if it is assumed that aggression is aggression is aggression, having perhaps already noted the wide variety of different types of aggression.

One consequence of this is the frequent failure to appreciate the different conditions and processes through which aggression may come about. The basic theories of aggression postulate psychological mechanisms which are virtually devoid of reference to social context and as such can scarcely be expected to adequately deal with aggression in a social context. What follows from this is that a social psychological explanation of aggression needs to include knowledge concerning the circumstances of aggression. It is simply not enough to develop ideas about general processes involved in aggression such as frustration.

Norms and aggression

It must be acknowledged that much of human action is guided by societally imposed schemes of appropriate action, that is, by standards of normal behaviour (see Chapter 3). Social scientists use the concept of 'norms' which really refers to the conglomeration of customs, practices, laws, common beliefs, social standards, religious tenets, and so on, which are, by and large, consensually adopted by groups of individuals. These provide guidelines and standards by which action can be judged. Obviously these normative standards vary from culture to culture, nation to nation, and across geographical and other boundaries. Even within one nation there will be sub-groups of people who may have rather different normative standards from the entire nation. For example, teenagers may have substantially different standards in respect of certain things from those of the older generation.

This is relevant in that it is difficult to understand aggression without reference to societal standards of acceptable action. Everyday experience tells us that acts are not judged simply on the basis of their consequences. Some acts which might seem violent are allowed by social norms, some apparently similar acts are not so accepted, and some actions which are acceptable according to the norms of one sector of society are not acceptable according to the norms of the wider community. For example, the use of force by the police and armed forces in many circumstances is within the bounds of what is normatively approved, despite strenuous condemnation by some. Deliberately breaking a child's arm because it is wakeful at night would be normatively prohibited. It is difficult to see how both of these could be explained by one single theory.

It is possible to identify at least three different types of social situation involving aggression which manifest distinct relationships between social norms and social action. These distinctions further strengthen the argument for a socially based analysis of aggression. They are:

1. *Conformity to norms.* In this situation the norms governing action direct the individual to aggress; for example, the norms which lead soldiers to kill in wartime. These include loyalty to one's country, one's comrades, and one's manhood as well as concepts of 'duty' and 'service'. Although the killing may well be further guided by rules of war, this aggression is socially accepted and may be rewarded by military honours and distinctions. It is not subject to punishment (so long as appropriate practices have been adopted) and is not punishable as such by even the enemy under international rules.
2. *Sudden release from norms.* In this situation, even though the individuals subscribe to norms against violence, and the situation is

one in which aggression is prohibited normatively, these normative constraints cease to operate. Hooliganism may be seen in this light.

3. *Direct opposition to norms.* In this situation, norms are rejected. In a revolution, for example, this occurs both in terms of the new social order that the revolutionaries wish to impose which contradicts the old order, and in terms of rejection of norms which essentially maintain the status quo. For example, it is a normatively based statement to suggest that one does not use violence in order to gain power in a democracy. The revolutionary has to oppose that norm directly since otherwise the revolution could not succeed.

This simple scheme helps to flesh out our understanding of aggression within society and further emphasizes the need to see aggression in its fuller social context so that the meaning of an act of aggression becomes a central feature of our social psychological analysis.

A more fully social examination of aggression

This section looks at how a social psychological understanding of a violent situation is possible without reference to inbuilt mechanisms. It also illustrates how ignorance of the social situation in which actions take place leads to misconceptions and inadequate theoretical formulations. It is based on a study of what we conventionally refer to as 'rioting'.

In recent years, considerable public attention has focused on inner-city disturbances. These have often been associated with race and appear to involve mindless and extreme violence, judging from newspapers. Such situations challenge social psychologists to explain why apparently senseless acts occur involving thinking people. Given that riots appear to be nothing other than a total breakdown of social order, how can we explain rioting from a social psychological point of view? It would seem at first sight to be the very sort of situation which theories of aggression should cope with – if we conceptualize riots as being essentially violent processes.

When trying to use the theories of aggression studied so far, problems rapidly appear and our levels of explanation seem to be very remote. For example, taking the theories which assume that aggression is an innate drive leaves us struggling to explain why riots are rare, confined to relatively small numbers of people, confined to geographically rather limited areas, and seem to be bound by historical factors. Theories that suggest that aggression results from frustration or other noxious events again cause problems. For example, how could an incident involving, say, the police and a black family be a noxious stimulus or even a frustration sufficient to cause a large number of people to become involved in violent collective action when many other noxious events and frustrations have no such consequences? Considering social learning theory introduces the difficulty of how rioting is socially learned. We might be able to claim that throwing a brick can be learned from observation, but it stretches disbelief to imagine that how to behave in a riot has previously been learned through observation as this implies that there are 'rules' for rioting. This runs counter to the social myth that rioting is mindless.

There is another possibility. Could we be trying to explain social phenomena which have not been sufficiently explored using theories which deal with entirely different issues? Given that the term 'riot' has a social representation as irrational, spontaneous indiscipline and the general abandonment of social mores, it is essential to evaluate the adequacy of this picture. After all, it might merely be yet another social stereotype without foundation.

Reicher (1984) investigated the riot which occurred in St Paul's, Bristol, in 1980. He wrote of the events:

> Indeed, perhaps the most remarkable feature of the whole episode was the backdrop of normality against which the so-called 'Battle of Bristol' . . . was played out. As police cars were burnt and officers stoned, cars flowed through the area, people walked home, families did their shopping, neighbours watched and chatted about the events (Reicher, 1984, p. 195).

He went on to explain that although the police officers and newsmen were the targets of attack, there was not a single individual otherwise who was attacked in the streets by the crowds and there was no malicious damage to any private house. Those civilians who were hurt were apparently injured by the police or as a result of being accidentally injured as a secondary consequence of the crowd's attack on the police. This is a radically different conception of crowd violence from the one to be found contained in the popular imagination. Reicher explains the events in St Paul's in a rather different way from the way the theories of aggression might choose to see them. This is not at all surprising, given that he is describing a radically different social phenomenon than most notions about crowd behaviour would have us believe. He is describing a social reality rather than a popular myth based on naive psychologizing.

Reicher's reference point is social identity theory. Quite simply, this says that individuals form their self-identification by reference to the social environment which provides a social and historical context for how the individual sees himself. In the context of the St Paul's riot, being a member of the St Paul's community defines what is permissible action. Actions were determined by reference to that social identity. So just as one would not expect the police to attack each other, neither does one expect a member of the St Paul's community wilfully to injure or damage the property of another identified socially as belonging to that community. The police were attacked because they were seen as attacking key aspects of the community, such as places where the community's social life was carried out. So instead of needing to explain a failure of social norms, the 'riot' fully conformed to the most important social norms. Furthermore, rather than implying a need to explain the discontinuity of the 'riot' with normal social behaviour, Reicher's explanation assumed that the rioting has substantially the same explanatory concepts as everyday life.

Co-operation

Many of the psychologists who had researched aggression (and especially violence in the mass media) chose to turn their attention to what they labelled 'pro-social behaviour'. This they saw as righting the balance which had been too much concentrated on destructive aspects of social behaviour. Common sense, let alone careful observation, would suggest that a key characteristic of humankind is the kindly, caring, co-operative, and helping relationships which humans frequently form. In shifting their attention in this way, social psychologists had picked up a very old theme in the history of psychology (as well as sociology) and in a sense turned full circle. The social nature of humans was a prime concern of many nineteenth-century writers. The idea of 'sympathy' (for example, in the work of Herbert Spencer, Charles Darwin and William McDougall), whether it is seen as emotional correspondence or as happiness and sadness at the fate of others, is clearly the antithesis of the destructive forces which have dominated conceptions of aggression.

In many ways there are very close parallels between how the positive features of social behaviour are explained and the ways in which explanations of aggression have been constructed. A very important approach, resurrected by biologists in modern times, has been to understand altruistic acts (and other social tendencies) in terms of natural selection. Spencer, especially, saw society as if it were something like a living organism and so prone to evolutionary forces. Unfortunately, this has its problems, especially when considering actions which are bad for the individual but good for society. The biologists (or socio-biologists) have to explain how evolutionary changes which benefit society can be transmitted through the individual's genes – quite unlike the usual evolutionary process in which chance genetic changes which favour the individual's survival are passed on to that individual's offspring. The difficulty is that altruistic actions which put society above the individual may result in the destruction of the individual (see, for example, Caplan, 1978). So the warrior who shows outstanding bravery in saving comrades is more likely to be killed than others not showing that trait. As a consequence the warrior cannot pass on his bravery genetically. Celibacy, which serves functions of communities rather than the individual, is also difficult to understand genetically. (Notice that it only makes sense to worry about the genetics of this if patterns of social behaviour are indeed genetically determined. If they are not the puzzle disappears.) There is the suggestion that altruism-related genes survive, for example, because altruism is usually directed towards kin who share similar altruistic genes. Thus it is the gene which survives, not the person carrying the gene as such. So if the strength of our altruism is greatest towards our immediate kin (as common sense suggests it is) rather than towards strangers, the social function of altruism is the continuation of genetic material very similar to one's own. With the survival of the gene, there remains a pool of altruistically 'programmed' biased individuals.

But the problems of such an approach, by and large, are similar to the biological approaches to aggression. They would include the following:

1. Human altruism is a long way removed from any possible animal homologues such as signals warning of predators in herding species.
2. Human altruism may well be vital to the continuation of societies but there is no reason to assume that this requires genetic survival value to be involved. There is no reason why everything which is of value to society needs to be genetically built in. Humans are quite capable of realizing the implications of danger to the survival of the group.
3. Altruism seems to be governed by many social factors which seem not to be reducible to biological blueprints.

The genetic approach to human social behaviour also suffers from being prone to supporting particular social ideologies. For example, if one assumes that social practices are functional and notes sex divisions in the animal kingdom, then this is close to accepting that traditional sex role divisions in society are natural and necessary.

The social psychology of altruism is poorly developed compared with the attention paid to aggression. To some extent it also lacks a clear terminology to employ. 'Pro-social behaviour', 'helping behaviour' and 'altruism' are often used interchangeably. Obviously they are behaviourally identical and to distinguish between them would require an analysis of motives. This had little appeal to experimental social psychologists committed to the analysis of behaviour.

The importance of a fully social psychological analysis of altruistic behaviour is evidenced by a classic series of studies by Latané and

Darley (1970). They placed people in situations in which helping others was a likelihood in order to see whether or not people would help. The researchers had been bothered by the reports of the murder of Kitty Genovese. Thirty-eight people witnessed her being stabbed to death but not one of them tried to help directly or by calling the police. Darley has spoken of the background to their research:

> This seemed to prove ... that people were becoming terribly indifferent to one another, particularly in the cities. A great many articles were written on the dehumanization of man, and there was the suggestion that we needed to think about a new kind of man, 'homo urbanis', the city dweller, who cared only for himself. There was a focus on speculating on the personality flaws of people who could stand and watch while others died. It was almost as if we were reverting to the kinds of explanations used in the sixteenth century, that people were possessed by devils to do such cruel things (Evans, 1980, p. 216).

No one can be blamed for jumping to such conclusions especially as they match our myths about city life. Latané and Darley chose not to accept such judgements at face value. They reproduced key elements of the murder situation experimentally and created in the laboratory (and sometimes in the field) controlled experiments in which an emergency occurred (for example, there is smoke pouring through a duct as if there were a fire, or someone collapses on a train). These emergencies either happened in front of a lone individual or the individual is in the presence of others who fail to respond. Despite common-sense theories about safety in numbers, the researchers found that the presence of others *inhibits* helping behaviour. The individual faced with the situation alone is the most likely to do something. The Kitty Genovese situation then becomes not abnormal but a normal human social process.

Why should helping be commoner in situations with fewer witnesses? One could suggest any number of factors, such as embarrassment if a mistaken interpretation of the situation had occurred, but Latané and Darley carried out a number of variations on their procedures to eliminate as many alternatives as possible. On the basis of their work they concluded, first, that people cognitively evaluate situations for meaning and that these interpretations partly determine what course of action they will take. So if the individual thought that they were being filmed as part of a *Candid Camera* stunt they would not act in the same way as if they felt a genuine emergency was taking place. Second, that the sense of personal responsibility to do something was greatest when few people were present and least when many people were present. They coined the phrase 'diffusion of responsibility' to describe the process by which people accept responsibility personally when alone or share the responsibility mentally among all those present when there are many of them. If one cannot share the responsibility with others then intervention is most likely.

This work is another fascinating example of how a careful social psychological analysis of a situation can displace other explanations of a phenomenon. Without the experimental method, Latané and Darley would not have established that the presence of others is an important inhibiting factor in the involvement of bystanders in emergencies. Equally, if they had not been committed to the view that there may be a perfectly reasonable explanation of what would appear to be selfish and irrational behaviour, then they would have leapt to the type of conclusion which claims that either people or cities, perhaps both, are sick or bad. The social psychological explanation shows how inadequate common-sense explanation can be at times.

Concluding comments

In this discussion of aggression and altruism we have explored a wide range of levels of theorizing about profoundly important questions related to human nature and the nature of human society. In both aggression and altruism we see how modern social psychological theories are a distinct advance on biological or psychological explanations, while at the same time being distinctive in both conceptualization and assumptions. To put it another way, social psychology is not simply common sense – it is a way of analysing situations which may result in new insights.

Biological theories have not been reviewed enthusiastically. The reason is obvious. Too often they rely on claims which, even if they had a vestige of validity, would be so far removed from the situations they are supposed to explain as to be basically of little worth. One is considerably pressed to come up with explanations of, say, football hooliganism or wife-beating based on the idea that they are directly or indirectly in our genes. They are also often prescriptions for a pessimistic view of society.

Little understanding is gained of human nature by concentrating too much on the animal metaphor. Certainly part of human nature and the organization of human society comes from the fact that we are animals of a particular type. However, this may be mundane as an explanation of human life. For example, human life might be very different if people, say, photosynthesized food and needed only mineral sources and sunlight or gave birth to offspring capable of looking after themselves within hours.

Purely social psychological theories of aggression and altruism have a dynamic quality which is missing from other types of explanation. Mechanisms built into society are more able to explain both change and stability than biologically keyed-in factors would be capable of.

7

SOCIAL COGNITION

In the history of social psychology there have been theories which stress the emotional life of people and theories which investigate the processes of thinking. Some theorists suggest that the key to human social behaviour lies in uncovering hidden irrational urges and emotional states. Others take a cooler view and argue that the most important issues in social psychology are revealed by studying the way that people think about the world. In the last 15 or so years, this calmer perspective, *cognitive social psychology*, has become more prominent.

Cognitive social psychologists assume that most important social psychological questions are best dealt with by studying the processes of *cognition*, or thinking. In particular, they have set the task of understanding how humans make sense of the social world. People do not merely react to outside stimuli or express inner emotional urges, they also make sense of and give meaning to their surroundings. Walking down the street, we notice all sorts of people going about their business: a tired woman may be pushing a pram towards a supermarket entrance; a policewoman directing traffic, and a shabbily dressed man tunelessly playing a mouth-organ beside a cap placed on the pavement. Assumptions are made about these people and about what they are doing. Assumptions can be made about these people because they and their actions appear meaningful. Cognitive social psychology has to explain how such sights are given meaning, and how this meaning affects our thinking about the social world.

Two main lines of research and theory characterize cognitive social psychology. One is *attribution theory*, which derives from the work of the European psychologist, Fritz Heider, who emigrated from Austria to the United States. This tries to understand how we make judgements of social causation. The other is *schema theory*, deriving from the work of the British psychologist, Sir Frederick Bartlett. This explains social thought in terms of its organization of mental elements. Despite being separable traditions, both concentrate on the way individuals make sense of their individual social worlds and, in doing so, tend to ignore the extent to which human thinking is shaped by culture.

Attribution theory

Origins

Fritz Heider is commonly held to be the founding figure of modern attribution research. Although he published experiments, he wrote in a literary style which seems to conjure the leisurely, unspecialized academic world of a lost age. Born in the old Austro-Hungarian empire, he wrote his doctoral dissertation just after the First World War. However, *The Psychology of Interpersonal Relations* (Heider, 1958), which has become almost the bible of attribution theory, was not published until Heider was over sixty and had been working in the United States for over 25 years. It represents the culmination of ideas which had preoccupied Heider throughout his career. For such a profoundly influential text, it was curiously old-fashioned on publica-tion, being full of references to philosophy and literature in a way that recalls the psychology of the previous century. Although including experimental studies, Heider made his points without reference to the hundreds of experiments and technical language which 'dutiful' modern psychologists are trained to see as their stock-in-trade.

It often helps to understand an innovatory perspective if one knows what it opposes intellectually. In common with most major theoreti-cians, Heider was arguing against existing ideas as much as proposing a positive theory. His first target was Freud's psychoanalytic theory. The very first paragraph of *The Psychology of Interpersonal Relations* states that 'our concern will be with "surface" matters, the events that occur in everyday life on a conscious level, rather than with the unconscious processes studied by psycho-analysis in "depth" psychology' (Heider, 1958, p. 1). For Freud, behind ordinary thinking, and pushing it in surprising directions, were the unconscious urges of a 'sexual' (libidi-nous) and destructive nature. Heider would have none of this. Ordinary thinking had to be understood on its own terms, and deeply hidden significances avoided. He saw that the immediate and obvious aspects of everyday life could be 'just as challenging and psychologically significant as the deeper stranger phenomena' (Heider, 1958, p. 1).

Heider's second target was the movement then popular in social psychology which saw the social group as the focus of analysis. By contrast, Heider (1958, p. 1) chose to 'centre on the *person* as the basic unit to be investigated'. It was not group behaviour which concerned Heider, but the individual's perception of the social world and, in particular, perceptions of other individuals. According to Heider (1958, p. 3): 'What determined John's attitude to Jim has not been investigated as thoroughly as John's attitude toward a group or the attitude of the group toward John'. Thus, the very title *The Psychology of Interpersonal Relations* contains an implicit criticism of social psychology's emphasis upon relations within groups. This emphasis, which was so characteristic of the social psychology of the 1940s, was to be reversed in the wake of Heider's work.

Heider (1958, p. 4) proposed a psychology based on a 'common-sense or naive psychology'. This meant that professional psychologists should build upon the psychological notions of ordinary people. In everyday life, we make judgements about why others behave in the way they do. That is, attributions are made about the *causes* of actions. In fact, the world would not be meaningful without attributions of causality. Heider made the study of such attributions a central part of his common-sense social psychology. He distinguished two different sorts of attributions of causality: 'It makes a real difference whether a person discovers that the stick that struck him fell from a rotting tree or was hurled by an enemy' (Heider, 1958, p. 16). The attribution would be an *impersonal* one if the person believed that the stick just happened to fall from the tree. However, the attribution would be *personal* if it was believed to be the deliberate action of another. Determining why events happen is, according to Heider (1958, p. 16), a basic property of thinking: 'Attributions in terms of impersonal and personal causes . . . are everyday occurrences that determine much of our understanding of a reaction to our surroundings'.

Heider claimed that two factors drew him to the position he took. First, he had always wished to be a painter. From an early age he had been fascinated by shapes and forms and his analysis of interpersonal relations, indeed, reflected this. Metaphors from the psychology of visual perception were to play a large part in his psychology. For example, the attribution of causality was described in the language of perception, employing such terms as 'figure' and 'background'. As John tries to understand why Jim did something, John tries to separate the figure (or the actor, Jim) from the background field (or the social situation in which the actor is placed). Separation is not always successfully achieved as there is a tendency for John to misperceive Jim's actions, believing Jim intended more than he did. In a few words greatly influencing later attribution theorists, Heider (1958, p. 54) wrote, demonstrating that enduring interest in perception:

It seems that behaviour in particular has such salient properties it tends to engulf the total field rather than be confined to its proper position as a local stimulus whose interpretation requires the additional data of a surrounding field.

The second major influence on Heider's thinking was the shortage of food and heating in Austria in the winter of 1918–19 just after the end of the First World War. Heider had suffered, as he sat wearing coat, scarf and gloves, trying to keep warm enough to continue work on his doctoral thesis. Under these conditions of shortage he noted that 'people became touchy and petulant' with one another, and this aroused his interest in human relations (Heider, 1980, p. 10). Amazingly, Heider was not to be inspired by this experience of hardship to study the effects of deprivation or warfare upon human relations. His psychology was to ignore wider societal issues, concentrating rather on the smaller worlds of individuals reacting to each other. It was the petulance and touchiness which had intrigued him, and not the major historical forces which were transforming the life of Europe.

So Heider's psychological picture of everyday perception was a calm miniature rather than a torrid grand masterpiece. His psychology avoided both the wider themes of group psychology, which connected individuals to the histories of their societies, as much as it avoided the turmoil of grand psychoanalytic theory. Stripping away the wider context of behaviour and determinedly refusing to acknowledge a hidden emotional life, Heider set social psychology the task of understanding the meanings one individual sees in the actions of another.

The expansion of attribution theory

In the 1960s attribution theory became a standard theme in experimental social psychology. The original emphases of Heider were preserved, including the emphasis on interpersonal relations and the perceptual metaphors. Above all, the assumption that social perceivers (that is, everyone) have an overwhelming need to explain events was central. These new cognitive social psychologists saw their task as devising experimental situations which examined in detail the circumstances in which perceivers attribute different sorts of causes to events. This desire to submit all hunches to experimental test marked out the new generation of attribution theorists from the old pioneer. Another change of intellectual style also occurred: the philosophical themes in Heider's work all but disappeared in this later American attribution theory. Perhaps this loss of philosophical awareness allowed the loose use of concepts, which, according to critics, has fatally hindered the development of the theory (Fincham and Jaspars, 1980; Kruglanski, 1979; Locke and Pennington, 1982).

Much of attribution theory hinges upon the distinction between two sorts of causal attribution: personal and situational. This does not quite match Heider's distinction between the personal and impersonal causation but later attribution theorists were not overly concerned with the difference between explaining willed actions and accidental un-willed events. It was the different sorts of explanation which people might offer for deliberate actions which interested them. In particular, when would naive psychologists (people) make a psychological attri-bution of causality, and claim that someone was acting in a particular way because of their personal characteristics, rather then because of the situation in which the action took place? For example, if a friend is angry with you this may be attributed to your friend's personal characteristics (they may be a notoriously bad-tempered individual), but there may be an alternative situational explanation (you may once again have borrowed money without paying it back).

This concern with the naive personality theories of everyday psychol-ogy was developed in one of the earliest post-Heiderian attribution theories. Jones and Davis (1965) proposed the notion of *correspondent inference*. Social perceivers make correspondent inferences, if, when witnessing an action, they infer that the actor has a stable disposition which corresponds to the action. Thus, if one perceives that a friend is angry and then infers that the reason is that this person is normally grumpy, this is a correspondent inference. A personal explanation of the action has been made, because the cause has been attributed to the friend's personal quality of grumpiness.

Jones and Davis were concerned to discover the sorts of knowledge people require before making a correspondent inference. They stressed the importance of whether action was in-role or out-of-role. A person who acts according to a defined social role might be presumed to be displaying less of their own personal feelings in their actions, than someone who is transgressing social standards. Thus, a person in the role of bus passenger might be obeying the normal standards (norms) of travelling by public transport, by sitting quietly in their bus seat. In observing such an individual, we are not inclined to attribute such unremarkable behaviour to correspondent inference such as an inner docile personality. To make such a correspondent inference would force us to conclude that the vast majority of bus passengers possessed this one particular personality type. On the other hand, if we observe a passenger behaving oddly, (shouting obscenities and running up and down the gangway) the temptation is to explain the behaviour as a quirk in the psychological make-up of an eccentric individual.

Jones *et al.* (1961) formally tested this basic notion of correspondent inference. People listened to a tape-recording of a simulated job interview, having been led to believe that the interviewers were looking for an applicant with certain personality characteristics. The 'bogus' applicants, knowing full well the desired characteristics, either displayed these characteristics or pointedly did not. When applicants behaved inappropriately, then observers more often made correspondent inferences and explained the out-of-role behaviour in terms of personal characteristics. On the other hand, more social attributions were chosen to explain the behaviour of the conforming applicants fulfilling the interviewers' criteria. A similar phenomenon occurs when attributing 'true' attitudes. A speaker, expressing views contrary to those of an audience from which little may be gained, is perceived as expressing their own real attitudes. By contrast, suspicion greets the speaker with something to gain from 'buttering up' the audience by supporting its view (Eagly *et al.*, 1978).

In these sort of experiment the subject is cast in the role of the naive psychologist who has to decide what inferences one can make about an observed individual's 'real' personality or attitude. One might say that professional psychologists created a naive perceiver in their own image. This was taken one step further in Harold Kelley's (1967) model of social perception. In analysing their experiments, professional social psychologists tend to use complex statistical formulae, which enable them to determine the relative contributions of different variables in causing the observed outcome. Kelley claimed that people do more or less the same when attributing causality, as they assess the effects of different influences on the event. The social perceiver makes calculations which are seen as rudimentary versions of the sophisticated analyses which experimentalists regularly perform.

According to Kelley, in deciding whether to attribute an action to personal or situational causes, a social perceiver has to take into account three basic factors: distinctiveness; consensuality; and consistency. These three terms are illustrated in McArthur's (1972) experimental test of Kelley's model of causal attribution. People were given descriptions of actions and had to state the cause of the events. The actions were the sort of small-scale interpersonal events the study of which Heider would have approved. One of them was 'John laughed at the comedian'. A personal attribution for this is that John laughed because John is a happy-go-lucky fellow who readily collapses in helpless mirth. A situational explanation would draw attention to the comedian: John laughed because the comedian was hilarious. The choice of attribution is affected by the other information available about John's and other people's typical reactions to the comedian.

1. *Distinctiveness.* This refers to whether John normally engages in the action in question. His laughing at this particular comedian would be

highly distinctive if normally he watches comedians stony-faced. However, the action lacks distinctiveness if they usually make him laugh. Thus, one can see that the attribution of personal causation (making a correspondent inference) depends upon the perceived action having low distinctiveness. One would not attribute John's laughter to a humorous disposition if this was the first time he had even smiled at a comedy act.

2. *Consensuality*. How funny do other people find the comic? If practically everyone finds the comedian funny, then laughing is highly *consensual*. In this case, if John were one of millions being convulsed with laughter, then we may not attribute his laughter to his personal disposition.

3. *Consistency*. A further piece of information might be necessary in addition to distinctiveness and consensuality. For instance, if John has no special tendency to laugh at comedians and this particular comedian is not especially popular with audiences generally, we might be interested in the extent to which John's actions are consistent. Does he always laugh when this particular comedian appears on the screen? If yes, we might prefer the personal attribution that John laughed because he is a fan of this nondescript performer. If he normally watches this comedian with indifference, the social perceiver might prefer situational explanations. Perhaps for once the comedian had some decent jokes from a new script-writer. Alternatively, John, surrounded by empty beer cans and friends laughing uncontrollably at the comedian's efforts at the jokes, might have found the particular atmosphere contagious, and been unable to stop himself from laughing.

This hypothetical example of John and the comedian illustrates the sort of information which a social perceiver might seek out if attributions are to be made. To use Heiderian concepts, the action cannot be understood merely in its own terms but needs to be set as a figure in a wider perceptal field. In this sense, the common-sense psychology of the naive perceiver is analogous to the model of scientific psychology of the profesional researcher who needs to investigate systematically the reactions of other subjects in this and other situations before formulating a theory about the laughter of John.

Critics of attribution theory have claimed that the theory is not merely a description of the way people understand events. It also implies that the naive psychology of the social perceiver is a bit too naive when placed alongside professional psychological analyses (Billig, 1982; Buss, 1979; Gergen and Gergen, 1981; Semin, 1980; Semin and Manstead, 1983). In this way, it would seem that attribution theory implicitly criticizes the naive psychology of the ordinary person, and it promotes its own techniques as providing the most effective means for understanding the everyday social world.

Biases in attribution

The evaluative implication has arisen out of the emphasis theorists have placed upon discovering *biases* in social perception. There has been considerable experimental investigation of the possible 'errors' in the attributions made by ordinary people. Much of this research is summarised in Nisbett and Ross's (1980) sad catalogue of the failings of the ordinary perceiver. Three of the best-known biases are: fundamental attribution error; actor–observer differences; and false consensus effect. As with so much in attribution theory, these are subject to disagreement. Some social psychologists (following Nisbett and Ross) suggest that attribution biases are characteristic of ordinary social perception; others claim the biases only occur under certain circumstances; and still others argue that the apparent biases are not really biases at all.

Fundamental attribution error

This essentially enlarges on Heider's comment that 'behaviour engulfs the field'. In simple terms, the error is the tendency to offer personal explanations over situational ones – we are over-hasty in ascribing personal characteristics to the actors we observe. Someone losing their temper is more likely to be judged to be short-tempered than as a reasonable individual provoked by circumstances beyond the limits of patience. We may forget that people often act according to the constraints of their roles and misinterpret their role-determined behaviour as reflecting their inner personal selves, rather than the prescribed parts they play in the everyday dramas of ordinary life.

Ross, Amabile and Steinmetz (1977) demonstrated how we can allow personal characteristics to engulf the social situation. People played the role of either questioner or contestant in a quiz game. The questioners were instructed to think of 'challenging but not impossible' general knowledge questions to ask the contestant. Observers watched as the questioners invented difficult questions, which had the contestants flummoxed. The observers were asked to evaluate the general knowledge levels of questioners and contestants. Consistently the observers rated questioners as being superior to the contestants as if the constraints of the situation were being ignored. Most of us know unusual facts which are unfamiliar to others. Being a questioner, in this situation is intrinsically easier than being a contestant who has no

chance to demonstrate their own personal fund of little-known information. The observers seemed to overlook the fact that, had the roles
been reversed, the former questioners would appear ignorant compared
with the now smoothly competent former contestants, asking challenging, and virtually unanswerable, questions. In other words, perceivers
'consistently fail to make adequate allowance for the biasing effects of
social roles upon performance' (Ross, Amabile and Steinmetz, 1977,
p. 485).

Actor–observer error

It has been argued that in at least one situation the fundamental
attribution error breaks down. When attributing causes to our own
behaviour, behaviour does not engulf the field. We are more likely to
attribute situational causes. If asked why we are laughing at the
comedian, we do not reply: 'I'm laughing because I'm a cheerful sort of
person', but 'This comedian is just incredibly funny' (Nisbett *et al.*,
1973). However, there is some evidence that if we can see our own
behaviour in just the same way as we see that of others, then the
behaviour may once again engulf the field. Storms (1973) showed people
video-tapes of themselves in conversation with someone else. When
asked to explain why the conversation took the form it did, people were
likely to make the sorts of personal attribution which they normally
avoid when describing their own behaviour. The video-tape allowed
them to step outside their own selves and to see themselves as another
person would.

It must be stressed that some social psychologists believe that the
actor-observer bias, like the fundamental attribution error, has been
much exaggerated and that the differences between attributing causes
to our own actions and those of others is not so clear-cut (Monson and
Snyder, 1977; Quattrone, 1982; 1985).

False consensus effect

One reason for attributing one's own behaviour to situational causes is
the belief that most reasonable people would behave in the same way.
People do not like to think they laugh at a particular comedian because
they are frivolous; they prefer to believe that the average, reasonable
person would be equally amused. An error occurs if we overestimate the
extent to which other (reasonable) people will act as we do. Ross, Greene
and House (1977) asked students to walk around their university
campus wearing a large sandwich board proclaiming 'Eat at Joe's'. They
also estimated the percentage of other students who would be willing to
walk around advertising Joe's culinary delights. Of those who agreed to
wear the board, 62 per cent thought other students would do the same.
Those who refused thought that the majority of the students would also

refuse. Thus both sets of students, irrespective of their actual behaviour, believed that they were in accord with the consensus of other students. Accordingly, it has been suggested that people tend to overestimate the extent to which their own actions are consensual.

This sort of experimental evidence has convinced some professional social psychologists that their amateur counterparts are rather inadequate at explaining social events. The naive perceiver may try to juggle with different sorts of information about an act, but cannot compute all this information as accurately as the professional psychologists. For example, Nisbett and Borgida (1975) claim that the experimental evidence reveals 'bleak implications for human rationality' and Nisbett (1981) has argued that it is profoundly mistaken to make 'the untutored lay individual the arbiter of reasonableness in inference'. However, one should not dismiss naive psychology in the belief that scientific attribution theory has shown how everyday life should be properly understood. The limitations of attribution theory itself have an important bearing on this issue.

Limitations of attribution theory

Attribution theory assumes that making causal attributions is a key feature of everyday life: people are desperate to know the causes of events. In this, the attribution theorists have created a model of people in their own image. Certainly, professional psychologists seek the causes of ordinary actions, but do ordinary perceivers experience the world similarly? Semin and Manstead (1983) asked the basic question: when do people make causal attributions? Their answer: predominantly when there are breaks, or hitches, in social events. When something untoward occurs people are likely to look for causes. However, routinely people do not stop to ponder over normal everyday events.

This critique can be taken further by considering the actor-observer effect. What does it mean to be asked the question 'why are you doing that?' The very question contains a hint of accusation. We are being called upon to explain ourselves, and thereby to offer a justification for our actions. If we laugh at a comedian and someone asks 'Why are you laughing at that?' we may immediately feel attacked. The implication may be that we are laughing at a racist, sexist or otherwise offensive joke, or perhaps that we are sniggering at a comedian consensually agreed to be lamentably unfunny.

This illustrates that 'why' questions in everyday life can imply justification and blame. The 'why' question, instead of leading to a dispassionate computing of different sorts of information, might very well lead to an argument or even row: Why shouldn't I have a laugh? You're always laughing at trash, etc. Instead of everyday life typically being composed of naive psychologists, blundering through their psychological computations, we find practised arguers, ready to display the rhetoric of excuse and blame (Billig, 1987). Such arguments as the hypothetical one about laughing at the comedian are not merely concerned with the facts of social causation, but are about something much wider, which Heider specifically removed from his own focus of enquiry. They revolve around not merely the facts of an action but also its morality. The argument about the joke would be a debate about what people *ought* to laugh at, and, because of this, the original question 'why are you laughing at the comedian?' appears so challenging. In this context, the question implies we are doing something wrong.

Some have argued that attribution theorists, preoccupied with perceptions of causality, have ignored the importance of attributions of responsibility in everyday life (see Hewstone, 1983). According to Fincham and Jaspars (1980), social psychologists have asked of their experimental subjects ambiguous questions in that they seem to be inviting the subjects to assign responsibility as well as causation. Certainly in everyday life our enquiries about the causality of actions are typically posed in order to assign, or escape from, blame. Fincham and Bradbury (1987) asked young married couples at two points a year apart about the state of their marriages: he invited them to attribute causes to matters which were not going well. The attributions of blame which the wives made at the first interview were a good predictor of their marital satisfaction as reported at the second. Such statements as 'it's his fault that we don't go out together, that we don't have enough money, and that I'm miserable' are not simple assignations of causations. One might well accept that the actions of two people are necessary to *cause*, in a technical sense, problematic situations. However, one might think that just one of the two is *responsible* for the unsatisfactory pattern – 'It's his fault!'

Accepting that everyday notions about causality are bound up with notions of morality and responsibility suggests that some errors of the naive perceiver may not be quite so erroneous after all. In one of the classic demonstrations of the 'errors' of the naive perceiver, Walster (1966) presented subjects with a hypothetical example of a car rolling down a hill, because the owner had not left it parked satisfactorily with the handbrake on. The greater the damage caused to others, the more people assigned responsibility to the owner. Some attribution theorists have claimed that this shows biases in ordinary perception of causality (Fiske and Taylor, 1984). After all, how could an action's cause be affected by its effect? The cause was just the same, whether or not anyone was injured by the runaway vehicle. However, if people are talking about morality and responsibility, then the judgements may not be erroneous. Walster's subjects may not have been making hastily inaccurate calculations of causation, but may have been reflecting social views of morality. They may have been saying in effect that people ought to be responsible for the outcomes of their actions and they should suffer if they have caused, through their negligence, suffering to others. Indeed, the legal system, which in many respects embodies conventional morality, recognizes this. For example, punishment for dangerous driving resulting in the death of others is typically greater than if the same negligent driving had no harmful consequences. To say that judges are wrong in making such decisions is not to make a scientific statement, but a moral one: it is a criticism of the moral basis of the judgement.

This implies that attribution theory, following Heider, has been too narrow in its approach. Theorists have tended to presume that they are studying general principles of social judgement. Biases are assumed to be universal, affecting all social perceivers, regardless of social background, and they are seen as inherent properties of the perceptual process. In fact, if one follows Heider in disregarding much of the social context to look at small aspects of an interpersonal nature, the assumption of universal biases is difficult to escape. However, it is highly questionable if one looks at broader issues. For example, the evidence about social causation can be seen in terms of the cultural assumptions of modern industrial society. The distinction between personal and situational explanations, and the presumed bias towards the former, do not necessarily reflect facts of human nature. They can alternatively be seen in terms of current social assumptions about people and morality. The judgements of responsibility and causality can be seen as 'social representations' (Moscovici, 1984a) of the social world. Social representations refer to a culture's general beliefs and theories about the social world. Perhaps it might be true that modern people tend to share a social representation of the world which stresses personal action and responsibility (rather than naive sociological explanations about social causation); the evidence is not altogether clear-cut, especially in terms of perceptions of major social events. Studies which have examined lay explanations suggest that people recognize social causes of poverty and unemployment. Certainly there are personal attributions (such as idleness and fecklessness) but generally people also recognize the societal, or lay sociological, factors which give rise to poverty and unemployment (Furnham and Lewis, 1986; Nilson, 1980). Most importantly, there seem to be cultural differences in the balance between personal explanations, which hold the poor responsible for their own fate, and societal ones, which pin the blame upon the injustices of society. The proportion of personal attributions seems to be higher in the United States, especially amongst Republican voters, than in Europe or Australia (Furnham and Lewis, 1986).

If there are cultural differences between and within modern industrial societies, then one can expect even greater differences between a modern society and a traditional one. Indeed, the assumption that people offer either personal or situational attributions may itself be a modern assumption (or modern social representation). In Westernized societies very few fatalistic explanations are given of causality. A fatalistic response is neither personal nor situational, but might suggest inevitability: 'It's just the way things are' or 'It's all God's will'. In industrialized society people may have a materialistic view which leads to few metaphysical or fatalistic explanations. However, in other cultures, or at other times, spiritual considerations may play a much greater part in the way that personal relations are experienced and understood.

The Book of Exodus recounts the flight from Egypt of the Children of Israel. A central theme is Pharoah's refusal to allow the Jews to leave his kingdom. A personal attribution of the cause of his refusal might stress his vindictiveness, whereas a situational one might point to the economic gains from having Israelite slaves. The Bible offers a distinct explanation for Pharoah's intransigent conduct, unfamiliar to modern analysts of political events: 'God hardened the heart of Pharoah'.

This example suggest that in religious societies spiritual forces, not the behaviour of others, may engulf the field. Alongside the naive psychologist must be placed the not-so-naive moralist and the everyday theologian. The attribution theorist, in creating the naive perceiver in the image of the professional psychologist, is forgetting the roots of causal attributions in culture. Analysis from cultural life would direct the social psychologist away from the path mapped out by Heider: the big issues about society would have to be looked at, rather than just John, Jim and the comedian who causes them such bother.

Schema theory

Origins

Schema theory is a wider approach to cognition than attribution theory. The latter concentrates upon perceived causation; in contrast, the former looks at general assumptions which social perceivers might have, and how such assumptions affect the way that they experience their worlds. How social perceivers process information about the world is its principal concern. Fiske and Taylor (1984, p. 13), who have conducted a considerable amount of experimental research into cognitive schemata, define a schema as 'a cognitive structure that represents one's general knowledge about a given concept or stimulus domain'. Knowledge is not 'filed' randomly in the mind, but is organized into more or less useful structures. The central assumption is that such knowledge structures crucially affect the way that incoming information about the relevant concept or stimulus domain is processed.

Put at its most basic, schema theory can be seen as a reaction against a naive view of perception, held early by psychological philosophers such as John Locke and Condillac, who maintained that our senses give us a true image of the outside world. We open our eyes and the outside world strikes our retinas, like a photographic image on the film of the camera. Schema theory, by contrast, stresses that perception is not quite that simple. All our perceptions are mediated by cognitive structures, which automatically impart organization to the incoming stimulus. To put it bluntly, there is no perception without conception.

The notion of a schema entered the psychology through the work of the great British psychologist, Sir Frederick Bartlett. Before the Second World War, Bartlett conducted a number of experiments which demonstrated how schemata affected memorization. One very famous experiment (Bartlett, 1932) involved reading a complex Indian folk tale, 'The War of the Ghosts', to one person, who then repeated the story to another, who in turn repeated the story to a third person, and so on in an elaborate version of 'Chinese' whispers. The experiment was designed to illustrate how in the transmission of information changes occur. What information was lost and what retained tended to follow certain broad patterns. In the first place, the story was always repeated as a story: the sense of narrative structure was never lost. It was as if the subjects heard the words and slotted these words into an overall 'story' cognitive structure. However, story detail was lost. Bartlett noted that many of the unfamiliar themes were weeded out. His British subjects tended to ignore the ghostly, metaphysical themes of the original story, and make it altogether more homely. In other words, the new information of the story was assimilated to previously held knowledge structures. By assimilation to such schemata the story could be remembered, although it became fundamentally changed, and Anglicized, in the process.

Further experiments expanded on how the perception and memory of the outside world might be influenced by previously held cognitive schemata. In one experiment Bartlett had students draw a shape from memory. Their reproduction of the shape was affected by how they had categorized it originally. Those for whom the shape resembled an anchor made drawings which were more anchor-like than the original. Significantly, only one student drew the shape accurately, having correctly identified the original drawing as a pre-historic battle-axe. Bartlett concluded that his subjects were not attempting to reproduce the visual image as such, but were reproducing the schema under which it had been automatically categorized.

The art historian, E. H. Gombrich, showed how Bartlett's idea of schema could be applied to the arts. Gombrich (1968, p. 62) suggested that an artist who wishes to paint the world as it is does not naively observe things, but is guided by schemata, or prior knowledge, about the world: 'He begins not with his visual impression but with his idea or who concept'. This can be seen in the work of Albrecht Dürer, the sixteenth-century German artist and engraver, whose pictures of animals have become synonymous with detailed realism. Gombrich shows that Dürer cannot be said to have reproduced what was really there, but his pictures often reveal what he thought he saw. His etchings reflect the biological knowledge of the time: his woodcut of a rhinoceros is influenced by medieval assumptions about the nature of dragons. Gombrich (1968, p. 72) added that even Leonardo da Vinci made errors in his anatomical drawings: 'Apparently he drew features of the human heart which Galen made him expect but which he cannot have seen'.

Gombrich draws from Bartlett's theory of schemata the conclusion that even artists, trained to observe the outside world, are fundamentally influenced by schemata. Indeed, schemata often enable an artist to develop a distinctive style or, at least, to develop the aesthetic traditions within which they are working. Nor is this peculiar to painting or etching whose so-called biases can be contrasted to the accuracy of photography. The same process can be seen at work in photography. The assumptions and social concerns of the photographer can determine the nature of the eventual photograph, for a photograph is no more devoid of schematic influence than is a painting. Like a painting, it does not represent an objective view of the world, untouched as it were, by human thought:

> The photographic image shows the perception of a social agency, whether it is an advertising firm, a left-wing newspaper or a rock group promoter. Its partiality may be personal, economic, artistic or ideological. That social agency's expectations, aims, assumptions will have led to selection, highlighting, censorship, beautification, uglification, all these being part of the formal and informal stock-in-trade of the photographer (Beloff, 1985, p. 17).

If the camera is no naive recording of the world, so then, the eyes of the ordinary social perceiver are not naive cameras.

Schema theory and the biases of categorization

The burst of experimentation in schema theory came in the 1980s, although some of the key studies had been conducted a good few years earlier. Schema theorists have not deliberately shut themselves off from the big problems of the world. Indeed, the analysis of prejudice has been a major theme. The notion that we impose prior conceptions upon our perceptions suggests that we make prejudgements. These, according to some theorists, constitute the essence of prejudiced judgements.

The idea that we impose meaning upon our perceptual data means, at the minimum, that the outside world has to be interpreted. The process of interpretation can be illustrated by an early study in social psychology already discussed in Chapter 3 (Cantril, 1959). As the result of a radio play for a period of time, over a million Americans believed that the United States was being invaded by Martians who were sweeping across the country, gassing the population and destroying all cities. The majority of listeners, who believed the play to be a genuine report of a Martian invasion, did not passively receive the information. Instead they sought out other sources of information such as neighbours and other radio stations. The most common immediate reaction was to rush to the window to look outside. By doing so they would obtain perceptual information, which did not indicate that there were Martians stomping up the street. However, the perceptual field, with its lack of Martian figures, still needed to be interpreted. Cantril gives three different reactions:

> I looked out of the window and everything seemed normal. 'They haven't reached our section yet,' I thought.

> We looked out of the window and Wyoming Avenue was black with cars. 'People are running away,' I thought.

> There were no cars in my road. 'There's a traffic jam, on account of the roads being blocked,' I thought.

In each case, the visual field could be interpreted as providing evidence for the prior conception that the Martians were invading. It did not matter whether the street was emptier than normal, full, or just the same. It all could be interpreted as pointing to the reality of the invasion. We might say that the schema of a Martian invasion was directing the interpretation of the information. In this case, the panic was not occurring because people, in some fit of madness, had taken leave of their senses. Indeed, the panic took root because they were using their senses to provide evidence for their prior conception. And, as schema theorists suggest, this is an all too common occurrence and is not confined to the sort of dramatic occasion which Cantril was studying.

The Bartlett experiments suggest that schemata do not merely guide the interpretation of perceptual data, but also influence what data is selected for attention. In the early 1950s there was a greaty deal of research to show that perception was selective (see Erdelyi, 1974, for a review). This is a point which later schema theorists have taken up. We cannot possibly attend to all the information which our senses are capable of providing us. As Taylor (1981, p. 87) writes, 'given a complex environment, people must develop shortcuts for organizing information'. Schemata provide such shortcuts, for they determine what information is encoded and available for attention, and what is discarded. Thus, as we rush down the street, we have our own internal civil service working away inside our brains: incoming information is efficiently sorted into important files, to be brought to the 'minister's' immediate attention; less important files can be stored and recalled at leisure; and much is chucked out as unworthy of further consideration. According to schema theorists, the schemata provide the system by which this cognitive civil service operates.

Central to this process of *selective perception* is categorization. The incoming information has to be categorized as belonging, or not, to familiar categories. As we continue rushing down the street, the enormous, red, moving blob in our perceptual field is automatically categorized as a bus. It is not something which we normally think about, but is something which the internal civil service, with quiet efficiency, does for us. However, schema theorists stress that this necessary process of categorization involves a distortion. The individual features of the categorized object may be lost, as it is perceived as just another example of the well-known category. Under normal circumstances, we do not see the distinguishing features of a particular bus and we fail to notice the sun shimmering on the roof or the damage to the rear wheel arch. This information is available if we choose to select it. Instead, in our hurry, all we see is a 'bus'!

The link between categorization and distortion was illustrated by an experiment by Henri Tajfel (1981), whose pioneering work had made a deep impact upon the cognitive approach to social psychology, especially in Europe. He presented people with eight lines of differing lengths. They saw the lines one at a time, and then had to estimate the length of the lines. In one condition, a label, 'A', was attached to the four shortest lines, while the four longest lines were labelled 'B'. Tajfel found that the mere imposition of the labels changed the judgements of the subjects. People tended to judge that the four short lines, in other words all the 'A' lines, were much more similar in length than they were in actuality. Similarly they exaggerated the similarity of the four long lines, the 'B' lines. They also exaggerated the differences between 'A' and 'B' lines, by judging that the longest of the short lines and the shortest of the long lines were much more dissimilar than they were. In short, people underestimated differences within the categories and overestimated the difference between categories.

Tajfel suggested that this process applies to social perception. Having categorized a person as belonging to a particular group (for instance, 'the French'), we may mentally exaggerate the similarity of this person to all other French people. Moreover, we may tend to believe that the French are very different from other social categories, for example, the Germans of the Swedes. The consequences of categorization (maximizing similarities within categories and differences between categories), according to Tajfel, underlie stereotyped judgements and reflect a basic mechanism for the creation and maintenance of prejudices (see Chapter 9 for a fuller exposition).

Schema theorists tend to claim that categorization is a more basic process than that of causal attribution. To categorize an object is to say what it is and has to precede perceiving what caused it to do something. Under some circumstances the categorization can imply a causation. For example, to categorize an event as an 'accident' or a 'miracle' is to make a statement about its causes. To Tajfel, categorizing these events should involve cognitive distortions analogous to the distorted judgements of lines. The 'accident' or 'miracle' is perceived as resembling other accidents or miracles and, as such, will be seen as distinct from deliberate actions or naturally occurring events.

Mervis and Rosch (1981) suggest that most categories contain 'prototypes', or typical examples, such as an image of the typical accident or the typical French person. A stimulus is included under the category heading depending on its similarity to the prototype. The stimulus need not have all the features of the prototype, but merely enough of them to distinguish it from stimuli which should be categorized differently. There will be problem cases, where the boundary is uncertain: should we really call the crash caused by the angry, drunken driver an accident? In Mervis and Rosch's words our categories are 'fuzzy-edged', even though, at the centre, they may contain clear, prototypical examples.

One implication of this is that normally the act of categorization does not merely involve the imposition of a neutral label, as it did in Tajfel's line experiment. The imposition of a label conjures up related images, particularly of prototypical examples. These images can then affect our experience of the instance which is being categorized. The term 'images' may be too simple for what may be a whole network of meanings and assumptions – in other words a *cognitive schema*, whether for accidents, miracles or French people. Person schemata may direct attention about how to evaluate an individual and what to expect from their behaviour. Event schemata may contain all sorts of information about appropriate behaviour. Schank and Abelson's (1977) concept of scripts (see also Chapter 2) suggests that if we categorize a particular building as, say, a court of law, this gives a fair idea how to behave in such a building. We follow a courtroom script, which guides appropriate conduct in such a building. Without stored schemata containing whole masses of scripts everyday routine behaviour would be impossible. At a loss as to how to react, we would be perpetual strangers in a foreign land.

As in attribution theory, the schema theories highlight biases involved in making social judgements. Tajfel's work shows that there are distortions in the act of categorization itself. Others have said that schemata lead to a *confirmation bias*. Perceptual data are selected within the framework of cognitive schemata, and consequently, the perceiver tends to take in information which confirms the schemata. A racist individual might possess a cognitive schema which denigrates gypsies for being dirty. Such a person may then categorize every dirty caravan site as being a gypsy encampment. Clean caravans will be assumed to belong to 'respectable' holidaymakers. Thus, the initial schema governs both the selection and interpretation of information, which in turn, leads to the confirmation of the schema. One schema theorist (Snyder, 1981b) describes it as 'Seek and ye shall find'.

Biases can also occur when retrieving information from memory (Rothbart, 1981). According to schema theorists, we tend to remember information which confirms the initial assumption. Our racist may well have a ready story of examples of dirty gypsy encampments. On the other hand, that rather pleasant site which he chanced upon the year before last, may have already slipped his memory; and there is little to instruct the inner civil service to set in motion a search for the lost file. Furthermore, already coded and stored information can be recoded to conform to schematic assumptions. Snyder and Uranowitz (1978) found that giving the information that someone was homosexual led to a reappraisal of memories about that person. Suddenly, memories were reinterpreted and signs of the person's homosexuality were now found as easily as they had previously been overlooked. If this sort of seeking and finding occurs with information about others, then, according to Greenwald (1980), it happens with added force when we are thinking about ourselves. The ego, according to Greenwald, acts as a determined censor, defending our own images of ourselves. Information, uncomfortable to our own self-esteem, is weeded from our consciousness. We become the heroes of our life-episodes, remembering our funny jokes and devastating ripostes. The images of ourselves are protected by the careful and smoothing ministrations of that internal civil service, which runs the schemata quietly and efficiently.

Critique of schema theory

The schema approach portrays a rather unflattering view of the individual thinker. As Fiske and Taylor (1984, p. 12) write, cognitive social psychologists have produced an image of the naive perceiver which assumes that 'people are limited in their capacity to process information, so they take shortcuts wherever they can'; and, of course, these shortcuts involve distorting simplifications as the complexities of reality are reduced to the simplicities of social schemata. At worst, this simplification might appear to involve an element of charlatanry, as the social perceiver, in continual acts of bad faith, tries to make the assumptions of the schema come true.

Billig (1985; 1987) has claimed that cognitive social psychologists, especially those concentrating upon the process of categorization, have used a 'bureaucratic' model of thinking. Thought processes are regarded as pigeonholing and filing information as efficiently as possible, in order to drive away the spectre of disorder. This suggests that cognitive social psychology has produced a model of the thinker as essentially a non-thinker. Cognitive processes are followed unthinkingly and can lead to unthinking errors. Langer *et al.* (1978) provided evidence of this. According to Langer (1978, p. 40), we typically process the information of our daily lives with our minds a blank: 'Unless forced to engage in conscious thought, one prefers the mode of interacting with one's environment in a state of relative mindlessness, at least with regard to the situation at hand'. Yet there is a theoretical danger that needs to be avoided: we miss features of the way that people experience their social worlds by taking the 'mindless thinker' as our model of thinking.

Like attribution research, so much of the research in the schema approach is conducted from the 'standpoint of the individual'. Great attention has been paid to the ways that the experience of the individual might lead to the construction and development of schemata and how individual experience might affect the processing of incoming information (Taylor, 1981; Taylor and Crocker, 1981). This emphasis has led to a neglect of a basic point, which Serge Moscovici and his collaborators have emphasized (Moscovici, 1982; Jodelet, 1984), that, by and large, schemata are not created out of individual experiences. One may have a schema about people and events with which one has had no direct experience. Most British people have schemata about the kings and queens of times past but no direct experience of them. Moreover, there is a commonality between the schemata held by individual British people. Because they will be generally held, they are what Moscovici calls 'social representations'.

Attributions of causality can be seen alternatively as social representations. For example, the citizenry of a modern industrial society may share certain beliefs, image, prototypes and theories about poverty. Murray Edelman (1977) claims that people today generally accept two contrary myths about poverty. On the one hand, they talk about poverty in a way which blames the poor (the personal attributions of attributional theory would figure largely in the discourse of this mythology). On the other hand, they show pity on the poor and, using the language of situational attributions, criticize the social structure for creating poverty. One might say that the social representation of poverty contains these contrary themes, which are often, according to Edelman, intermingled when people start talking about the issue.

Moscovici's criticism of schema theory involves more than a recategorization of schema as social representations. He wishes to reverse the emphasis in cognitive social psychology on the standpoint of the individual perceiver. For too long, according to Moscovici (1984a; 1984b), social psychologists have confined their attention to asking questions about the effect of social knowledge on the individual perceiver. One needs also to ask questions about how such knowledge, or mythology, circulates within a society; how it originates and how it is transformed. In other words, one needs to examine the social contexts and social processes of schemata. This project does not merely involve investigating how members of a society come to hold grand beliefs about society and morality. It also means looking at the social origins of the small naive psychological theories which so interested Heider.

Bartlett came to dislike the word 'schema' because he thought it implied a mental rigidity: people who possess schemata might be thought to be unable to think about the world, but become dominated by their own assumptions. Bartlett (1932, pp. 200–1) wrote that we need to look at the way it is possible to 'turn round one's schemata'. Our views on the world might be influenced by culturally received schemata or representations, but this does not mean that we must be trapped by these schemata. The example of Dürer and his schematic representation of the rhinoceros can be reconsidered. It may be true that Dürer was influenced by schemata or social representations when he drew the animal with an armoured back and with scaly legs, but he also contributed to the transformation of the culture. His works served as a prototype for a new category of representative art. The paintings of Dürer affected the later art, but not through slavish obedience to a visual stereotype which prevented the development of art.

However, the process of changing schemata is not confined to creative genius. There is a further, not mindless, form of thought for which something else, beyond labelling into categories, is required – negation. For thoughtful and deliberative consideration of issues the capacity for negation is essential. As we have seen, attributional questions are asked in particular contexts and consequently bear a hint of criticism, leading to self-justification. In order to criticize and to answer criticisms one must be able to negate views: perhaps to unpick, or turn around, the categorizations of the critic, in order to offer one's own justifications. When one is in a social exchange, answering or offering criticisms, one is offering arguments and not mindlessly filing information into categories. One of the ways of studying how social cognition operates in creating change is to observe how people argue (Billig, 1987) since here may lie indicators of how schemata, social representations, and attributions may have flexibility and can change. Social representations are not so neatly organized as to impart a simple, unified view of the world. 'Common sense' contains its own contrary themes: 'Look before you leap' and 'Make haste while the sun shines'; 'Too many cooks spoil the broth' and 'Many hands make light work' (Billig *et al.*, 1988). It is the presence of such culturally produced contradictions (contrary schemata) which enables us to think: we can argue with ourselves, just as we can argue with others, about whether this particular situation should be categorized under the common-sense heading about the 'too many cooks' or whether it should be pigeonholed along with 'the many hands' mythology. At these times, we might hear our internal civil service doing something that it is rarely allowed to do in the experimental situations of the cognitive social psychologists: it is arguing about the outside world and about its own procedures. And as criticisms are offered, and criticisms criticized, then the business of social thinking really gets under way.

Concluding comments

Different approaches to social psychology often suggest different images of the person. For example, attribution theory tends to create the impression that the person is a rather detached scientist, whose prime task is to work out why events occur: the person observes events and then assigns causes to these events. The image of the 'person as scientist' has been extended in some more recent versions of attribution theory to become the 'person as lawyer'. The person is still seen to be assigning causes. But, in addition, the 'person as lawyer' is also prepared to pass sentence on those who are adjudged to have caused wrongful acts to occur. Both images – the person as scientist and the person as lawyer – present a somewhat cold image of the ordinary person, as if in daily life we are unemotional scientists or dispassionate judges. The image of thinker, which comes over in schema theory, is even colder: the thinker is rather like an unthinking, and unfeeling, filing clerk, packaging the world into neat administrative bundles.

However, a somewhat different image of the person is found in the 'rhetorical approach', which sees argument as an important aspect of thinking (Billig, 1987). Here the person is seen as discussing and arguing about what to do, how to judge others, and so on. Causes are not coldly and unemotionally affixed to events, but social life is filled with the sound of passionate discussions about why things happen and whether they should happen. In other words, we do not stand back from life, pinning causes on events and judgements on actors, but we are involved in life, arguing, disputing and being perplexed about what goes on in the world.

At first sight this shift of an image from the 'person as scientist' to the 'person as debater' might seem to indicate a change in the way that social psychologists study social life – a shift towards examining language. Certainly, if one is interested in the way people think about the world, attention must be paid to the language they use to talk about and describe social life. In particular, social psychologists should pay attention to the sorts of language people use when they argue about social life.

There is a further implication. The image of the person as a debater brings back the role of emotions in thought. Both attribution theory and schema theory present a view of thinking which is essentially unemotional. The person as scientist or information processor goes about their business of understanding the world in an unemotional way. In fact, emotions are seen rather to get in the way of thinking. The image of the 'person as scientist' in particular suggests that emotions are to be separated from thinking about the social world. However, in the ordinary language of thinking, emotions and thoughts are not so easily separable. Let us reconsider the example of how people go about explaining the existence of poverty. Attribution theory suggests that the 'person as scientist' might arrive at a conclusion having assessed social trends and observed the behaviour of the poor. Having done this, or having believed that they have done this, the person might then affix a causal label – 'governmental policy is causing poverty'. However, in debate, or perhaps in newspaper headlines, people might express themselves with much greater force: someone might claim that 'the government is allowing children to die of hunger'. In this cry, there is much more than the expression of causality, or the application of a causal schema. There is an emotional and moral force to the cry: deep anger is expressed, as criticisms are directed against the government and its supporters. In this way, the assignment of causality is both part of an argument (against the government) and an expression of emotion.

All this is achieved through language. It is only because we possess language that we can express thoughts in which accusations, feelings and beliefs are so subtly intermixed, so that simple statements can express a complexity of meaning at any one time. Such complexity can be seen not merely with statements about causality, but, also, as will be seen in the following chapter, in the ways that people express their attitudes.

8

ATTITUDES AND ATTITUDE CHANGE

Earlier in this century, the North American psychologist Floyd Allport claimed that attitude is social psychology's most distinctive and indispensable concept. The idea that people may be distinguished in terms of the their possession of enduring evaluative dispositions which guide their thinking and behaviour is a powerful one. It allows people to be differentiated according to their political, religious and other preferences, and predictions to be made about the way these preferences affect voting or attendance at church. Put simply, attitudes are taken to be indispensable because they seem to account for much of the regularity and predictability in the social world.

What are attitudes?

Attitudes and attitudes

Some might object that they do not need a psychologist to tell them about attitudes because they already know about them. And in a sense they would be right. We talk about attitudes all the time. We worry about our friends' attitudes to their parents or the disadvantaged. And we are told that we have the wrong attitude if we are rude to the boss.

Now there is an important issue here. There are actually two words which look and sound the same – attitude and attitude. One of these terms we use in our everyday talk, and the other one we use in social psychology in some rather different ways. It is easy to get confused, and even psychologists do it. The scientific and everyday uses are difficult to disentangle. Social psychology has developed by drawing on and refining our everyday language for social phenomena and rarely have distinctly and expressly social psychological terms gained much usage. At the same time modified and refined terminology filters back, adding new shades of meaning and once in a while entire new words to our everyday world (Moscovici, 1976; 1984a).

During modern elections, public opinion polls have increasingly dominated news coverage, sometimes at the expense of substantive issues. People seem to be as interested in what *other people think* as in the important questions of how their lives are going to be run. More striking is the widespread understanding of the *technical* language of attitude measurement such as sample size, reliability and validity, as well as issues of question wording which have been learned from the media. There is a close relationship, then, between psychologists' and everyday notions of attitudes; each influences the other.

The cultural specificity of attitudes

Before defining attitudes more precisely it is worth reminding ourselves of their historical and cultural context. The influential attitude theorist, William McGuire (1985), has suggested that there have been four great eras of attitudes and persuasion: fourth-century BC Athens, first-century BC Rome, the Italian Renaissance, and most places in the twentieth century. Only in these has persuasion, and therefore attitudes, played a central economic, social and political role. At other times being skilful in persuasion was unimportant and a science of persuasion unimaginable.

This may seem strange as we assume people have always had their own specific preferences and desires. Indeed, are attitudes not the sort of reasoned response we think distinguishes people from coffee machines and geraniums? However, our understanding of human nature is conditioned by our society's particular model of people. Modern Western society is characterized by mass advertising of both consumer products and politics. This advertising is all about the refinement of preferences and the shifting of opinions, and its success depends on its being able to generate new attitudes towards products and candidates.

Attitudes are only important in circumstances where there is a substantial element of choice. Muslims have a negative view of eating pork, but this represents a universal attitude, not one which will vary from person to person. It would not be casual or easy for a Muslim to obtain, prepare and eat pork in Islamic countries. Attitudes towards politicians are by and large, unimportant to the course of political life in anything but a democracy. Consumer capitalism, with its vastly enlarged range of consumer choice, requires that individual preferences are manipulated in the hope of creating markets or maximizing market shares.

Furthermore, the notion of the importance of attitude thrives in conditions where there is a very individuated notion of persons. We tend to take this for granted in our culture, which places an enormous emphasis on the uniqueness of each person and largely treats decisions as things that individuals rather than groups do. However, there are cultures where things are very different. For instance, some social anthropologists have suggested that Eskimos do not characterize emotions as internal states as Westerners do. Westerners talk of bottling up indignation or letting it go; Eskimos do not characterize it as the feeling of the individual speaker but as something directed at another. Displays of emotion are almost always communal. That is, if one Eskimo weeps, they all weep; when one laughs they all laugh (Carpenter, 1966; Solomon, 1976). Individual feeling, intentions, and so on, play a very small part. It follows, then, that for Eskimos the notion of attitudes as personal, mentally represented, preferences will not be well developed.

Defining attitudes

Having been alerted to the duality of 'attitude' as both a technical and everyday term, and to the fact that it has a historically and culturally located range of interpretations, can it usefully be defined? We have to be careful to avoid definitions which prejudge the facts, for example incorporating notions of the unchanging nature of attitudes. There is always a very real danger of inadvertently incorporating assumptions in the guise of a definition (Eiser, 1986). However, a recent definition offered by McGuire (1985, p. 239) has much to recommend it; attitudes are 'responses that locate "objects of thought" on "dimensions of judgement" '. That is, when people are 'responding' (speaking or acting in some other way) they are taking some idea or object of interest and giving it a position in an evaluative hierarchy. It allows for transitoriness in attitudes as much as permanence. Furthermore, it avoids requiring attitudes to be deeply emotionally tied. A final advantage is that it treats attitudes as mental constructions not as real objects to which evaluations are attached.

Attitudes and behaviour

Having established a more precise understanding of what attitudes are, it may seem that they provide a powerful method of predicting how people will behave. Once we know people's attitudes we also know what they will do – people who have very positive attitudes to chocolate will buy and eat it, for example. Unfortunately things are not this simple

and an important qualification needs to be made to McGuire's definition. As noted, he defines attitudes as 'responses that locate "objects of
thought" on "dimensions of judgement" '; yet it would be more correct
to say that responses are *expressions* of attitudes. The need to make this
distinction becomes clearer if we think of the following simple
example. You go to see a film with a friend. Afterwards, walking home,
you chattily observe that it was the most appalling film you have ever
seen in your life – bad script, awful acting. Then you ask your friend
what he thought of it. Now there is a problem here; people often feel
themselves under pressure to agree with strongly stated views of this
kind. What your friend tells you about the film may be different from
what he really privately thinks. That is, the *public* attitude may be
different from the *private* attitude. Worse still, the public attitude may
change if your friend is talking to someone else who is, say, not keen on
films by that director. The private attitude may even change to come in
line with the public attitude. This presents researchers with a problem.
If they are dealing with just an expressed attitude there is a danger that
the ramifications of situational determinants and public–private mis-
matches will be ignored. Indeed, there are a large number of studies
which show that people may act in a way which is rather at odds with
what one might naively expect from how they fill in an attitude scale
(Wicker, 1969). But is there any reason to assume that attitudes
expressed on questionnaires reflect anything about attitudes publicly or
privately expressed in other circumstances?

The classic demonstration of variation between these things was
conducted as long ago as 1934 by La Picre. He visited 184 restaurants and
hotels across the United States in the company of a couple of Chinese
extraction (La Piere himself was a white American), with the intention
of having dinner. Only once in 184 attempts did they fail to be served,
and from this one might conclude that the restaurateurs were not
prejudiced against minority groups. However, a letter from La Piere sent
to these same establishments asking whether they would 'accept
members of the Chinese race as guests' generated a very different
picture. Ninety-two per cent flatly said no, and the rest said it would
depend on the circumstance!

Although the issue of attitudes not correlating with behaviour is
frequently raised, this terminology is misleading because expressing
attitudes is itself a form of behaviour. Roughly speaking, the problem is
one of the lack of relation between what people say and other sorts of
activity they engage in. We *say* that we are Christians when asked our
religion by a nurse in hospital, but when Sunday comes, faced with the
effort of a long walk to church, we may not put it into practice. It is
sometimes easier to say what we believe is expected rather than risk
embarrassment by telling the truth.

Resolving the attitude–behaviour problem

Social psychologists have come up with various responses to this problem. Here we will discuss two principal approaches and deal with examples of each in turn: techniques which can be used to try to bring expressed attitudes into line with 'genuine' attitudes; and suggestions that the connection between a person's expressed attitudes and what they will do in practice is rather more complex than is often assumed.

One dramatic technique for trying to get honest answers from people is the *bogus pipeline*. Jones and Sigall (1971) reasoned that if people could be duped into thinking that a researcher has *infallible knowledge* of their attitudes they would be truthful. In this situation there would be no point in lying for, if they did, they would be immediately exposed.

The experimenters devised a rather devious set-up to convince experimental volunteers that they knew would be found out if they lied. The volunteers were connected to apparatus consisting of lots of electrodes and a panel of flashing lights, with a big pointer which could move along a scale from agree to disagree. Crucially, the researchers had surreptitiously ascertained certain of the participants' attitudes in an earlier study. Consequently, the researchers could ask the participants questions which they *already* had the answers to, and make it look as if the *apparatus* was measuring their attitudes. From the point of view of the participants it looked as if they were wired up to a gadget which could magically reflect their attitudes – 'a lie detector', as it were.

In these circumstances, there is little point in presenting a 'cleaned-up', socially acceptable version of one's attitudes since it 'will not wash'. For example, a study of attitudes to women's rights (Faranda *et al.*, 1979) found that, when asked about women's rights using the usual pencil and paper attitude scale, members of both sexes expressed similar attitudes. However, when wired up to the bogus pipeline, the men admitted much less sympathy toward women's rights than did the women. It appears that the bogus pipeline had led them to reveal attitudes that they would have otherwise kept to themselves in the context of a social psychological study.

The other approach to the problems thrown up by La Piere's study is to rethink presuppositions about the relationship between the attitudes people express and what they actually do. One of the most influential moves in this direction comes from Martin Fishbein and Icek Ajzen in the theory of reasoned action (Fishbein and Ajzen, 1974; Ajzen and Fishbein, 1980).

Their explanation of the findings of the La Piere study is dependent on the following suggestions. There is something very *different* happening when people are asked in a general enquiry whether they would accept members of the 'Chinese race' from when a smartly dressed and obviously very cultured Chinese couple turn up accompanied by a white man. The former measures *general attitude*, while the latter concerns feelings about a *specific couple*. Furthermore, without seeing the couple, respondents were probably guided by a negative *stereotype* or *image* of Chinese people which the couple did not resemble at all. Moreover, think of the embarrassment and disturbance to other guests that would be involved in turning the couple away. Fishbein and Ajzen's model has to maintain the basic idea that attitudes are important determinants of behaviour while accounting for apparently discrepant findings like those of La Piere. Their ideas can best be introduced by way of a concrete example (see Smith, 1987). Imagine that there is the prospect of a strike in the local lawnmower factory. Will one of the workers, Jane, go on strike or not? Fishbein and Ajzen claim that we need to consider two things very carefully. First, that the *intention* to go on strike is more important to explain than the actual act itself. Often the act will follow from the intention. However, other circumstances could get in the way – perhaps some unforeseen event occurs, such as illness. That doesn't alter the *intention*, but it does *prevent* the behaviour. Second, that the way attitudes influence behavioural intention depends on a complex evaluation of the *consequences of behaving*. Put simply, whether people do something will depend on whether they think it will bring rewards, whether it will make them look silly, and so on. Thus, does Jane think that striking will bring her more money and does she believe her workmates will support or criticize her?

In the theory of reasoned action behavioural intention will be affected by two principal factors: social expectations and attitudes themselves. Moreover, both these factors can be analysed further. We can see why this is so if we consider Jane's reasoning about going on strike. Starting with her attitude, a central component is her desire to be paid better – shortage of money may make a pay rise very important to her. However, when thinking about striking, assessments will also be made of its likelihood of success. That is, even if a pay rise is desperately needed Jane may not strike if she thinks the strike is doomed to failure.

The other dimension in Jane's reasoning concerns her social expectations. Decisions of this kind are not made in a social vacuum; what other people think proper is strongly involved. People weigh up costs and benefits, but they also want to preserve their reputations. Issues of keeping face and maintaining dignity are often as important as material rewards and economic gain (Harré, 1979). For Jane, then, there are two considerations here: what other people (her workmates, her family) think of her going on strike; and how seriously she takes their views. For Fishbein and Ajzen, the reason why many studies of attitudes fail to predict behaviour is that they do not take all these separate considerations into account. Predicting what Jane will do involves, at the very least, assessment of how much she values the reward; how likely she thinks she is to get it; what she thinks others think about her striking; and how much she is bothered about what they think.

If all of these and more are precisely measured, according to the theory, behaviour ought to be precisely predictable. Nothing in psychology is ever this neat, but there have been notable successes using this theory. These include predictions about such behaviour as smoking (Fishbein, 1982), contraceptive use (Pagel and Davidson, 1984), and infant feeding choice (Manstead *et al.*, 1984). Eiser ,(1986, p. 61) sums up the state of play as follows: 'with suitable matching of levels of specificity, high correlations between measures of attitude and behaviour can be found'.

Attitude change and social cognition

During and after the Second World War social psychologists sought to establish the basic variables that make a communication persuasive. Best known was that carried out by Hovland *et al.* (1953) in the United States. This and other studies pointed to the importance of four basic variables: attractiveness, credibility, power, similarity. Roughly speaking, communication was persuasive when it came from individuals or groups who were attractive, credible, powerful or similar to the recipient of the communication.

There is nothing greatly surprising about this list — most of us have a reasonably intuitive idea about what is persuasive. We put on smart clothes for job interviews, we take note of credible people like scientists, and we are aware of the effectiveness of politicians who 'have the common touch'. However, even if their efficacy is established, there is still a further question for social psychologists to ask, namely *why* they are effective in changing attitudes. In asking this question researchers have started to move beyond these rather global notions to take a finer-grained look at how people respond to persuasive messages (Fiske and Taylor, 1984). The approach to this in the 'Hovland tradition' tended to seek global principles for structuring persuasive messages. Furthermore, the aims of these early researches included finding means of communicating effectively through the mass media. As a consequence the effectiveness of written communication was of more concern than interpersonal persuasion. Issues like whether it is best to include all sides of the argument, to make your point before or after opposed opinions, and to try to persuade over a good meal were typical. The aim was to develop *general* principles in persuasive communication. Frustratingly, social life refused to throw up such ready solutions and the complexity of the research findings defeated simplistic attempts to create a foolproof technology of persuasion. One lesson from this is that analyses of individual communication may be needed in preference to endeavours towards finding precise and general laws.

Attributes and influence

A theory which provides a finer-grained account of the influence of basic communicator variables is attribution theory (see Chapter 7). To recap, the basic idea of attribution theory is that people come to understand the social world in rather the same way as scientists come to understand the natural world. That is, they try to infer causes for events. In this case, the events in question are people's actions. Scientists ask what made the atom break into a positron, neutron and two neutrinos?; ordinary people ask what caused Jim to go off in a huff? and what makes Sally such a prig? Broad patterns exist in attributions of causation. In particular, the split between factors internal to the person and those which are external warrants consideration.

Communicative effects can be examined in terms of attributions of causality. Here there are three different classes of causal attribution we can make – to the object, to the environment, and to the individual. Government ministers who announce support for the legalisation of marijuana will be viewed differently if they have consistently advocated liberal causes (individual cause), or their prime minister has recently advocated a similar position (environmental cause), or if it has recently been proven that marijuana has no deleterious consequences (object cause). How convincing the announcement would be depends on a 'Well they would say that, wouldn't they?' decision. If one expects the person to advocate the position it carries less force than if no such explanation can be given in terms of personal characteristics.

This idea has been tested experimentally. For example, Wood and Eagly (1981) gave people transcripts which were supposedly the arguments made by a person called Jim for the restriction of pornography. Some participants were told that Jim had a history of supporting freedom of speech and the availability of pornography, and others that Jim's background was against freedom of speech and against pornography. Considerable effort was made to present Jim as a real person – they gave participants snippets of information about his past and quotes from things he had supposedly written or said. In line with the experimenters' prediction, the participants found Jim much more convincing if his history was such that they could not explain his views away as just what you would expect from someone like that.

Studies of this kind do not imply that people are unreflexive and unaware information-processing mechanisms. Attributions are not immutable labels which, once applied, fix a speaker's credibility for ever. As some sociologists have stressed, people are not 'social dopes' who are helpless victims of the attributions of others (Garfinkel, 1967; Heritage, 1984). Instead they are both skilful manipulators of how they want to be seen and are aware of how others are trying to present themselves. People have considerable tacit understanding of the processes of attribution (Pollner, 1987) and they often try to enhance their credibility by anticipating the perceptions of the other person.

For example, politicians in interviews often say things like 'I used to be a strong/fervent/committed believer in X, but now . . . '. This technique tries to avoid the audience's attributing the cause to long-standing dispositions since this would make it much harder to convince them. But the audience often sees through strategies like this and makes a subject attribution despite attempts to circumvent it.

Cognitive response analysis

Cognitive response analysis is basically uncomplicated. Petty and Cacioppo (1986) propose that a message's persuasiveness depends on what people think about it. This may sound simple-minded, but by suggesting that there are two routes to persuasion they add precision to our understanding. The routes are the central and peripheral ones:

1. *The central route.* Here the recipient of a communication first generates and then weighs up arguments for and against a particular point of view. This involves actively elaborating and evaluating the message. In essence, the more arguments the person elaborates in favour of the position the more their attitudes are likely to be influenced toward it. The converse is also true so that the more counterargument one elaborates the greater the rejection of the message's point of view. The overall attitude change will be a function of the relative number of counter-arguments and supporting arguments.
2. *The peripheral route.* Here the person is influenced not by high-level cognitive elaboration of the message, but by more peripheral processes. For example, the influence might work through simple emotional associations which are not really thought out, or by making simple inferences from the context without thinking about the content of the message. Much advertising demonstrates this with appeals to stylishness, motherhood, fear of isolation, and other links which are hinted at. Alternatively, the peripheral route can work through wider cues taken from the context. An example of this is assuming that a message is correct without further thought simply because the speaker is highly credible.

Cognitive response analysis makes quite subtle predictions about the influence of a number of different variables on attitude change. Communicator credibility provides a good illustration of how the theory explains attitude change via the central and peripheral routes. It has generally been found, as one would expect, that more credible communicators generate the most attitude change. Naturally credibility is defined in terms of secondary criteria such as social status, power, expertise, and authority – to define it in terms of effectiveness would be a tautology. One of the striking features of cognitive response analysis is that it predicts that there are cases when speakers with *less* credibility may be more effective at persuading an audience.

Think about this example. Someone strongly in favour of an increase in student grants listens to a high-credibility communicator, a top politician, making a powerful speech in favour of such an increase. This is quite comfortable; the person may feel their position is well represented, will hear arguments comfortably similar to their own, but better presented, and will not think much about the arguments. However, if a lower-credibility communicator, perhaps a flatmate, makes the same points the person will probably not feel so well represented or comforted, or may feel the need to marshall more support, and so elaborate more arguments to themself. As a consequence of this elaboration of arguments in favour, the individual will move to a more strongly pro position. Conversely a high-credibility opponent, say the Education Minister, arguing that the grant should stay the same, will be a greater threat than a flatmate making the same points. The Education Minister will have opinions based on knowledge, evidence, discussion, debate and research, so will have a major undermining effect on other positions. Consequently the person has to elaborate more arguments against and, ironically, the Minister will have less influence than the lower-status flatmate.

Hass (1981) tested these predictions by exposing people with strong feelings on a particular issue to either high- or medium-status communicators talking about it. Cognitive responses were measured by asking participants to write down all the arguments that came to their minds. These were then rated by the participant as pro, neutral or anti. It was found that attitudes had changed more in the *medium*-credibility condition than in the high-credibility one. These findings confirm just what cognitive response theory suggests. They are dependent on the considerable involvement of the subjects in the issue and, as much, do not conflict with the classic demonstrations of the effects of credibility on attitude change in which subjects responded to issues which did not concern them greatly. The effects of communicator credibility are essentially due to being motivated or not to do the argumentative work oneself.

The process, then, is different by the peripheral route. Here people are uninvolved with the issues or even unattentive. In this situation, argue Petty and Cacioppo, factors such as attractiveness and credibility have their greatest impact. If one is engrossed in the actual arguments, the communicators' attractiveness and credibility are usually unimportant. Where the evaluative and critical faculties are not engaged, acceptance of the advocated position may follow based on aspects of the communicator. This was confirmed by Petty *et al.* (1981) who found that uninvolved people are more likely to be affected by attractiveness and similar variables.

Despite its achievements, cognitive response analysis is not without its problems (Eiser, 1986). First, it is only a partial theory of attitude change. Specifically, although it describes the effect of elaborating pro and anti arguments, it does not say *why*, for example, people generate pro as opposed to anti arguments. Second, it has been claimed to treat people as too thoughtful – do people really spend time generating arguments when they hear messages, even one on topics they are highly involved with? Third, does the generation of arguments itself cause the attitude change, or do people generate such arguments to rationalize change which has taken place for some other reason? Given the importance that people place on self-presentation (Goffman, 1959) and accountability (Heritage, 1984; 1988) people may need to make arguments of this kind simply to maintain the rational and credible appearance of their positions.

Attitudes, persuasion and the analysis of discourse

One problem with the theories of attitude change from the social cognition tradition is that they treat persuasion as something very abstract. There are arguments, which have a certain quality, and there are communicators, who have certain basic features such as credibility or attractiveness. The recipient computes these features together in either an involved or a lazy manner, and the outcome is some change of attitude. This underplays the rhetorical nature of persuasive communication (Billig, 1987; Potter and Wetherell, 1987). Indeed, Billig (1988a) argues that attitudes only come into existence when some contentious issue is at stake. The implication of this is that attitude and persuasive talk in natural situations cannot be ignored, particularly when dispute and argument are found.

Research on political oratory has examined the way talk can be structured in real life in order to persuade. How do politicians rally support for a cause? How do they persuade others of their views? What makes really charismatic orators so effective? Are they really special, possessing a natural gift for persuasion?

Some researchers have come to see the topic of political oratory rather differently. Max Atkinson (1983; 1984a; 1984b; 1985) and, more recently, Heritage and Greatbatch (1986; see also Grady and Potter, 1985) make the following suggestions about political oratory. First, skilled oratory and charisma are not to do with the personality of the orator but result from the way orators use language. That is, they are a phenomenon of rhetoric; something anyone could do if properly trained. Second, there are public, observable clues to the effectiveness of oratory. In particular, audiences applaud and cheer, or they boo and heckle. That is, there is an immediate evaluation of the effectiveness of oratory that can easily be measured. Third, the effectiveness of political oratory arises from the skills used in everyday conversation. In fact, high-quality oratory is, in certain crucial respects, like an ordinary conversation. Atkinson resurrects the traditional term *claptrap* – literally the trapping of applause – to characterize this skilled manipulative oratory. He based his research on video-recordings of political party conferences. All those sections where speakers received applause were transcribed using a standard system. This enabled detailed examination of the kinds of oratory which bring about applause, so as to establish broad relationships between audience approval and rhetorical technique.

Trapping the clap

In ordinary conversation people usually know in advance when the speaker will stop and it is their turn to say something (Sacks *et al.*, 1974; Levinson, 1983). Such anticipation is possible because of cues from the speaker including the intonation of voice, the syntax, the sorts of words used, and certain gestures. These allow everyday conversation to run more or less smoothly. Atkinson argues that similar skills are needed by an audience to applaude appropriately. If they are unable to predict effectively the appropriate gap there will be a delay between the speaker's point and the applause, which will seem half-hearted or reluctant. In fact, the interval between the completion of the applaudable utterance and the onset of the applause is typically zero or even slightly anticipates the speaker's final words. This suggests that applause is being accurately placed. Atkinson looked for features which signal the points when the audience could 'show their appreciation'. He found several.

Namings

Thatcher: I am however (0.2 [*seconds pause*]) very fortunate (0.4) in having (0.6) a <u>mar</u>vellous deputy (0.4) who's

wonderful (.) in <u>all</u> places (0.2) at all times (0.2) in all
things.
(0.2)

Willie White – law: ----------------(8.0)--------------- :
Audience: x-xxXXXXXXXXXXXXXxxx-x

                                            (Applause)

In the above extract (taken from Atkinson, 1984a, p. 50) we can see that
the completion, the point where the audience should come in, is
signalled very clearly. The person to be named is identified very early in
the passage ('deputy'); a few words are said about him. And then he is
named. All this is carefully paced out so the audience can grasp it, just
like the 'hip hip' in 'hip hip hooray'.

There are three other interesting aspects to this passage. First, note
the 'however' at the start of the extract, which signals a change of topic
and encourages the audience to pay attention. Second, observe the use of
'fortunate', '<u>mar</u>vellous' and 'wonderful' which cues speakers that
applause is likely to be appropriate. In Atkinson's data one of the largest
classes of applause is directly after speakers have made positive
evaluations of this kind. Third, the duration of the applause is about 8
seconds. It seems that this is the length which is considered proper;
longer bursts are seen as exceptionally enthusiastic; shorter bursts as
lukewarm or ambivalent.

The applause that follows namings, of course, is not the most exciting
for researchers studying persuasion. Applause following a specific point
made by a speaker is much more interesting. Laying aside namings,
mid-speech applause follows specific types of oratory – in particular
attacks, criticisms and boastings. All of these are situations where a
strong evaluative assessment is made. The sort of statements include:
'they're idiots', 'their policy is a disaster', 'the X group of our party are
traitors', 'we're wonderful', and 'our policy is brilliant'.

Three-part lists
It is immediately apparent that criticism or boasting are not sufficient to
generate applause – unskilled orators demonstrate their failure in this
regard with boring inevitability. Utterances must be organized in
certain recognizable ways if they are to get applause. Take the following
extract (taken from Atkinson 1984a, p. 62), which shows Eric Heffer, MP,
addressing a Labour Party Meeting.

Heffer: The National Executive decided (0.8) that we <u>agreed</u> in
            <u>PRINCIPLE</u> (0.8) that we <u>MUST</u> <u>AGAIN</u> <u>TRY</u> AND
            <u>GET</u> SOME <u>CONSTITUTIONAL</u> <u>AMEND</u>MENTS
            (0.5)
    ①→ BE ↑ <u>FORE</u> YOU
            (0.2)

②→ <u>AT</u> CONFERENCE
   (0.2)
③→ THIS ↓ <u>WEEK</u>
          [SO THAT YOU CAN <u>STILL</u> MAKE]=
Audience: xxxXXXXXXXXXXXXXXXXXXXX
Heffer: = [YOUR <u>MINDS</u> UP
Audience: XXXXXXXXXXXXXXXXX (*TV editor's cut*)

The passage is strongly advocating a particular position. However, one of the immediately striking things about the language of this extract is that the oratory leading up to the start of the applause is audibly split into three parts through a mixture of pacing and intonation. We see that there is rising (↑) intonation in the first part, level intonation in the second, and falling (↓) intonation in the third.

Research on lists in ordinary conversation shows that they commonly consist of three grouped items (Jefferson, ,1989). Conversants sometimes get stuck after producing two parts and grope around for the third: 'he's sleek, muscular and, er, er, healthy'. Listeners generally do not start speaking after the first two parts of a list, but wait for the third. Moreover, lists with *more* than three parts are often interrupted after the third. In general, three-part lists are the norm – they are expected in everyday talk. In political speeches audiences tend to treat the third part of a three part list as a completion point. They give plenty of warning so are a good signal to the audience to prepare to applaud. Normally completion is signalled by several cues acting together – for example, Heffer's falling intonation signals completion as do his hand gestures which become more emphatic with each part.

Contrasts
More common and successful is the use of contrast structures or contrastive pairs. The following extract (taken from Atkinson 1984a, p. 75) shows this.

Callaghan: [. . . in this election I don't in<u>tend</u>
      Ⓐ {   (0.8)
          [to make the most promises
             (0.8)
             [I in<u>tend</u> that the next Labour government
             [(0.2)
      Ⓑ { shall ↑ <u>KEEP</u>
             [(.)
             [the most promises
Audience: Hear [hear
Audience: [x-xxXXXX-(*tape cut after 6.0 seconds*)

The extract combines a boast with a criticism, but the complexity of structure makes it a puzzle for the audience. An anomaly is raised in the first part because don't most politicians make lots of promises? The second half solves the difficulty – Callaghan is not going to make empty promises. By mirroring most of the important terms in the two parts and by stressing and rising intonation on the crucial contrasting term 'keep' the contrasts are highlighted. All this gives the audience a very strong guide to exactly when the evaluative assessment will be complete, and, therefore, the perfect time to applaud.

This by no means exhausts the types of rhetorical device that orators use to help generate applause (Heritage and Greatbatch, 1986: Atkinson, 1985). The crucial point, though, is that oratory is not something that wells up mystically from the inner person, it requires skills which can be learned and are open to analysis.

Evaluative assessments in conversation

Interestingly, the general organization of applause closely parallels one of the most recurrent patternings of ordinary conversation. Pomerantz (1977; 1984) has shown that when a speaker makes an evaluative assessment of something others seem obliged to make an assessment of their own displaying their own preference. The following extract (taken from Pomerantz, 1985, p. 65) is a good example:

A: Isn't he cute.
B: O: :h he: :s a: :DORable

Indeed, speakers who fail to add their own assessment are often interpreted as disagreeing or having alternative views of their own. The constraints of conversational expectation become particularly poignant when people are receiving compliments – they are caught in a tricky dilemma. On the one hand, they are party to an assessment so they really ought to add their own upgraded assessment. On the other hand, if they do this they may seem to appear smug or boastful. Conversationalists resolve this dilemma, in a number of ways, most effectively by reassigning the praise to some other person or object or returning the compliment to its author, as in the following extracts (taken from Pomerantz, 1977, pp. 102, 105):

A: You're a good rower, Honey.
B: These are very easy to row. Very light.

A: Yer <u>look</u>in good.
B: <u>Great</u>. So'r <u>you</u>.

This work allows us to see that applause is just like taking a turn in an everyday conversation. When one party, in this case the orator, offers an assessment, the other party, in this case the audience, offers its own upgraded assessment.

The conversation analysis approach has situated the study of persuasion in naturalistic studies of everyday interaction and moved away from looking at attitudes as discrete cognitive entities to looking more generally at the use of evaluative expressions. The interaction between orator and audience is here understood in the same terms as everyday exchanges. The focus is not on attitudes as essentially private mental entities which generate behaviour, but as public displays expressing evaluations in a manner highly sensitive to the social context.

Concluding comments

This has implications for how attitudes should be conceived in psychology. Earlier we noted how the idea that people possess sets of enduring, mentally encoded evaluations of things is assumed to be necessary in social psychology. That is, attitudes are a major source of consistency in people's discourse and activities. However, recent studies have found that evaluative discourse is considerably more variable than can be accounted for using such a conception. Consequently, attitudes have been reconceptualized in terms of discourse and rhetoric (Billig, 1987, 1988a; Potter and Wetherell, 1988; Smith, 1987).

For example, studies in New Zealand documented a number of different levels of variation in racist attitudes (Potter and Wetherell, 1987; Wetherell and Potter, 1988; forthcoming). Two points from this work are particularly telling. First, the evaluations of a single speaker vary enormously. This makes it particularly difficult to reconcile with the idea that those evaluative claims are a product of consistent underlying attitudes. Remarkably Thurstone (1928), an originator of attitude measurement, dealt with these variations as if they were simply errors in measurement, though Sherif *et al.* (1965) in the 1960s considered the range or latitude of acceptable attitudes as an important feature of commitment (or ego involvement) on an issue. Second, it has been recognized that in natural discourse there is no straightforward means of distinguishing evaluative from factual statements (Potter and Wetherell, 1988). The whole logic of attitude measurement is that scales can be used to compare different people's attitude's to the same object. However, since in natural discourse people offer their evaluations in the course of factual descriptions it becomes highly questionable whether people are indeed responding to the same object. In a very real sense, people construct in their discourse different objects and their evaluations appear in the manner of these constructions ('Scots are mean', 'blacks are taking our jobs', and so on).

The general conclusion of this work is that people appear willing to modify their evaluations and descriptions on a moment-by-moment basis in accordance with the exigencies of the current context. Furthermore, evaluations are tied to specific contextually produced versions of the attitudinal object rather than the sort of abstract and idealized formulations common in attitude scales. Discourse analysts have shifted the focus from a search for underlying entities (or even realities) such as attitudes to a detailed examination of how evaluative expressions are produced in discourse and what contextually appropriate purposes they serve.

This chapter has reviewed two broad approaches to attitudes and attitude change. The first, exemplified by the theory of reasoned action and cognitive response analysis, is squarely within the social cognitive tradition in social psychology. Attitudes are here understood as very much technical constructs. They are entities whose role is to mesh with other theoretical ideas within this tradition; they are particularly useful for giving neat encapsulations of participants' positions and providing a simple index of persuasion. In this sense, the reality of attitudes as entities that can be touched is less important than the theoretical coherence they provide.

The second position, exemplified by Atkinson's work on oratory and Pomerantz's work on assessments, takes its inspiration from areas of micro-sociology such as ethnomethodology and the work of Goffman. Rather than attempt to produce integrative theories of motivation, persuasion and cognitive processes, it has been concerned more to do justice to some of the more subtle phenomena of a social interaction and in particular everyday conversation. In this perspective attitudes are not seen as abstract constructs, nor are they seen as genuine entities possessed by individuals; rather they are viewed as one of the concepts that ordinary people use to make sense of their worlds.

Both these perspectives have their pros and cons, of course. In the longer term it remains to be seen whether one or other will gain ascendancy in social psychology or perhaps whether creative dialogue between the positions leads to something entirely new.

9

GROUPS AND INTERGROUP RELATIONS

Plato, in his dialogues, describes how Socrates would stop and argue with young men on the streets of ancient Athens. Profound philosophical questions, such as the nature of virtue and truth, and the goals of education were discussed. Both Socrates and his opponents had a great love of debate and argument. However, in the dialogue *Meno*, Plato describes Socrates' encounter with the fiery Athenian, Anytus. The discussion concerned the Sophists, who had come mainly from neighbouring Greek states, to seek their fortunes by teaching and practising the art of public speaking. Socrates forever criticized the Sophists, claiming that their skills were morally inferior to the art of philosophizing. Yet, Socrates' views were mild compared to those of Anytus. Socrates asked Anytus what he thought of the Sophists. The swift and sharp reply was that Anytus would have nothing to do with such foreigners. When Socrates asked whether any Sophist had done him any personal injury, Anytus exclaims:

> Heavens no, I've never in my life had anything to do with a single one of them!

> So you've had no experience of them at all? asks Socrates.

> And don't want any either, Anytus retorts.

Socrates then put it to Anytus that as he had no dealings with the Sophists, he could not claim to know what they were like. Quite unembarrassed by the implications of this, Anytus replied:

> I know their kind, whether I've had experience or not (Plato, 1965, pp. 146–7).

At a distance of over 2,000 years, the modern reader can easily recognize Anytus's attitude. He is literally showing prejudice against

the Sophists, for the term prejudice means 'prejudgement'. Anytus had
made up his mind about the Sophists without any personal experience.
He knew what they were like, and did not need any evidence to convince
him in his beliefs about Sophists.

Anytus's beliefs were characteristic of prejudice in other ways. He
was not merely expressing a bias against one or other of the Sophists but
was making a sweeping judgement about all of them when he said that
he knew their kind. Moreover, there is an undercurrent to his opinions,
which is very recognizable from modern everyday experience. Anytus,
from a long-established Athenian family, casts aspersions against
foreign immigrants. He talks of 'decent Athenian gentlemen', implying
that the foreign upstarts were destroying the traditional good Athenian
ways. In voicing his prejudice, Anytus defends the goodness of his own
group (his ingroup), while he castigates the group of others (the
outgroup). This ingroup–outgroup distinction is very important in the
modern study of prejudice.

There is a further theme in Anytus's outpourings in that he not only
expresses a particularly unflattering, and unjustified, view of the
Sophists, but he does so with vehemence. His opinions are beyond
reasonable discussion. Whereas most of Socrates' opponents loved a
good debate, Anytus was not open to argument: he did not want to
change the opinions which he held so forcefully. He even lost his temper
when Socrates tried to reason with him. Socrates was blamed for stirring
up trouble, and, most incredibly, for being 'too ready to run people
down' (Plato, 1965, p. 150). Then Anytus stomped off, obviously in a
huff and full of his own self-righteousness. He carried off his own
prejudices and let the others get on with their philosophical arguments.

The characteristics of prejudice

Plato's sketch of Anytus depicts vividly the sort of person social
psychologists would have little difficulty in categorizing as prejudiced.
For example, the three characteristics of prejudgement, bias against
groups and vehemence are central to the definition of prejudice given by
Gordon Allport in his classic work, *The Nature of Prejudice* (1954).
Allport (1954, p. 6) offered a simple initial definition of prejudice as
'thinking ill of others without warrant': because the ill thought is
unwarranted and not based upon evidence it is a prejudgement. Allport
makes two qualifications. First, prejudices normally concern prejudgements against groups: the prejudiced person holds an unflattering view
against a whole group and then stigmatizes all individuals who are said
to be members of the group. Second, not all prejudgements, not even
those against groups, are, strictly speaking, prejudices. According

to Allport (1954, p. 9), prejudices are prejudgements which are 'not reversible when exposed to new knowledge'. Anytus's comments about the Sophists qualify as prejudices on all three counts. He makes hostile statements about the Sophists without any personal knowledge and sweepingly dismisses a whole outgroup. Moreover, his views are impervious to change as he closes his ears to anything good about the Sophists. The social psychological concept of prejudice indicates that prejudiced people make erroneous and irrational judgements against outgroups. In this respect three particular features of prejudiced judgements can be noted: the tendency to over-generalize; the magnification of differences between ingroups and outgroups; and the expression of values.

Over-generalization

Allport suggests that racists tend to believe that *all* black people, or *all* Jews, or *all* Turks, share certain characteristics, thus making generalizations about the group, overlooking individual variation within the group. (The term 'over-generalization' should not be taken to imply that there is any 'grain of truth' inherent in racist ideas. 'All embracing' might be a better term.) The characteristics attributed to groups are often called *stereotypes*. In an early social psychological study of attitudes, Katz and Braly (1933) found regularities in the characteristics attributed to different ethnic groups by white American respondents. The results showed that the traits of laziness and dirtiness were associated with blacks, meanness and ambition with Jews, cruelty with Turks, and so on. The combination of traits which were regularly associated with a particular group formed the stereotype of the group. Although some later studies (Gilbert, 1951; Karlins, *et al.*, 1969; Brigham, 1971; Dovidio and Gaertner, 1986) suggest that stereotypes may not be quite as clear-cut as they used to be, they each confirm the basic notion of Katz and Braly: different clusters of traits are regularly associated with different ethnic and national groups. It should not be forgotten though that stereotypes may be contradictory yet equally firmly held; witness the phrases 'working like a black' and 'as lazy as a black'! There is nothing inherently true in stereotypes.

The connection between stereotypes and over-generalization is clear. If a person believes that the French are excitable or that the Germans are efficient, or that the Sophists are alien tricksters, then that person is liable to believe that individual members of these groups are excitable, efficient or tricksters. Evidence suggests that prejudice may often operate more subtly than this in that not *all* members of the other group are judged in this way. It may be asserted that the *typical* member of the group possesses the characteristics in question, rather than *all* members

(McCauley, *et al.*, 1980; McCauley and Stitt, 1978; Jackman and Senter, 1980). The variability of character is still minimized, say, among the French and their 'excitability' overestimated. General stereotypes influence the way we think and talk about individual members of the group: 'knowing' that the typical French person is excitable, we are liable to prejudge the character of individual French people we chance to meet.

Magnification of differences between ingroups and outgroups

Tajfel (1981) stressed that stereotyped judgements were not just judgements about a group, they were *intergroup* judgements. Each prejudiced judgement about an outgroup is also an implicit statement about the ingroup and the relations between the ingroup and the outgroup. The case of Anytus can be used as an illustration. When the choleric Athenian was running down the Sophists, he was not just saying that the Sophists constituted a bad lot: he was implying that the Sophists' immorality should be contrasted to the morality of the traditional Athenian gentlemen. This process is particularly clear in the case of gender stereotypes: judgements about women are, implicitly or explicitly, judgements in comparison to men and *vice versa*. For example, Eagly and Steffen (1984) showed that women are thought to be caring ('communal') and men dynamic ('agentic') (see also Deaux and Lewis, 1984; Deaux *et al.*, 1985). These judgements only make sense if women are thought to be more caring *than* men, and if men are thought to be more dynamic *than* women.

In other words, a stereotyped judgement separates groups. If over-generalizations are made about an outgroup, then the generalizer is exaggerating the differences between the ingroup and the outgroup. The man who assumes that all women are emotional is exaggerating gender differences. In consequence, according to Tajfel, the over-generalizations of stereotyped judgements lead the believer to assume that outgroups are relatively homogeneous (all/most/typical women are emotional) and, in this way, different from the ingroup. Linville *et al.* (1986) provide evidence which suggests that people make fewer over-generalized, stereotypical judgements about the group they are members of. For example, young people know full well the variety of young people – that some are fashion conscious, some rebellious, some ambitious, and so on. However, these same young people, mixing less with the elderly, make more global statements about what 'old people' are like. In contrast, older people are more liable to lump the young together in over-generalized judgements. The effect is to heighten the contrast between the ingroup and the outgroup: after all, *we* are a group with a variety of characters, whereas *they* are all the same. Again, there is magnification of the difference between *us the ingroup* and *them the outgroup*.

Stereotypes and values

Most stereotyped judgements express values, whether directly or indirectly, for the traits which are used to stereotype groups generally are not neutral but express a moral evaluation. This can be seen clearly in some of the traits used by the American students studied by Katz and Braly in the 1930s. When blacks were categorized as being 'dirty' or 'superstitious', the white students were not paying a compliment. Similarly when Jews were described as mean, again a moral evaluation is implied. The fact that the students chose to single out Jews for the alleged 'meanness', rather than everybody else for being 'spendthrift', tells us something about the moral values of judgers, or prejudgers. The moral dimensions in stereotyped judgements are sometimes quite subtle. Thus, the English person who suggests that the French are excitable may be implying that the French are *too* excitable, otherwise their excitability would hardly be worth mentioning.

A problem with much stereotype research is that the subjects are required to make judgements in the abstract, not in a context in which the moral evaluations can be discerned. Some of the traits used in stereotyped judgements may seem, at first sight, to be innocuous enough. For example, whites often associate the traits of 'musical' or 'athletic' with black people. However, the traits ascribed to a group must be understood in relation to those which are withheld. Ascribing the traits of 'musical' and 'athletic' to blacks in the absence of the traits of 'scholarly' or 'intelligent' can carry with it a derogatory implication: the group in question is good for singing, dancing and running about, but not for serious careers, which demand intellectual study. Similarly, the traditional stereotype of women as 'caring' can be used, not merely to praise obviously desirable qualities, but as an implicit criticism, because other traits are lacking. The judgement could be expanded to state that because women are 'caring', they lack the necessary toughness and dynamicism for successful and well-remunerated careers. What this means is that stereotyped judgements involve more than the ascription of adjectives such as mean, excitable, and lazy to target groups. Trait attribution to 'outgroups' must be understood in terms of wider beliefs or 'social representation', about what is and is not desirable conduct (Mosocovici, 1984a; Jodelet, 1984).

Prejudices are not merely erroneous in extent, exaggeration, and in content – if that was all they would be easily changed by experience. Prejudices by their nature are resistant to change: they represent just those unfounded beliefs to which people cling tenaciously. Moreover, these beliefs are not neutral, but often express deep moral values. Because the errors of prejudice are not easily corrected and tend to be self-confirmatory, it may be insufficient to bring a prejudiced individual into contact with members of the outgroup. Anytus himself was actually talking to Sophists, and he certainly classed Socrates, despite also being an Athenian, as one of the blighted breed. However, the conversation, far from undermining Anytus's prejudices, ends with him as convinced as ever of his own rightness.

Nor is there anything peculiar about this example of contact failing to undermine prejudice. Studies of intergroup contact have shown that people can take their prejudices with them when they meet members of outgroups. Thus, housing whites in a multi-racial housing estate need not diminish prejudices (Deutsch and Collins, 1951; for an excellent survey of recent evidence on the effects of intergroup contact on intergroup prejudice, see Brown and Hewstone, 1986). Gender stereotypes provide perhaps the most vivid reminder that contact may reinforce rather than undermine prejudice. A man can live with a woman in a situation of utmost physical intimacy, but there is no guarantee that assumptions about what women want, need or are capable of achieving will be discarded.

In consequence, the major social psychological question has been to discover why prejudices might be resistant to change, and what it is that makes people cling to beliefs. Three broad approaches to this question have been identified (Ashmore and Del Boca, 1981): the motivational, the cognitive and the socio-cultural. Each will be considered in turn.

Personality and motivation

A simple way of looking at the origins of prejudice is to blame 'quirks' in the psychological make-up of bigots. Perhaps Anytus was bitterly jealous of the worldly successes enjoyed by the Sophists or maybe his home life was miserable and he convinced himself that the foreigners had the sort of carefree sex life which he craved. Such speculations have in common the view that the cause of Anytus's prejudice is presumed to lie in his needs or in the structure of his personality. It may not be profitable to speculate about the inner personality of a long-dead Athenian, about whose personal life little is known. However, it seems a natural starting point to seek an explanation of the intensity of prejudice in the characteristics of individuals.

Such assumptions are the root of several psychoanalytically-influenced accounts of prejudice. Taking their theoretical framework from Sigmund Freud, a number of theorists have suggested that unconscious and hidden desires lie at the root of prejudice. For example,

Erich Fromm (1941) saw racism as deriving from an unconscious fear of the responsibilities of freedom, causing the racist to seek refuge in the certainties, but irrationalities, of fascistic beliefs. Jean-Paul Sartre (1954), the French novelist and existential philosopher, expressed a similar view. Wilhelm Reich (1975) (a practising psychoanalyst and member of the Communist Party) argued that the root cause of racist and anti-semitic beliefs lies in the inadequacies of a person's sex life. It is easy to scoff at ideas such as those of Wilhelm Reich, with their suggestion that a good sex life 'cures' prejudicial tendencies. However, all these theorists wrote in the shadow of Nazism, the most irrational and deadly of modern political movements. Arthur Koestler (the novelist and critic) was briefly in the same Communist Party group as Reich in pre-war Berlin. Although later Koestler admitted that Reich's ideas might seem absurd, he stressed that at the time they seemed quite plausible to those who were observing irrationality on a mass scale in Nazi Germany. Whole nations were succumbing to an irrational political movement, spouting the mumbo-jumbo about superior and inferior races, marching in their uniforms, and saluting a leader and his absurd philosophy. It seemed natural for observers like Reich and Koestler to think that there must be something lacking in the lives and personalities of these people. These early psychoanalytic theories were based more upon hunches, rather than systematic empirical evidence. Following the Second World War, there was a concerted effort by a group of researchers in the United States to test the assumption that underlying prejudiced beliefs were deep-seated psychological motivations. The final report, *The Authoritarian Personality* (Adorno, *et al.*, 1950) became both an immediate classic in the psychological study of prejudice and the object of considerable critical debate.

The investigators sought to find the personality characteristics which predisposed people to favour fascist politics. Their starting-point was a questionnaire designed to measure anti-semitic attitudes, but then they examined whether the anti-semites would also hold prejudices against other groups, such as blacks, homosexuals and foreigners in general. A strong relationship was found between the anti-semitism and antagonistic attitudes towards other minority groups. Adorno *et al.* concluded that prejudiced people tend to express negative views towards outgroups in general and not confine themselves to a specific group such as Jews. Such people who chauvinistically support their own group while downgrading any group perceived to be different were said to be *ethnocentric*. In-depth interviews were then carried out with small numbers of very highly and lowly prejudiced individuals. The questions dealt with their family backgrounds, relationships with their parents, their dreams, hopes, fears, and so on. The investigators began to get the impression that the highly prejudiced subjects were rigid people who had grown up in strict, rather formal families. Above all, it was thought that the prejudiced people had an extreme respect for conventional authority. Following this, the investigators developed an opinion scale, concerning attitudes towards authority (for example, whether children should be taught to be obedient; whether rules should be obeyed; and whether rule-breakers should be strictly punished). The scale contained questions on a range of moral issues, but none concerned ethnic groups. When they administered the questionnaire, Adorno *et al.* found that prejudice against Jews, blacks, and foreigners in general correlated highly with attitudes towards authority. The most prejudiced subjects were the most 'authoritarian', just as Anytus so vehemently defended 'traditional' standards, that is, those of his parents, against the foreign Sophists.

Adorno *et al.* were not merely concerned to discover the attitudes held by a prejudiced person but also to relate these to this syndrome of the 'authoritarian personality'. Their explanation, based on psychoanalytic theories of personality, claimed that prejudiced people had a particular style of upbringing. 'Authoritarians' had strict parents, who demanded respectful obedience. 'Authoritarians' would tend to speak about their parents in very idealized ways, as perfect parents. Because psychoanalytic theory states that the emotions of love and hatred often are intermingled, it was suspected that hostile feelings towards the parents were lurking beneath the surface of outward respect and admiration. In-depth interviews produced evidence of such hidden hostilities – some talked openly about parents who were 'perfect' but then let slip stories about physical beatings or their anger against harsh parents.

Authoritarian personality theory argues that prejudiced people are raised to treat their parents as paragons of every virtue and, consequently, need to repress and deny any hostile feelings towards them. In Freudian theory feelings which cannot be expressed openly, or even admitted to ourselves, do not disappear. Instead they are often directed at new targets. Consequently the ambivalent feeling which prejudiced individuals have towards their parents are partially diverted so that while the parent receives outward love and exaggerated respect, the hostile feelings became displaced onto targets perceived as inferior. Other shameful feelings also have to be repressed. Furthermore 'authoritarians' tend to deny their own sexuality, seeing it as something to be ashamed of. These feelings become displaced onto other targets: it is others, never oneself, who have these desires. In later life, figures of authority in general (in addition to parents) become the recipients of exaggerated respect. The repressed hostility becomes focused on minority groups and those who transgress conventional moral codes.

The basis of 'authoritarianism' was held to lie in an inability to admit complex, ambivalent feelings. Emotions had to be either all or nothing: the parents had to be perceived as completely wonderful, inferiors as completely reprobate.

Not only do 'authoritarians' see social relations as hierarchical (people categorized inferiors or superiors) but these hierarchies are viewed rigidly. Because of their inability to handle ambivalence, 'authoritarians' are unable to appreciate the complexities of the social world. They deal with the world in terms of stereotypes, generalizing about (presumed) characteristics of minorities by making sweeping statements about '*the* blacks' or '*the* Jews'.

Criticisms of personality approaches to prejudice

Adorno *et al.* (1950) had an immediate impact on research into prejudice. The opinion scale measuring authoritarian attitudes (called by Adorno *et al.* the F-Scale, or Fascism Scale) was used in thousands of studies. Although it became a standard psychological measure, there was a number of major criticisms of various aspects of the study. Experimentally minded social psychologists were unhappy about the in-depth interviews and the psychoanalytic themes in the theory. Survey methodologists pointed out that the opinion scales (including the F-Scale) had not been constructed as carefully as might have been expected and there is now general agreement that the opinion scales were methodologically far from perfect (Hyman and Sheatsley, 1954; Kirscht and Dillehay, 1967; for a defence of the study, by one of the original authors, see Sanford, 1973). However, the important issue is not methodology in itself, but what conclusions can be drawn from the theory of authoritarianism.

Probably the most incisive of recent criticisms are those discussed by Altemeyer (1981), who, having learnt from the mistakes of Adorno *et al.*, sought to construct new scales of authoritarian attitudes. Painstakingly, over a number of years, Altemeyer sought to discover what attitudes were correlated with authoritarian views, and, in this, he reversed the procedures of Adorno *et al.* While the original study started with racial attitudes and worked towards the concept of authoritarianism, Altmeyer began by examining authoritarian attitudes themselves. His results suggested that authoritarian attitudes were not as tightly bound to racially prejudiced attitudes as Adorno *et al.* had thought. Moreover, he failed to produce the clear-cut evidence of underlying motivations and childhood experiences necessary to confirm the *Authoritarian Personality* theory.

The differences between Altemeyer's findings and the original Adorno *et al.* study may not be due to methodological advancements but indicate something much more important – that the nature of prejudice has changed. There is something rather dated about the authoritarian personality; it may describe a type of person from an earlier time. Evidence suggests a possible decline in authoritarianism since the 1940s. Lederer (1982) compared the levels of authoritarianism in American and West German schoolchildren. Just after the Second World War there was widespread authoritarianism but by the 1970s it had decreased substantially, especially in West Germany. In fact, the decline in West Germany was so great that the German children were less authoritarian than the American children. Children who had been brought up in a Nazi state, then, had much higher levels of authoritarianism than did a later generation raised in the post-war West German democracy (see also Himmelweit, 1986, for evidence that levels of authoritarianism may have declined in Britain). The social climate, then, influences authoritarianism. Social factors, over and above individual family experiences, may create the motivational state of authoritarianism. The original theory implied that authoritarians transmit authoritarianism to their children who will, in turn, produce the next generation of authoritarians. However, it seems that social factors determine whether authoritarian attitudes dominate in a particular society.

There is the further point that the link between authoritarianism and prejudice may change over time. It may well have been strong in a pre-war Germany when both authoritarian social attitudes and particular forms of racial prejudice were rife, but in post-war society, with authoritarianism in decline, the link may have changed. For example, the sharp decline in authoritarianism in West Germany does not necessarily mean that the new 'non-authoritarian' generation lacks racial prejudices. Prejudice, especially against migrant workers, is common among German schoolchildren (Schonbach, 1981). Smaller numbers of authoritarians do not result in correspondingly fewer racially prejudiced people.

This was demonstrated by Pettigrew (1958), who found that in South Africa and the southern United States only a small percentage of the population could be described as authoritarian; however, the bulk of whites in both places held strong negative stereotypes about blacks. The authoritarians may have been particularly strong racists, but there was a considerable number who were not also authoritarians. Perhaps it might be thought that authoritarianism best explains a particular form of extreme racism. Psychoanalytic insights illuminate the nature of the personalities which hold particularly virulent racist attitudes (Sherwood, 1980). However, further caution must be exercised since not all extreme racists are necessarily authoritarians. Adorno et al. (1950) had originally hoped to predict those inclined towards fascism. It has become clear that not all members of fascist parties are authoritarians (who are very rigid, *inhibited* people, who seek desperately to *control* their emotions). Fascist parties have always attracted many people who *express* their violent racism in *uninhibited* ways, thereby showing a very different motivational structure from authoritarians (Billig, 1978). Instead of disappearing with the decline in authorianism, fascist parties such as the National Front in Britain have recently attracted young males seeking the excitement of violence, but who contemptuously disregard traditional figures of authority, such as the police, teachers and religious leaders. These young violent types are dangerously racist, but their anti-authoritarian attitudes often clash with those of the older, more authoritarian members of the party (Billig, 1981).

Members of fascist parties are today only a small proportion of the population in countries such as Britain. Racists are much more widespread. One danger with motivational explanations is that they can lead to an underestimation of the extent of prejudice. Many more people hold prejudiced attitudes than can be described as full-blown authoritarians. One should not expect authoritarianism to account for much other than why a few extremely prejudiced people cling to their beliefs. Prejudices found among those without the inhibitions and insecurities of the authoritarian are based more on cognitive and cultural factors.

Cognitive bases of prejudice

The cognitive approach to the study of prejudice takes issue with the assumption that prejudiced thinking is only found in people of a particular personality disposition. Instead, it traces the origins of prejudice to the act of thinking. People are not prejudiced because they have irrational hatreds: they are prejudiced because they make pre-judgements which are essential to the process of thinking. In this way, the cognitive approach assumes that prejudice is involved in the processes of thought itself.

Cognitive social psychologists (see Chapter 7) claim that people use schemata to organize their perceptions and experiences. Schemata provide the assumptions and prejudgements which then shape incoming experiences. In consequence, authoritarians are not unusual in possessing schemata, nor in having prejudgements about people and groups. The ordinary processes of thought often serve to promote over-generalizations and then to protect or reaffirm such over-generalizations.

Authoritarians may categorize others as being socially superior or socially inferior and this may be peculiar to their particular cast of mind. However, the process of categorization is not. As Tajfel (1981) has emphasized, the act of categorization is a basic cognitive phenomenon.

We need to group together objects under different labels – for example, to distinguish chairs from tables, cats from dogs. We also have ways of categorizing people, by grouping them in social categories. Language is fully of such categories (male/female, Catholic/Protestant, rich/poor, and so on) which provide convenient ways of understanding the social world. One cannot pay attention to every detail of every individual one meets, yet one makes assumptions about people. This is often done by fusing social categories. For example, one might notice another passenger in a railway carriage. Immediately, without conscious thought, the passenger is probably categorized in terms of gender and age, so that, for instance, he is registered as a middle-aged man. Perhaps his clothing is noticed next. If he is wearing a smart suit, one might assume that this is a businessman. As the passenger produces a copy of *The Times*, we feel confirmed in our hunch that here is a rather well-heeled conventional individual, likely to vote Conservative.

We are not basing our judgements on direct experience, but have pre-judged the individual, using categories which simplify the social world. We are acting on the over-generalization that middle-aged males, wearing sober suits, are likely to have particular sets of values and attitudes. In short, we are stereotyping much as an authoritarian person does about ethnic or racial groups. It could be, in fact, that the passenger is a working-class man dressed in his best suit for a family wedding and that the kiosk at the station only had *The Times* left when he arrived. In this case, we would revise our view of the individual in question, but this will probably leave our assumptions about middle-class male behaviour untouched. The cognitive approach suggests that we all show prejudices because we use over-generalized assumptions, or prejudgements, about human social groups. Moreover, as Tajfel (1981) argues, these over-generalized prejudgements oversimplify the world in a way which might encourage us to exaggerate the differences between males and females, working and middle-class, French and Germans and, above all, between our ingroup and outgroups.

The mere act of categorization alone is not sufficient to produce prejudice, according to the definition proposed by Allport mentioned earlier. The prejudgements must also be resistant to change. Ordinary people, just as much as authoritarians, can cling to prejudgements, not because they are emotionally committed to such prejudgements, but because the processes of thinking can lead to biases. Cognitive social psychologists have shown the self-fulfilling nature of assumptions about the social world. It is easy to reinterpret events in the light of our assumptions. This selective interpretation of the world is by no means confined to authoritarians, but is more general. We have to interpret and make sense of what we see, and use our pre-conceptions to impart meaning. Consequently, we frequently 'see' what we expect to see.

Duncan (1976) showed how racial stereotypes can affect the way that people interpret the social world. Actors were trained to play a scene in which one man appears to push another. The scene was deliberately ambiguous as to whether the pushing was playful or aggressive. In the experiment the race of the actors was varied. White subjects were more likely to attribute aggressive motives to the man who pushed when he was black than when he was white. Since the same action had been seen, it was the race of the actor which had determined how the action was interpreted. Probably without realizing it, the subjects were being influenced by the assumption, or stereotype, that black males tend to be aggressive. A similar finding was reported when schoolchildren were shown ambiguous sketches involving black and white figures (Sagar and Schofield, 1980). Again, the actions of blacks were much more likely to be interpreted by white subjects as being aggressive than as playful.

Perception is not merely a passive process, in which the sights and sounds from the world flow into the brain. Snyder (1981a) had conducted a series of experiments which illustrate bias in the way that information is accumulated about others. In one experiment subjects were instructed to interview someone in order to determine their personality (Swann and Snyder, 1978). Some subjects had to decide whether the person was an extrovert and other subjects whether the person was an introvert. Each subject chose 12 questions to ask in the interview from a list of questions. The type of question chosen indicated that subjects biased their search for information. For example, those subjects deciding about extroversion tended to pick questions such as 'What would you do if you wanted to liven things up at a party?'. This biasing effect of expectancies is not confined to the issue of personality determination and includes personality traits or characteristics based on group membership such as race, sex or sexual preference (Fiske and Taylor, 1984, p. 386). Not only can the prejudgements be self-fulfilling (Hamilton and Trolier, 1986), but on occasions we have the power to influence others to act in a way which fulfils our prejudgements. Word *et al.* (1974) examined the way white students behaved when asked to interview white or black applicants for a job. Whites tended to be uncomfortable interviewing blacks, and gave them shorter, curter interviews. Not unexpectedly, applicants seemed to be affected by the way they were interviewed. In the longer, friendly interviews the applicants seemed more relaxed than in the shorter interviews typically given to the blacks. In a second study, actors played the parts of interviewees, using scripts based on the interviews from the first study, but with white and black actors using the same script. Video-tapes of these performances were shown to subjects, who had to rate how well or badly the interviewee appeared to be performing. The actors acting out the scripts which had originally been produced by the black applicants were rated as less satisfactory irrespective of the race of the actor. In other words, the behaviour of the interviewer affected the behaviour of the applicant. Having been made nervous or given less of a chance to present themselves well, the black applicants performed less well. In real life there would be a further round to the self-fulfilling prophecy. The black would not have got the job through no fault of their own, and furthermore, the interviewer, believing that the interview had been fairly conducted, would have 'evidence' that blacks are not as suitable as whites for the job. The now strengthened expectancy would apply with more force to the next unfortunate black interviewee.

Of course, experiments are artificial and omit many of the complex subtleties of naturally occurring interaction. Essed (1988) reports a detailed analysis of a real interview session for a high-ranking Civil Service post. In this the white male interviewer seems to be searching for information to confirm his expectancies of black females. The interviewer persistently asks the well-qualified, professional woman whether she would miss discos if she were posted abroad! The woman is disconcerted by these questions and the session does not run with the smoothness which might have been expected from a similarly well-qualfied and ambitious white male.

Criticisms of the cognitive approach

At this stage it might be thought that the cognitive dynamics of prejudice are a natural part of thinking. Some cognitive social psychologists have taken this line, which suggests that we must categorize the social world, and in doing so, we inevitably build up stereotyped assumptions, which become protected by our cognitive biases. Hamilton (1976) suggests that it is a 'depressing dilemma' that our categorizations lead to stereotypes. Similarly Allport (1954, p. 21) wrote that people have a 'propensity to prejudice' because of a 'normal and natural tendency to form generalizations, concepts and categories, whose content represents an oversimplification of the world of experience'. However, this assumption that prejudice is inevitable has been criticized by social psychologists adopting a rhetorical or discourse-analytic perspective (Billig, 1985; 1987; Potter and Wetherell, 1987). They suggest that the cognitive social psychology has overlooked the fact that people can argue about and discuss their own assumptions (that is, there is a reflexivity about human thinking). In addition, prejudices and stereotypes are, above all, expressed in language and so are linguistically constructed. That being so, it is an over-simplification itself to suggest that language oversimplifies the world, for it is because of language that human beings can develop sophisticated views of the world. And it is because of language that one can be reflexive about one's own activities. Indeed it is obvious that the same human mind that expresses prejudice is capable of expressing much more tolerant and understanding views. After all, the language categories which permit us to make generalized statements about gender, race and nationality also enable us to criticize these same statements and to argue for the virtues of tolerance. Selection interviewers, for example, may learn to, or be educated to, ask questions which do not perpetuate stereotypes, beliefs and myths, as well as to avoid forms of questioning which upset or otherwise put members of minority groups at a disadvantage. It is too simple merely to state that human beings have a propensity for prejudice, when the expression of tolerance is also possible, both in theory and in practice.

Socio-cultural factors

The cognitive approach suggests that individuals, left to their own cognitive devices, piece together a meaningful picture of the world and, needing to use short-cuts and generalizations, often add two and two together to make five. However, stereotypes do not emerge because isolated individuals have all chanced to make the same errors of judgement when thinking about social groups. Stereotypes and pre-judgements are socially shared, so are part of the culture in which they are to be found. Anytus was not an isolated individual about whom people might say: 'There goes old Anytus – he's got some strange views'. Plato drew his portrait of Anytus quite deliberately in the dialogue so that a strong current of thinking in Athens was embodied dramatically by this single figure. In fact, Anytus was powerful in the political life of Athens, by no means a crusty and isolated old man. Nowadays prejudice tends to be expressed in subtle ways, rather than in crude, bigoted statements. There is a norm against prejudice and people, consequently, do not wish to appear prejudiced (Billig, 1988b; Billig *et al.*, 1988). There is a formula found time and time again in conversations about race: 'I'm not prejudiced' declares the speaker before launching onto a stream of 'buts' which express the very prejudices which are being denied (Billig, 1986; Van Dijk, 1984; 1987; Reeves, 1983; Seidel, 1988; Wetherell and Potter, 1986). Some investigators have suggested that this indirectly expressed prejudice constitutes a 'new racism' to be contrasted with the more old-fashioned, uninhibited racism far less concerned about the accusation of prejudice (McConahay, 1981; 1982; 1986; Weigel and Howes, 1986). Because such views are common, they are part of the shared 'wisdom' which provides the 'facts' to support their views. Being 'social facts' they are not seen as prejudice by those who hold them. In this way the believers see themselves as 'reasonable' or 'factual', rather than recognizing their own prejudices. An example of this is the way in which equal legislation is redefined by sections of the public to be something that it is not. So, for example, some people will claim not to be racist and claim that whites are the underdogs because the law gives blacks particular advantages. For example, they believe, erroneously, that white pub landlords cannot refuse to serve blacks because they could be prosecuted under the racial discrimination law, but black pub landlords could refuse to serve whites. The appeal is to 'fair play', but in actuality this is a socially constructed 'fact' which helps maintain antagonism towards blacks.

That stereotyped beliefs might be part of the culture of a group does not mean that stereotypes, and indeed cultures, are static and unchanging. Perhaps one of the most dramatic social psychological demonstrations of changes in stereotypes and images of groups was provided by the boys' camp studies of Muzafer and Carolyn Sherif (Sherif, 1966; Sherif and Sherif, 1979). The researchers took over a boys' residential summer camp, attended by approximately 24 boys carefully selected to be without any particular personality problems. There were several stages to the studies. In the first stage, the boys, who were all strangers to one another, arrived at the camp and settled into the round of communal activities. The boys seemed to become friendly with those who shared the same interests as themselves – the sporty types stuck together, for example. In the second stage the camp authorities announced that it would be simpler to run the activities if the boys were split into two groups. As far as possible friends from the first stage were put into different groups. From then on, the two groups slept in different dormitories, ate at different times and undertook their activities separately. The researchers found that the boys quickly identified with their groups. Former friends were dropped as norms developed suggesting that group members should not fraternize with members of the other group. Before the competition was initiated, the groups developed their own mini-cultures and routines, adopting symbols of identification such as their 'group colour'. In other words, there was pride in the ingroup. After a few days of such separation the camp leaders announced a series of competitive events between the two groups. Points would be awarded to the winning team for each event, and the team with the most points would be awarded a prize at the end of the camp. During the period of competition hostile stereotypes about the outgroup quickly developed, as relations between the groups deteriorated. There was constant name-calling and even occasionally fighting. Actions performed by ingroup members were interpreted positively, but the same actions performed by members of the rival group were given no benefit of the doubt. In just a few days the boys had created strong stereotypes about a group which had not hitherto existed, and which was comprised of individuals, many of whom had been their friends just a few days before.

In one of the studies, the researchers added a final stage. They tried to get the groups to co-operate on joint projects, to achieve 'superordinate' goals: these were goals which both groups wished to achieve, but which neither could achieve on its own. For instance, both groups had to co-operate to pull a truck carrying food for a picnic or to organize a film show. After the joint activity to achieve the superordinate goals, it was found that some of the most extreme stereotypes had been somewhat attenuated. However, the group biases were by no means as easily eradicated as they had been established. Unhappily, the researchers had to send some of the boys home still clinging to their beliefs about how awful the other group had been.

The study also illustrates how the intergroup divisions and the institutionalized competition led to the development of stereotypes. Thus the prejudices seem to follow, rather than cause, changes in the way of life of the boys in the camp. In this respect they mirror real-life incidents, in which eruptions of prejudice follow political decisions. For instance, during the Second World War, the Russians were the brave allies of the British and Americans, battling courageously against the common enemy of Nazism. As soon as the war ended the Russians became the next potential enemy, and 'common-sense' attitudes fell into line with the changed political climate.

Henri Tajfel extended this work by arguing that group competition is not necessary to produce hostile intergroup stereotypes and feelings. The importance of grouping people and the ensuing identification with that group is that people are distinguished from the relevant outgroup (Tajfel, 1981; Tajfel and Turner, 1979). A series of laboratory experiments was conducted which show how people identify with the flimsiest or most minimal of group categories (Billig and Tajfel, 1973; Tajfel *et al.*, 1971; Turner, 1987). Subjects were merely told that they were in 'group X'. They did not know who else was in their group, nor who was in the other group. They were asked to allot money to anonymous others, who were only identified by their group label. Under these deliberately artificial conditions, people showed a definite preference for ingroup members and a bias against outgroup members. Merely telling people that they were in a group develops some sort of loyalty, even though the groups only existed in the imagination. Tajfel (1978; 1981; 1982) went on to develop *social identity theory*, which discusses how social identity determines much social behaviour. If one identifies with a particular group and the general societal view of that group is favourable, then, normally, all is well since one can rest content with a comparatively secure, socially valued, social identity. However, if the society does not value the group then things are less comfortable and the motive to change things may be aroused. A number of different strategies are open to a group and its members whose social identity is not valued. Individuals may attempt to extract themselves from the group in order to pass into another more valued group. For example, upwardly socially mobile people often leave their roots completely behind them. They identify with the middle-class and adopt the habits, patterns of belief, and prejudices of their new group. In so doing they might talk about their former class in the most unflattering terms. An example is provided by Seymour Lipset, a noted American sociologist. One of his most famous essays is a description of the working- class as consisting of authoritarian, bigoted, rigid thinkers (Lipset, 1960). Readers of this essay may fail to recognize that Lipset himself came from a poverty-stricken, working-class background, but he had, of course, passed into the middle class.

Sometimes a group identification cannot be easily discarded, as in the case of a woman who wishes to make her way in a man's world, or a black in a white world. However, such people may adopt a style of behaviour which allows them to fit into the world of the majority group with a minimun of trouble. The woman may become 'gender blind', suggesting that gender does not matter, and trying to fit into the man's world without upsetting things too much. According to Tajfel, this would be an individual strategy, since the woman rejects identification with the wider group of women. The individual level of response may satisfactorily change the life of the individual, but may do nothing for accepted stereotypes. The successful woman in a man's world may even reinforce stereotypes. For instance, consider the successful woman who is loath to draw conclusions about discrimination against women from the experience of her own career, but prefers to draw the moral that women really can achieve things if they have the determination. She interprets in individual, not group, terms.

On the other hand, a group may react in group terms, and, in so doing, directly criticize the stereotypes and assumptions which are so demeaning. The example often cited by Tajfel is the black consciousness movement in the United States during the 1960s, when a determined attempt was made to reverse the demeaning stereotype of blackness by promoting slogans like 'black is beautiful'. The result was not a growth in blacks' adopting a 'white' perspective, but increased confidence in the desirability of black identity (Milner, 1983). This strategy must operate at a group, not individual, level, since the ingroup acts against the commonly held stereotype. In this way, such a strategy changes the cultural climate. The strategy not only concerns images or beliefs but attacks the patterns of life supporting these beliefs. It may confront the issues such as power, and particularly the power of an outgroup to make impositions upon an ingroup. Thus, radical feminists might seek to end the situation by which men, especially white men, have more social and economic power than women.

Therefore, in describing prejudices between groups, one should examine the wider socio-cultural context, and in particular, the power relations between groups. Thus, some strategies for social change might seek to alter stereotypes and assumptions within the existing balance of power while others seek to change these power relations and thereby radically alter the ways of life which provide the 'facts' which seem to fulfill these prejudices. By conceiving prejudice in this way the origins and maintenance of prejudice are relocated away from the emotional life of individual bigots. Prejudices are seen as linked to the wider history of power relations. This can be illustrated by returning for a final time to the story of Anytus. His prejudices against Sophists in general, and Socrates in particular, had a wider significance in the history of power in Athens. Plato was writing when the power of the state had been used against the Sophists. Socrates had been condemned and executed for his philosophy, and in the courtroom one of the principal accusers had been Anytus. Today, Anytus is remembered, thanks to Plato, for nothing more than his prejudices against the Sophists and for his complicity in a legal murder of the great enemy of prejudice.

Criticisms of the socio-cultural approach

The main criticism of the socio-cultural approach is not that the approach is incorrect. After all, it is clearly the case that prejudiced assumptions about other groups can be contained within an ingroup's cultural heritage. The main problem is that the socio-cultural approach can be applied in too simple a way, such that social psychologists might think that they have explained everything that needs explaining, when, in point of fact, they may have explained very little. For example, one might say that racist or sexist attitudes are a product of contemporary culture. This may be very true, but it is not the sort of explanation which closes the matter once and for all. In fact, rather than being an explanation, such a statement raises all sorts of interesting problems, which themselves need to be investigated. One would want to know how racist or sexist assumptions are expressed in the culture and how they are transmitted.

Earlier, the experiment of Duncan (1976) was briefly discussed. This suggested that white American students were likely to interpret the behaviour of blacks as being aggressive rather than playful. Duncan hypothesized that the stereotype of blacks aggression had created an expectancy in these subjects. He also hypothesized that this stereotype was regularly expressed in the mass media. In this way, the cultural climate, which includes the mass media, had affected the expectancies and interpretations of individual members of the culture. Duncan's experiment in itself says very little about the cultural creation and transmission of the stereotypes of black aggression. It then becomes important to look at the way that images and beliefs about black people are transmitted in the press and on television. Thus, detailed studies of the mass stereotypes of the culture are required, as well as investigations about how individuals interpret what they read in newspapers and what they see on the television. The same is true for the complex images which people might have of women. Essed's (1988) description of the prejudice faced by the black woman applicant is a case in point. We can accept that the interviewer was not consciously ill-mentioned and also that his thinking was filled with assumptions which he had mostly picked up from his culture. Yet, it remains essential to study how such assumptions are 'picked up', so that the subtly complex ways in which a culture is transmitted and reinforced can be understood.

In one sense, studies like that of Essed (1988), and indeed that of Duncan (1976), do show this. It is a mistake to think that such studies produce data which are then to be explained by some sort of causal factor, which we will call 'culture'. The reactions of the interviewer and the reactions of Duncan's subjects were themselves part of the culture itself. For instance, the interviewer was not merely being prodded along by mysterious, external forces, which we can call 'cultural factors'. The interviewer was participating in the culture, and thereby ensuring the continuation of the culture. By fulfilling his own expectancies, he was doing more than providing confirmation of his personal prejudices; he was transmitting in both thought and action his own cultural traditions.

In this way, reactions, which are based upon stereotyped assumptions, are not explained simply by saying that they are 'determined by culture', because the reactions themselves determine the existence of the culture. If whites stopped making assumptions about black aggressiveness or about the lifestyles of black women, then the culture would be changed. The culture of prejudice can only continue to exist if it is used and thereby transmitted. Therefore, the socio-cultural approach does not constitute a series of explanations of prejudice which suggest that the major questions about prejudice have been satisfactorily resolved. Rather, the socio-cultural approach suggests that researchers should keep examining the ways in which prejudiced assumptions are transmitted, used and, hopefully, sometimes discarded.

Concluding comments

This chapter demonstrates the importance of the social psychological approach to understanding intergroup relations. It certainly leaves little room to doubt that a full understanding of intergroup hostility, in particular, needs to concentrate on the interaction between the social and the individual rather than merely looking at the attitudes and personality of individuals. The role of cognitive processes in encouraging many of the features characteristic of prejudice in general, and racism and sexism in particular, is well understood thanks to the pioneering work of people like Tajfel. A complete understanding of prejudice does not come from this work alone but it does anchor our understanding in the appreciation of human cognitive processing and avoids presenting prejudice as the prerogative of 'sick' and peripheral bigots. It is also important in that it highlights the interplay between social thought and other aspects of social experience.

The socio-cultural approach draws attention to the need of social psychologists to break free of the constraints of a narrowly psychological approach. It requires that we extend explanations to cover issues such as political power and the development of increased self-valuation by minority groups in order to understand and appreciate the dynamic and changing nature of prejudice in society.

To understand Anytus we need to understand more than Anytus.

10

SO WHAT IS SOCIAL PSYCHOLOGY?

Now that a great deal of social psychological theory and research has been discussed, it may be helpful to draw together some threads. There is no possibility of integrating the vast range of issues into a 'grand theory' of social behaviour and experience here. The subject matter and theoretical perspectives of social psychology are far to diverse for that. But we can use earlier chapters as a base from which to discuss social psychology more broadly, to give 'insider information' about the discipline. At first, the detail of any discipline tends to dominate, obscuring the wider perspective, and making a coherent evaluation difficult. With apparently so much that is new and unfamiliar to assimilate, the task seems to be one of absorbing the material almost like a list of 'facts', and not one of forming a point of view. To treat social psychology in this way is to fail to appreciate the intellectual challenge of social psychology. To regard social psychology as snippets of knowledge to be regurgitated as appropriate and when circumstances necessitate, does the discipline and the student a disservice.

It is no easy matter to build an overview of a discipline on the basis of just a few chapters. Ideas need to be placed into a perspective, and it is the job of this chapter to provide some of the necessary elements for this. The 'thing' we call social psychology has to be examined in its social context since it is as much a social creation as anything it seeks to explain. As elsewhere in this book, we are presenting ideas to be worked with, not answers. There is no intention to present views of what social psychology is and should be which are fixed for all time. Hopefully, many of the issues raised here will be ancient history in 20 years' time, as social psychology evolves.

Social psychology as a social process

By now, it should be obvious that social psychology was not chiselled on tablets of stone by the hand of Mother Nature. The discipline is clearly a socially constructed set of ideas, practices and activities. In addition, the fact that social psychology is full of conflicts and controversies means that it cannot be seen simply as being the 'objective truth', whatever that may be. It can be as important to explain why a particular set of ideas is generally accepted at a particular point in time as to know the theoretical and empirical adequacy of those ideas. Social psychology cannot be isolated from the 'world outside' as it is part of and responsive to it. It also is capable of acting on that 'outside' world and to a degree changing it, as on occasions when the ideas of social psychology are adopted by people other than social psychologists. This means that social psychology is subject to much the same forces as shape other institutions in society.

The ways in which ideas emerge in the intellectual community are partly a consequence of a range of economic and social factors. Social psychological thinking is not simply the natural outcome of previous intellectual activity. To clarify this, one could compare social psychology to, say, a market research firm operating in the centre of Amsterdam just to see how such factors would operate. Thinking as social scientists researching such a market research company, we would probably wish to consider the following factors, among others, when describing its operation:

1. The clients of the firm: what do they want?
2. The training of the staff: who trained them and what were the assumptions of the trainers?
3. The financial climate: can the firm afford to be choosy about work?
4. The attitudes and ideologies of the staff: do they prefer working in the public service rather than for big business?
5. Social contacts both within and outside the firm: who talks to whom?
6. The organizational structure: just how are management decisions made?
7. The individual talents and abilities of particular workers: do these push the work of the organization in a particular direction?
8. Its location in Amsterdam rather than elsewhere: would it be a rather different organization doing different things in different ways if it were situated in a different culture, say, Singapore?

Similar factors also help determine the nature of social psychology. Social psychologists tend to carry out research for which funds can be obtained which, in their turn, often go to projects matching the needs and interests of funding agencies (frequently the government or government agencies, including the military). The training of social psychologists partly imposes ideas of what the appropriate subject matter is and what the best theoretical approaches are. The financial climate can affect social psychology in many ways. For example, the expansion of any academic discipline may be restricted by the shortage of funds in the university system. The attitudes and ideologies of social psychologists may make them wary of doing research for, say, racist organizations; or, because they value highly the methods of the natural sciences, they may model their own research on those methods. The communication networks among social pschologists may determine the ways in which ideas and priorities for research are transmitted, as well as the setting up of co-operative projects. The organizational structure of social psychology would include who owns and operates social psychology journals, who gets the job of editing them, whom they ask to review articles, and sometimes whom they invite to write them. All of these can affect what kind of social psychology is published and thereby obtains the 'status' of being worthwhile a contribution. The individual talents and abilities of individual social psychologists clearly have to be taken into account as some contributions to the discipline are significantly out of the ordinary. Finally the culture in which social psychology operates has a great bearing on its contents and even on whether it exists at all. Much of what is described in this book comes from North America and Europe. It is generated within these cultures and often appears specifically to meet the demands of Western cultures, and thus may be limited in terms of understanding 'Third World' issues.

Once considered in this way, social psychology seems a little less solid and more transitory. The issues tackled do not merely result from the intuitive conviction of brilliant, individual scientists struggling to grasp 'the Truth'. That is more the Hollywood film industry's view of science than a properly considered one. The questions asked by social psychologists and the research they do are the product of much more varied factors than the intellectual judgements of individuals.

The origins of social psychology

It can be easier to understand what social psychology is today if aspects of its history are highlighted. Perhaps the major issue in the history of social psychology is to explain why, during the twentieth century, there has come to be a loosely-knit corpus of people who would more or less readily accept the label 'social psychologist'. There is no intention to suggest that this is any sense an integrated body of people since they are likely to differ widely in terms of their theoretical viewpoints, their training, and the subject matter of their concerns. Indeed there are factions within social psychology who would be seen as in direct opposition to others. While the label 'social psychologist' is the common factor, there is also a social network which loosely organizes the parts of the whole together in the form of learned societies, or sub-divisions of them, devoted to social psychology. In addition, there are publications devoted exclusively to social psychology and people are given posts as 'social psychologists' by employers. To explain the origins of such a relatively amorphous body in a few paragraphs is no easy matter. However, it is important to attempt to do so since history explains many of the characteristics of social psychology.

Although the bulk of published work which could be described as social psychological in nature has been produced in the second half of the twentieth century, no one could seriously argue that the concerns of modern social psychologists were not at least echoed throughout history. Aristotle's *Rhetorica*, for example, reflects in an organized way practically every primary concern of modern social psychologists, and others, including Machiavelli, wrote about the social psychological nature of people. Nor can one dismiss the explanations of human social conduct to be found throughout literature.

However, there is something different about modern social psychology which is not found in these other writings. The most obvious manifestation of this is perhaps most simply described as placing a high value on the 'scientific approach'. This is not to enter the controversy of whether or not social psychology is or could be a science but merely to highlight how social psychologists orientated themselves in the academic community. The most obvious signs of the allegiance to 'science' was the commitment to the collection of empirical data, particularly that from 'controlled' experiments. This more than anything distinguishes 'social psychologists' from anyone else concerned with similar issues. It also provides a basis for social psychologists assuming the status of 'professionals' in the field. No one else had the 'expertise' for collecting such data although they had experience of social psychological matters through their day-to-day lives. Not surprisingly, as a consequence, there is a tendency among social psychologists to see their discipline as having a relatively short history. In one sense this is a self-serving history in that it retains for social psychologists a prime claim to areas of interest through their skills in applying 'the scientific method'. That is, it enhances the self-regard of the 'profession'. At another level, almost by the same token, the idea that social psychology has a short history is a truism if one wishes only to apply the label 'social psychology' where there are hints of the 'scientific'.

But when did social psychology, so labelled, emerge? It is probably reasonable to suggest that it began to emerge as a substantial grouping in the 1930s when the techniques for measuring social attitudes 'objectively' were being developed. Most social psychologists will acknowledge that the roots of the discipline go back a little further than this, to the late nineteenth century. Much of this reflects concerns which were brought to the fore during the Industrial Revolution and after – particularly the *apparent* sickness and instability of society. In France, Tarde (1983–1904) suggested that the fundamental social process is imitation and applied the concept to explaining criminality, while Durkheim (1858–1917) studied suicide and Le Bon (1841–1931) tried to explain crowd behaviour by reference to the primitive workings of a collective 'mind'. In Italy Sighele (1868–1913) and Lombroso (1836–1909) were also concerned with criminality and Pareto (1848–1923) explained how human action, by and large, stems from non-logical sentiments about which people invent pseudological justifications. In Germany, Marx (1818–83) saw the individual consciousness as being the result of the class struggle. In Britain, Darwin (1809–82) pointed out the survival value of a social instinct and Trotter (1872–1939) argued that human behaviour is that of a gregarious animal motivated by a herd instinct (see Sahakian, 1982, for a fuller discussion).

While few of the above ideas are current in modern social psychology, they are nevertheless precursors of a major theme in the development of social psychology – its role in dealing with social problems. If it is correct to say that social psychology substantially leapt forward to become a recognizable discipline in the 1930s, this was probably because it became practical to study various social problems by means of the then newly developed attitude scales. These enabled investigations of the manipulation of the social attitudes at a time when the mass media were an increasingly dominant feature of society with the introduction of radio and rising popularity of the cinema. Indeed, the first method developed by a psychologist to measure social attitudes was that of Thurstone who was receiving funds to study the effects of the cinema on the attitudes of young people, and in particular their racial attitudes. Into the 1940s and 1950s, studies of persuasion through communication were typical of social psychology. Continuing into modern times, topics like violence, pornography, leadership, the media and rioting have attracted considerable public funds to social psychology; one might suspect this to be because they link to the search for means of social control.

This simplifies things a little too much. It should not be forgotten that the term 'social psychology' is essentially a twentieth-century label. Certainly before the twentieth century there were no books bearing the title 'social psychology'. Then in 1908, the British psychologist, William McDougall (1908), and the American sociologist, Edward Ross, separately published books with the title *Social Psychology*. Their influence on modern social psychology is not at all great but the roots of social psychology in both sociology and psychology are highlighted by this temporal coincidence. McDougall's book was an examination of the basic instincts and the emotions which accompany them, and included a gregarious instinct. Ross dwelt on imitation and the mob mind. The sociological and psychological strands of social psychology remained substantially segregated (a carefully chosen word) during the twentieth century until the 1960s, and slightly less from then on. It requires little to explain this segregation. First, in universities, sociology and psychology were taught in separate departments in different faculties. In the twentieth century, psychology has predominantly been seen as a biological science, and sociology as an art or a social science. Second, the ideologies and methods of the two disciplines also differed substantially. For example, sociology tended to deal with large-scale social phenomena using grand theoretical frameworks. Increasingly during the twentieth century, it used survey methods in data collection. This contrasted markedly with psychologists who were concerned with scientific precision which they emulated using painstakingly carefully controlled experiments aimed at establishing causes of particular phenomena. There was little crossing over disciplinary boundaries. Indeed, there was almost a sense of antagonism between the two. Again there were exceptions. Some sociologists, such as Talcot Parsons and George Homans, incorporated psychology into their theories, just as some psychologists were capable of introducing a sociological perspective into their writing. Third, social psychology was a very minor aspect of each of the disciplines until comparatively recently.

Psychological social psychology

Psychological social psychology tended to fall into one of two camps – the atomistic and the holistic. The origins of the atomistic approach to social psychology lay in behaviourism, which dominated much of American psychology for the first half of the twentieth century, and whose main advocate was John Watson. His central theme was that psychology should be based on the objective observation of behaviour. Thoughts, feelings, and other 'internal' processes, not being available to direct, 'external' inspection, were invalid both as data and as explanatory principles. Bad as this might be in so far as it excluded much of what is interesting about human social nature, there was worse. Behaviourism imposed a system of analysis on psychology in general, and social psychology in particular, which was akin to the physical scientists' search for the atoms or elemental units of the physical world. This took the form of a quest for the stimulus which causes a particular response, in other words, what had to be done to the individual to generate a particular form of behaviour. Among the luggage which accompanies behaviourism was an adherence to experiments as *the* only valid method for psychological research.

Full-blown behaviourism was modified early on in social psychology, though its strictures lived on. One of the reasons for this was the early and continued interest of social psychologists in social attitudes, which are difficult to infer from behaviour alone without reference to so-called 'verbal behaviour' (a phrase which has tended to be detached from the thought processes to which it really refers). Perhaps the best example of behaviourism in social psychology appears in the work of Carl Hovland, which is discussed briefly in Chapter 8. He, along with colleagues associated with Yale University, studied the factors in communication which led to changes in attitudes. The research frequently divorced people from the social context in which communication takes place. A pastiche of this research would be one group of subjects reading one version of a persuasive communication and a second group reading a slightly different version. Relative changes in attitudes after reading the two versions would allow the stimulus causing the response to be isolated. Essentially the very complicated social processes of attitude change and communication were thereby reduced to a trivial stimulus and a very simple response. No wonder that this sort of research failed to provide a firm basis for understanding attitude change in the social world away from the social psychology laboratory.

Coexisting with behaviourism in social psychology (though, in Northern America especially, sometimes making concessions to it) was a much more whole-person-centred approach. In trying to see the whole individual, these other social psychologists inevitably identified a fuller picture of the social environment within which people are born, develop and define themselves. Not only this, they sacrilegiously allowed themselves to acknowledge that people think, feel and judge! It may appear a little strange that some social psychologists should be noted for treating people as people, but this has to be placed in the perspective of the opposing intellectual force of behaviourism which saw people as household dust – composed of minute elements and best ignored.

Many of the psychologists from the whole-person or holistic 'school' were greatly influenced by gestalt psychology. This has its origins at much the same time as behaviourism but had radically different methods and originated in continental Europe rather than in the United States. Gestalt psychology emerged out of the psychology of perception. Its major contributions were the realization that psychological processes are more than the sum of their parts (for example, the recognition of a circle cannot be explained away by a sum of distinct components since many different physical patterns are recognized as circles) and that there are 'laws' governing how the whole is perceived as an entity. Furthermore, the gestaltists often relied on descriptive reports of the individual's self-awareness (that is, phenomenological methods) for their data; this again radically differentiated them from behaviourist psychologists.

It is a mistake to assume that the detailed findings of gestalt psychology influenced social psychology substantially. It was more important because of the broad framework that it provided, and because of its influence on many social psychologists, principally the 'holistic trinity' of Kurt Lewin, Fritz Heider (Chapter 7) and Leon Festinger (Chapter 4). Much modern social psychology can be traced to their influence, especially the emphasis on cognitive or thought processes as a central concern.

The influence of gestalt psychology was not great in social psychology until the 1940s, many years after it had emerged in Europe. It was imported into American social psychology by emigrants from continental Europe, including Lewin and Heider, and was spread by their students. The gestaltists were not the only major foreign influence on American social psychology. Muzafer Sherif, from Turkey, had a profound influence, as Chapters 3 and 9 show, particularly in the way he used the experimental method to show important social phenomena such as norms and cohesion and in the way he combined an experimental approach with observation in the studies of the boys' camps.

Sociological social psychology

It is a little misleading to write of psychological and sociological social psychology as if they are distinct entities. Their differentiation does not mean that they have to be treated separately, but reflects the institutional split between sociology and psychology. It would have been better for social psychology had its parent disciplines been a better-matched pair as there are many gains to be had from unifying the two approaches.

George H. Mead (1934) is often identified as the sociologist who influenced sociological social psychology most, despite the fact that he described himself as a 'social behaviourist'! His contribution came to be called 'symbolic interactionism'. This argues that human interaction is set in a symbolic (largely linguistic) world rather than in one of causes and effects. In order to understand human interaction it is necessary to know how the symbols are used. If a man gives a woman roses it means an awful lot more than giving her a bunch of daffodils. Roses are not just things, and manhood and womanhood are radically different social existences which affect the symbolism in the giving of these flowers. Just imagine the symbolic interpretation of a man giving another man the same bunch of roses. Symbolic interactionism gave sociologists an approach to social life which was predominantly social psychological rather than psychologically or socially deterministic in its explanations. The symbols of interaction do not exist in an individual's psychological make-up, but only through relationships in the social world.

Symbolic interactionism did not dominate sociology as such. The developments in sociology after Mead's death often consisted of grand theories concerning structures and change in society, rather than in understanding the social individual. As the stranglehold of be-haviourism was loosening in psychology more and more in the 1960s, among some sociologists there was something of a reaction against old-fashioned grand theoretical approaches in the form of a small-scale sociology with more than passing allegiances to Mead's ideas. Goffman, for example, chose to see interaction in terms of the social 'scripts' which govern social behaviour, so taking the metaphor of life as a stage into the social sciences. Garfinkel's 'ethnomethodology' sought to describe how individuals made their social action sensible and orderly. 'Labelling theory' chose to explain how some activities become categorized in society as deviant rather than taking the social construct of deviance as being unproblematic and not requiring explanation. Even transactional analysis (developed by the psychiatrist, Eric Berne, and discussed in Chapter 5) acknowledged a debt to Mead's ideas on games in social life, although it was couched in terms that perhaps owed more to psychoanalysis.

More recent times

The consequence of these changes was that in the 1960s there were competing forces shaping social psychology. However baleful the influence of behaviourism on social psychology, the work in the sociological and psychological social psychology traditions had left the discipline broader and more firmly established. This was not simply a matter of building bridges between the two traditions since, to some extent, the parent disciplines had also changed substantially: main-stream psychology, in general, changed it vision of human nature to make thought paramount; while mainstream sociology concerned itself more and more with small-scale social phenomena.

Regrettably, it remains the case that most psychologists and sociolo-gists have relatively little knowledge of each other's disciplines. The training of social psychologists has largely been from within the discipline of psychology. In a limited sense, this need not necessarily prevent progress since the reality often is one of two distinct strands of a discipline using radically different frameworks to explain rather different things. Rarely have the two strands offered competing explanations of identical social phenomena. On the other hand, being unaware of alternative approaches may restrict social psychologists unduly.

It is not difficult to find the marks of the history of social psychology on the current discipline. The priorities, methods, and subject matter of many social psychologists can be understood in terms of how they are located in respect of the broad historical streams.

Defining social psychology

Perhaps it is a little unconventional to leave discussing formal definitions until mid-way through the final chapter of a book. However, to do otherwise risks presenting ideas by dictate since one can only arrive at a definition knowing something about the thing to be defined. Certainly one can only question a definition on the basis of having a broader perspective.

A definition of social psychology might seem to be the key to understanding what it is. However, this is a little too slick and has inherent risks. It is difficult to define social psychology's subject matter precisely, partly because its boundaries with other similar disciplines are fuzzy. Sociologists often appear to encroach into the territory of social psychologists, and social anthropologists as well as linguists tackle much the same issues at times. But anthropology, linguistics and sociology neither embrace social psychology completely, nor are they sub-divisions of it, a common situation in academic disciplines. Who can say what ultimately marks the distinction between physics, chemistry, biology and engineering? One might suspect that this says much more about the artificiality of disciplinary boundaries than anything else.

Definitions in social psychology, as well as the social sciences in general, frequently create more problems than they solve. They always need careful examination. Although students are told to 'define their terms', it seems unlikely that a terse phrase or two can adequately encapsulate the scope and nature of an entire discipline. The earlier chapters provide a far better idea of what social psychology is than that.

Social psychology seems to be about the relationships between people and groups of people. However, it has already been pointed out that there is nothing approaching a single, universally accepted, view of how to describe and explain these relationships. Indeed what is fascinating is the immense range of different viewpoints incorporated into this relatively short book. It can hardly be said that social psychology is a single coherent framework for studying social relationships – a Tower of Babel with a multitude of competing voices would be closer to the truth.

It is worth briefly examining why definitions can be so problematical in order to show why they should be treated warily. Definitions can incorporate unacceptable ideas in the guise of objectivity. A definition taken from a popular North American textbook of a few years ago (Baron *et al.*, 1974, p. 3) suggests that social psychology is 'that branch of modern psychology which seeks to investigate the manner in which the behaviour, feelings, and thoughts of one individual are influenced and determined by the behavior and/or characteristics of others'. There is nothing particularly bad about this definition and there was no special reason to pick it out for consideration in preference to a multitude of others. But it does show some features which, although not universal, can cause difficulties and it does seem to be located in the past in terms of its content.

First, it claims that the subject matter of social psychology is the individual. This may appear to be self-evident but it actually clashes with much that appears in the earlier chapters. To define the individual (or even the individual in society or the individual in the group) as the subject matter of social psychology, encourages the view that groups (families, church congregations, workmates, and the like) should be studied as collections of individual people, with their individual social psychologies somehow summed together. Even if we reinterpret this to mean something along the lines that in social psychology we study groups by looking at what happens to the individual within the group, we still have problems because the definition still directs us to a particular unit of analysis. A longstanding and unresolved debate in social psychology concerns whether groups can adequately be conceptualized as amalgamations of individuals. Another view is that the actions of groups cannot be reduced to compounded individual personalities and that group processes are a function of groups and not individuals as such. However, much social psychology (especially that influenced by North American ideas) has tended to concentrate on the individual as the appropriate unit of analysis.

While one might agree with the definition in so far as it *reflects* what has been typical in social psychology, it is hardly a definitive statement of what social psychology is or should be. The definition, in a sense, trails behind what has been done rather than justifies what ought to be. Although it is often difficult, at first, to conceive groups as being something other than collections of individuals, parts of social psychology cannot be understood otherwise. Chapter 3 complicates the matter even further by demonstrating the interplay between roles and rules which are only meaningful in relation to both groups and the individual group member. The point is that a definition can constrain thinking unnecessarily.

Second, it claims that the subject matter of social psychology is the 'influence' of people on other people in terms of behaviour or attitudes or beliefs. The idea that social psychology should concentrate on how one thing causes another is an assumption which is too easily slipped into the definition of social psychology without being questioned. Does social psychology only seek to discover what social stimulus leads to a particular social response? Inevitably, by emphasizing influence, the definition excludes that part of social psychology which is not about cause-and-effect links. For example, a researcher may seek to understand how people perceive different social situations such as, say, a first date or a first day at work; or perhaps to obtain information about attitudes towards a particular disease. None of these necessarily concerns influence but could aid our understanding of human social experience. Or, to take attribution theory (Chapter 7), in which the so-called biases in attributions of social causality are examined, the intent of this is to examine the nature of social perceptions of causality – the characteristics of the inference process – not what *causes* people to make particular inferences.

Why would one want to exclude from social psychology that which does not involve examining 'influence'? There clearly is no good reason, which further questions the value of terse definitions of social psychology.

Sometimes it is said that social psychology is what social psychologists do. Despite the superficially humorous edge to this, it does acknowledge that the definition of social psychology cannot be precise. In some ways, social psychology is merely a label applied to a broad agenda of issues, a curriculum if one prefers, which will change substantially over time. There are central themes which recur frequently but inevitably the boundaries, approaches and organization of social psychology are not fixed. It seems inescapable that the definition of social psychology will change as the discipline develops. For that reason social psychologists should not feel encumbered by definitions limited to the present historical context. After all, in one of the first books entitled *Social Psychology*, Ross (1908, p. 1) defined the discipline as the study of 'the psychic planes and currents that come into existence among men in consequence of their association'. Most modern social psychologists would have difficulty in recognizing their discipline from this quotation which reflects a previous stage of social psychology, not current issues.

What is a social psychological explanation?

Whatever one's view about definitions, social psychological explanations must be characteristically different from other types of explanation. But how? Social geographers may choose to explain the movements of populations of people in terms of pull and push economic factors affecting the individual such as over-population and expanding job markets. Would the social psychologist use exactly the same sorts of explanatory concept? Would they prefer to discuss the motives of individuals instead? What if electronics progressed so much that we could understand mother–child interactions in terms of the electrical activity of their bodies? Would such a physical analysis warrant the description social psychological? Probably not.

Identifying key features of social psychological explanations is complicated by the variety of different 'brands' of social psychological explanation which are to be found. These differ substantially from each other and sometimes compete. This is frequently the result of major theoretical differences between social psychologists.

One way of understanding the different types of social psychology, as well as what is and what is not social psychology, involves classifying explanations in terms of the three following dichotomies:

1. *Referent social/referent non-social.* The referent is the thing to be explained and it may be social or non-social in nature. Social referents include friendships, conformity, social attitudes, language, culture, and many others which are specifically concerned with interaction between people. Non-social referents might include visual perception, hearing, intelligence, reaction times, and many others familiar from psychology courses.
2. *Concepts social/concepts non-social.* The concepts used in explanations are broadly either social or non-social in nature. Explanations of why a person becomes a leader, for example, might postulate social mechanisms – for example, leaders share the dominant attitudes in the group. An explanation using non-social concepts might be that leaders tend to be those who have high levels of intelligence coupled with high motivation to achieve. (Though this is a psychological explanation, it is not particularly social since it does not concern itself with processes which have any necessary origins in social activity.) A social explanation has to be based on interactions between people.
3. *Individual perspective/group perspective.* The referent may be essentially an individual whose individual characteristics are *explained* or are *used to explain*. For example, explaining conformity to group pressures in terms of an individual's degree of gullibility (or

other personal characteristics, as discussed in Chapter 4) is an example of the individual perspective. It is about an individual's characteristics (gullibility) not about the characteristics of people in general. The alternative is to study conglomerations of people (spouses, groups, particular social classes, sexes, nations, cultures) without reference to the special characteristics of particular individuals. So to study doctor–patient interaction from the group perspective might involve understanding how doctors in general are trained to perceive their professional role.

The above are three separate and independent dichotomies. This implies that there are eight types of explanation ($2 \times 2 \times 2$) formed from these three dichotomies, as shown in Table 10.1. In actuality, only six of the eight types are social psychology, even assuming the widest possible definition. If we consider each of the eight in turn, it will become clearer why this is the case and what the view of social psychology is underlying the choice of material included in this book.

Table 10.1 Types of social psychology

	Concepts social		Concepts non-social	
	Individual perspective	Group perspective	Individual perspective	Group perspective
Referent Social	Type 1	Type 2	Type 3	Type 4
Referent Non-Social	Type 5	Type 6	Type 7	Type 8

- Type 1: *Referent social/concepts social/individual perspective.* This is typical social psychology stemming from the psychological tradition. A good example of this is to be found in Chapter 9 in the discussion of the authoritarian personality. The referent is social since authoritarianism supposedly describes a pattern of relationships with authority figures. The concepts used to explain authoritarianism are also social since they deal with the effects of the interaction between parents and children in creating the syndrome. The perspective is individual since it attempts to describe a characteristic which different people have in different amounts. Another example, not discussed earlier, would be the explanation of an individual's shyness in terms of an overprotective relation with one parent.
- Type 2: *Referent social/concepts social/group perspective.* This is typical of social psychology originating in the sociological tradition.

Most of Chapter 3, concerning roles and rules, falls into this type. Clearly this describes a social referent (the conduct of interactions between people; the concepts are social since roles and rules emerge out of interaction between people; and it involves the group perspective since roles and rules are things which people share a common perspective on. A further instance of Type 2 would be the influence of the school on the composition and dynamics of inter-racial friendships. This is the type where confusion between the sociological and the social psychological is very likely and marks a major point of overlap between disciplines.

- Type 3: *Referent social/concepts non-social/individual perspective.* This is typical of biological and similar approaches to understanding society. Chapter 6 reviews several examples of this type of work when it considers genetic explanations of aggression. In these, although the referent is social in that it deals with relationships between people, the explanatory concepts involve biological mechanisms which relate to the individual. A particularly good example is the attempt to explain differences in aggressiveness in terms of the possession of extra 'male' chromosomes.

- Type 4: *Referent social/concepts non-social/group perspective.* Again this is typical of biological and similar explanations to understanding society but there are examples discussed in this book. Tajfel's work of intergroup prejudice (Chapter 7) claims that the basic perceptual mechanism of categorization leads to prejudice against groups of people of which one is not a member. While intergroup prejudice is certainly a social referent, there is nothing social about the idea that categorization is a basic perceptual process. It is a psychological, not a social-psychological, concept. Another example is the attempt to explain cross-cultural differences in toilet training practices by means of Freudian psychosexual theory. This is a non-social explanation because it relies primarily on notions developed from the psychology of individuals.

- Type 5: *Referent non-social/concepts social/individual perspective.* This might include, for example, explanations of mental illness or suicide in terms of abnormal patterns of interaction within the family. There are many examples of such work in the psychological literature but one would be hard pressed to find many examples in the earlier chapters. That is because we have chosen not to include material which does not seek to consider social referents. However, Chapter 5, on interpersonal attraction, has examples which conform to this type. For instance, the 'attraction from afar' syndrome concerns a non-social referent since it would apply as well to a newsreader on the television as in any more directly interactive situation. It really refers to an internal state rather than interaction as such. In the example of Byrne's work, attraction is based on the degree to which the two individual's share attitudes knowingly, which makes the explanatory concepts social. It is from the individual perspective in that ultimately it tries to explain the extent to which one person will be attracted to another on the basis of variations in attitudes.

- Type 6: *Referent non-social/concepts social/group perspective.* Included in this would be attempts to explain the emotionality of adolescence in terms of the discontinuities or separation of the roles of young people and adults in Western society. But again this type of material is not represented in this book, again for the very good reason that it is about the influence of society on what is really a psychological rather than clearly social psychological phenomenon.
- Type 7: *Referent non-social/concepts non-social/individual perspective.* As example of this would be explanations of the reading difficulty, dyslexia, in terms of damage to a particular area of the brain. This is clearly not social psychology at all in that it neither explains a social process nor uses social concepts to explain that phenomenon. Clearly dyslexia may have profound influences on interpersonal relationships but the concept itself does not refer to anything particularly social in nature.
- Type 8: *Referent non-social/concepts non-social/group perspective.* Again this is not social psychology at all for very much the same reasons as for Type 7. An example of it would be explanations of sleeping patterns is new-born infants by reference to the need to consolidate the large amounts of learning children have to achieve.

Although at first sight these distinctions might appear to be a little dry and too fussy, they actually go some way towards clarifying what social psychology is and, perhaps of more immediate concern, this book's view of social psychology. There is no way in which Types 7 and 8 could be remotely classified as social psychology, and they very firmly describe much of the mainstream contents of any psychology degree. They do not pretend to be social and frequently lean towards the biological. The same cannot be said with equal conviction about Types 5 and 6. Really these are the areas of psychology for which consideration of societal influence is important and, in general, has been well recognized. Most psychologists pay at least lip-service to the influence of cultural and other social influences on basic psychological processes such as perception, learning, intelligence, and the like. They are also important because they highlight the fact that there is not a complete disjunction between the social psychological and the psychological. However, they are not essentially social psychological in character, it might be argued, because they do not directly try to explain relationships between people.

This leaves us with the first four types. Types 3 and 4, while referring to social matters, do not see the basis for the social in social interaction but in more purely psychological or biological factors. While there are examples of these types in the earlier chapters, they do receive considerable criticism and they are disproportionately few compared to examples of Types 1 an 2. They seem to reflect a stage in the development of social psychology where it is clinging firmly to its origins in psychology rather than developing its own explanatory processes.

Types 1 and 2, by contrast, show a social psychology capable of standing on its own, borrowing relatively little from psychology. They also tend to share as much with other social science disciplines as they do with psychology. While Type 1 seems to be closer to the great tradition of American social psychology dependent on the experimental method for its empirical data, and Type 2 more related to European social psychology and small-scale sociology, the matching is by no means perfect. The combination of these two types, with the possibility of a relatively independent social psychology with its own concerns and its own explanatory principles, seems a more satisfactory proposition than the bifurcation of streams of thought which, as we have seen, occurred in earlier times.

Moving towards a better social psychology

One reason why it is important to develop a clear understanding of the broad context of social psychological work is that stepping aside from the immediate subject matter of the discipline allows a clearer view of future directions for social psychology. It is also important in that one is freed from the belief that what is, is what should be. The social psychology of one generation of researchers may well fail the next.

Until just a few years ago, it would have been possible to caricature the typical piece of social psychology as follows: Dr Wayne Smith, assistant professor of psychology, at the All-American State University, having published seven journal articles on the effects of prolonged ventro-medial stimulation of the top left hand corner of the rat's brain on maze-learning ability, decided to branch out. It was his view that the skills that he had developed in his doctoral work could be used to unravel the 'laws' of human social behaviour. He reasoned that although people are a little more complicated than rats there were marked similarities between the two so he would not have to change his approach when dealing with human subjects. Actually the chairperson of his department had also encouraged him to accept a research grant from the US Navy which had become concerned about the effects of prolonged submarine service on the morale of sailors. Dr Smith was rather offended by his wife's 'totally naive' suggestion that he should spend a few days at the naval base to talk to some submariners. He explained to her that psychology is a science and that there is no way one could know what the cause and effect sequences were without proper experiments and that people could not be expected to be aware of the 'true' causes of their behaviour. Finally, because of the 'rigour' demanded by him of research, he decided to simulate a submarine environment in the department's psychology laboratory so as to achieve maximum control over the situation. This was easy enough because there was a fairly small room next to the main lab which he could use to simulate cramped underwater conditions. The psychological literature seemed to have no theories which could help him formulate rigorous hypotheses so he resorted to the 'pragmatic' approach of working from his hunches about life in submarines. He hypothesized that those most prone to claustrophobia would experience lower morale in submarines, and that higher morale would be experienced in submarines painted green rather than grey, because of the association of the colour with open spaces.

This research design pleased him greatly because it included two independent variables – claustrophobia proneness and colour – which made for an 'efficient' research design. Having toyed with the idea of keeping a group of 12 subjects in these conditions for a whole week, he rejected it on the basis that it would not be possible to control all of the variables properly because the group members could be saying or doing things which might substantially affect the outcome of the research. There was only one thing for it – to create artificial groups. So what he decided to do was to place a single subject at a time in the 'submarine' and, to reproduce the 'group atmosphere', play a standard tape-recording of people having a good time at a party in an adjacent large laboratory at a sufficient volume that the subject could hear it through the wall. After spending four hours in the 'submarine' the subject would be asked to rate on a five-point scale, from extremely to not at all, the extent to which they would like to join the party. This seemed to Dr Smith to be a very good 'index' of morale. Soon afterwards, he administered the Alabama Multiphasic Claustrophobia Proneness Inventory to his introductory psychology class. He used scores on this test to form two groups of subjects – those high on claustrophobia proneness and those low on claustrophobia proneness. A week later, at the next scheduled lecture, he reminded the class that it was a requirement of their course that they take part in research as subjects, otherwise they lost marks from their coursework. Pleasingly, all of the class agreed to take part, thus ensuring a 'representative' sample.

Dr Smith, under pressure to complete his first book, persuaded a postgraduate student to run the experiment for him. However, to ensure that the research was done rigorously, Dr Smith first of all randomly assigned the subjects to the experimental and control groups. Furthermore, in order that the postgraduate student could not bias the results, Dr Smith did not tell her his hypotheses, thus 'ensuring' maximum scientific precision. The results were very pleasing; although the colour variable did not have any 'effect', the results revealed that subjects high on claustrophobia proneness had a significantly greater desire to join the party in the large laboratory, thus demonstrating that claustrophobics had higher morale in submarine conditions! Wayne Smith felt confident in his recommendation to the US Navy that there was no need to repaint its submarines and that only recruits high on the claustrophobia proneness scale should be selected for underwater service. He was certain that the few tens of thousands of dollars spent on the research were more than offset by the savings on paint and the increased efficiency that improved morale would bring. The last heard of Professor Smith was his presidential address to the Society of Applied Psychology in which he pointed out the great strides forward made by social psychology as a science as demonstrated by such results as his which were a big advance on common sense and, what is more, counter-intuitive. Clearly psychologists do not simply restate the obvious in complicated terms!

Social psychology does not have to be like that. There is still plenty of it around, both new and growing dusty on library shelves, and the above caricature is still sometimes not far from the reality. Such ways of doing things are simply not good enough and it would be deplorable to fail to learn from the lessons of the past. We have already seen in previous chapters that social psychology, when it is tuned into, a careful analysis of social experience, can usefully and readily forgo the obsessions of Dr Wayne Smith and, by doing so, generate a degree of understanding which he would never achieve.

Social psychology cannot simple be regenerated from what has gone before, it also needs inputs which both stretch and change its horizons. The stamp of social psychology's dependency on the concerns and ideology of academic psychology is patently obvious. However, it is a mixed blessing because of the often poorly developed sense of the social in mainstream psychology.

In appreciating the potential of social psychology, it is essential to see how other academic disciplines can contribute and have contributed to it. Such links between social psychology and other disciplines have often been more obvious than actual. By this is meant that there is a common consensus that social psychologists have a lot to gain from related disciplines and a lot to offer them, too. This virtually goes without saying, but a glance at textbooks of, say, social psychology, sociology, economics and anthropology would revel relatively few cross-references to the other disciplines. While this might not be true for political science, which shared with social psychology from the early part of this century a major concern with persuasion and propaganda, this is exceptional. Furthermore, the training of specialists in any of these disciplines need not, and probably does not, involve training in the other disciplines. Whether this seems satisfactory is likely to depend very much on the perspective from which one begins. The laboratory-based social psychologists working on basic social psychological research projects probably would not be able to incorporate a great deal from other disciplines. The applied social psychologist may well find that the understanding coming from other disciplines extremely helpful in comprehending a social phenomenon. For example, understanding what might appear from media coverage to be a mindless riot in an inner-city area may be enhanced by incorporating the economic, the historical, the sociological, the political, as well as the social psycho-logical – and perhaps other things which simply do not fall easily into any of these other disciplines.

Social psychology and anthropology

One would expect that social anthropology, with its techniques for studying relatively small groupings of people in 'their natural habitat', might have had a lot of influence on social psychology. Historically, there have been some cross-influences between the two – for example, Freudian ideas were adopted by social anthropologists to explain cultural phenomena (and Freud borrowed social anthropological data as 'facts' for his cultural theories). Probably the general legacy that social psychology received from the social anthropologists (especially, per-haps, Margaret Mead, despite claims that her data are suspect), was the convincing evidence that culture is a major determinant of many human characteristics. For example, it became very clear that sex differences in terms of social and work roles are not immutable and that cultures differ radically from each other in the degree of differentiation between the sexes and in terms of the 'typical' behaviour of males and females. The biological presumption that male aggression is in some way genetically 'built into' men becomes difficult to support if there are cultures in which men do not demonstrate aggression or women are more aggressive than men.

Social psychology and language

In more recent times there has been a major cross-fertilization with disciplines which focus on language (linguistics, semiotics, literary theory). This has resulted from a growing realization that social interaction is overwhelmingly conducted through language and that casual, unconstrained conversation is in one way or another the primary feature of everyday life.

Social psychology and sociology
The split between sociology and psychology in terms of dealing with social psychological issues has already been outlined. Here the links are clearer and greater than between social psychology and any other discipline. The influence has at times been great, and recently sociological styles of doing research and the idea that one can use how people define and see their social worlds as data have gained a lot of ground in social psychology.

Social psychology and psychology
It is intriguing that much of what we call 'social psychology' is a group of issues which are 'left over' and not claimed by other branches of psychology. For example, there is a lot in developmental psychology, clinical psychology, industrial psychology, psycholinguistics, for example, which seems as social in nature as anything to be found in social psychology. Notice that one consequence of this would seem to be that many applied issues of a social nature are claimed by other branches of psychology and are lost to social psychology as such. Naturally, there are opportunities for social psychology to influence and to be influenced by these other branches, but often it would appear that there is an absence of interest in doing so. Certainly a lot of academic psychology (which includes physiological psychology, memory, perception, and so on) lacks much social input and is increasingly distanced from social psychology, for better or worse.

Where social psychology is located in relation to other social science disciplines, psychology and the biological sciences is hardly a factual matter. It is much more a matter of choice than this implies. Social psychology is not merely something that is, it is also what social psychologists want it to be. Individuals can make social psychology what they want it to be. What that particular image of social psychology should be cannot be decided in a totally detached fashion as the issues dig deep into questions of ethics and morality, politics and belief. While it is true that social psychologists easily forget these matters in the nitty-gritty of their day-to-day work, they are part of the broader perspective which is endemic in the approach we have taken throughout this book.

Concluding comments

Having taken a broad look at what social psychology is, one is left with the feeling that in many ways it is a rather strange beast. While it would seem that there is plenty of room for the discipline to reach out and grasp new fields with fresh approaches, at the same time it tends to be more tied to psychology than it is broadly based. Some of the many reasons for this are embedded in this final chapter and include matters such as the academic base of social psychology, its history and its ethos. Whether or not changes in social psychology can occur sufficiently to alter this can only be guessed. But there is not a shadow of a doubt that social psychologists can achieve more if they are freed from the orthodoxy of the discipline to a degree which makes them receptive to and creative of new ideas. The way things have been done is no criterion for the way they should be done. Being able to see social psychology broadly, away from the minutiae of variables, experimental manipulations, causes and effects, tests of significance, and the rest, is invaluable in establishing better priorities for social psychology. The detailed skills of social psychology are essential, but by themselves they take us nowhere. The priorities demonstrated in earlier chapters are merely one starting point.

REFERENCES

Adorno, T. W., Frenkel-Brunswik, E., Levinson, D. J. and Sanford, R. N. (1950). *The Authoritarian Personality*. New York: Harper and Row.

Ajzen, I. and Fishbein, M. (eds) (1980). *Understanding Attitudes and Predicting Social Behaviour*. Englewood Cliffs, NJ: Prentice Hall.

Allport, G. (1954). *The Nature of Prejudice*. Garden City, NY: Anchor Books.

Altemeyer, R. A. (1981). *Right-wing Authoritarianism*. Manitoba: University of Manitoba Press.

Ardrey, R. (1966). *The Territorial Imperative*. New York: Atheneum.

Aronson, E. (1972). *The Social Animal*. San Francisco: W. H. Freeman.

Asch, S. E. (1952). *Social Psychology*. Englewood Cliffs, NJ: Prentice Hall.

Asch, S. E. (1956). 'Studies of Independence and Submission to Group Pressure: A Minority of One Against a Unanimous Majority', *Psychological Monographs*, 70, 416–688.

Ashmore, R. D. and Del Boca, F. K. (1981). 'Psychological Approaches to Understanding Intergroup Conflicts' in D. L. Hamilton (ed.), *Cognitive Processes in Stereotyping and Intergroup Behavior*. Hillsdale, NJ: Erlbaum.

Atkinson, J. M. (1983). 'Two Devices for Generating Audience Approval: A Comparative Analysis of Public Discourse and Texts' in K. Ehlich and H. van Riemsdijk (eds), *Connectedness in Sentence, Discourse and Text*. Tilburg: Tilburg Papers in Linguistics.

Atkinson, J. M. (1984a). *Our Master's Voices: The Language and Body Language of Politics*. London: Methuen.

Atkinson, J. M. (1984b). 'Public Speaking and Audience Responses: Some Techniques for Inviting Applause' in J. M. Atkinson and J. C. Heritage (eds), *Structures of Social Action: Studies in Conversation Analysis*. Cambridge: Cambridge University Press.

Atkinson, J. M. (1985). 'Refusing Invited Applause: Preliminary Observations from a Case Study of Charismatic Oratory' in T. A. van Dijk (ed.), *A Handbook of Discourse Analysis, Vol. 3*. New York: Academic Press.

Ax, A. F. (1953). 'The Physiological Differentiation Between Fear and Anger in Humans', *Psychosomatic Medicine*, 15, 433–42.

Bales, R. F. (1958). 'Task Roles and Social Roles in Problem-solving Groups' in

E. Maccoby, T. M. Newcomb and E. L. Hartley (eds), *Readings in Social Psychology*. New York: Holt, Rinehart and Winston.

Bandura, A. (1962). 'Social Learning through Imitation' in M. R. Jones (ed.), *Nebraska Symposium on Motivation: 1962*. Lincoln: University of Nebraska Press.

Bandura, A. (1973). *Aggression: A Social Learning Analysis*. Englewood Cliffs, NJ: Prentice Hall.

Baron, R. A., Byrne, D. and Griffitt, W. (1974). *Social Psychology: Understanding Human Interaction*. Boston. Allyn and Bacon

Barrow, J. C. (1976). 'Worker Performance and Task Complexity as Causal Determinants of Leader Behaviour Style and Flexibility', *Journal of Applied Psychology*, 61, 433–40.

Bartlett, F. (1932). *Remembering*. Cambridge: Cambridge University Press.

Bass, B. M. (1981). *Stogdhill's Handbook of Leadership*. New York: Free Press.

Beloff, H. (1985). *Camera Culture*. Oxford: Blackwell.

Berkowitz, L. (1982). 'Aversive Conditions as Stimuli to Aggression' in L. Berkowitz (ed.), *Advances in Experimental Social Psychology. Volume 15*. New York: Academic Press.

Berkowitz, L. and Rawlings, E. (1963). 'Effects of Film Violence on Inhibitions against Subsequent Aggression', *Journal of Abnormal and Social Psychology*, 66, 405–12.

Berne, E. (1964). *Games People Play: The Psychology of Human Relationships*. New York: Grove Press.

Bettelheim, B. (1958). 'Individual and Mass Behaviour in Extreme Situations' in E. Maccoby, T. M. Newcomb and E. L. Hartley (eds), *Readings in Social Psychology*, New York: Holt, Rinehart and Winston.

Billig, M. (1978). *Fascists: A Social Psychological View of the National Front*. London: Academic Press.

Billig, M. (1981). 'The National Front and Youth', *Patterns of Prejudice*, 15, 3–16.

Billig, M. (1982). *Ideology and Social Psychology*. Oxford: Blackwell.

Billig, M. (1985). 'Prejudice, Categorization and Particularization: From a Perceptual to a Rhetorical Approach', *European Journal of Social Psychology*, 15, 79–103.

Billig, M. (1986). 'Very Ordinary Life and the Young Conservatives' in H. Beloff (ed.), *Getting into Life*. London: Metheun.

Billig, M. (1987). *Arguing and Thinking: A Rhetorical Approach to Social Psychology*. Cambridge: Cambridge University Press.

Billig, M. (1988a). 'Social Representation, Objectification and Anchoring: A Rhetorical Analysis', *Social Behaviour*, 3, 1–16.

Billig, M. (1988b). 'The Notion of "Prejudice": Some Rhetorical and Ideological Aspects', *Text*, 8, 91–110.

Billig, M. and Tajfel, H. (1973). 'Social Categorisation and Similarity in Intergroup Behaviour', *European Journal of Social Psychology*, 3, 27–52.

Billig, M., Condor, S., Edwards, D., Gane, M., Middleton, D. and Radley, A. R. (1988). *Ideological Dilemmas*. Sage: London.

Borgatta, E. F., Couch, A. S. and Bales, R. F. (1954). 'Some Findings Relevant to the Great Man Theory of Leadership', *American Sociological Review*, 19, 755–9.

Brehm, J. W. (1966). *A Theory of Psychological Reactance*. New York: Academic Press.

Brehm, J. W. and Sensenig, J. (1966). 'Social Influence as a Function of Attempted and Implied Usurption of Choice', *Journal of Personality and Social Psychology*, 4, 703–7.

Brigham, J. C. (1971). 'Ethnic Stereotypes', *Psychological Bulletin*, 76, 15—38.

Brown, R. and Hewstone, M. (1986). *Contact and Conflict in Intergroup Encounters*. Oxford: Blackwell.

Bruner, J. S. (1983). *Child's Talk*. Oxford: Oxford University Press.

Bruner, J. S. and Sherwood, V. (1981). 'Thought, Language and Interaction in Infancy', in J. P. Forgas (ed.), *Social Cognition: Perspectives on Everyday Understanding*. London: Academic Press.

Bryman, A. (1986). *Leadership and Organisations*. London: Routledge & Kegan Paul.

Buss, A. R. (1979). *Dialectical Psychology*. New York: Irvington.

Byrne, D. (1971). *The Attraction Paradigm*. New York: Academic Press.

Cantril, H. (1959). 'The Invasion from Mars' in E. Maccoby, T. M. Newcomb, and E. L. Hartley (eds), *Readings in Social Psychology*. London: Metheun.

Cantril, H., Gaudet, H. and Hertzog, H. (1940). *The Invasion from Mars*. Princeton, NJ: Princeton University Press.

Caplan, A. L. (ed.) (1978). *The Sociobiology Debate: Readings on the Ethical and Scientific Issues Concerning Sociobiology*. New York: Harper and Row.

Carpenter, E. E. (1966). *Eskimo Realities*. New York: Holt, Reinhart and Winston.

Christie, R. and Geis, F. L. (1970). *Studies in Machiavellianism*. New York: Academic Press.

Clore, G. L. and Byrne, D. (1974). 'A Reinforcement-Affect Model of Attraction' in T. L. Huston (ed.), *Foundations of Interpersonal Attraction*. New York: Academic Press.

Cramer, D. (1985). 'Psychological Adjustment and the Facilitative Nature of Close Personal Relationships', *British Journal of Medical Psychology*, 58, 165–8.

Cramer, D. (1988). 'Self-esteem and Facilitative Close Relationships: A Cross-lagged Panel Correlation Analysis', *British Journal of Social Psychology*, 27, 115–26.

Crook, J. H. (1968). 'The Nature and Function of Territorial Aggression' in M. F. Ashley Montegu (ed.), *Man and Aggression*. New York: Oxford University Press.

Crutchfield, R. S. (1955). 'Conformity and Character', *American Psychologist*, 10, 191–8.

Deaux, K. and Lewis, L. L. (1984). 'Structure of Gender Stereotypes: Inter-relations among Components and Gender Label', *Journal of Personality and Social Psychology*, 46, 991–1004.

Deaux, K., Winton, W., Crowley, M. and Lewis, L. L. (1985). 'Level of Categorization and Content of Gender Stereotypes', *Social Cognition*, 3, 145–67.

Deutsch, M. and Collins, M. E. (1951). *Interracial Housing: A Psychological Evaluation of a Social Experiment*. Minneapolis: University of Minnesota Press.

Dollard, J., Miller, N., Doob, L., Mowrer, O. H. and Sears, R. R. (1939). *Frustration and Aggression*. New Haven, CT: Yale University Press.

Dovidio, J. F. and Gaertner, S. L. (1986). 'Prejudice, Discrimination and Racism: Historical Trends and Contemporary Approaches', in J. F. Dovidio and S. L. Gaertner (eds), *Prejudice, Discrimination and Racism*. Orlando, FL: Academic Press.

Draguns, J. G. and Phillips, L. (1971). *Psychiatric Classification and Diagnosis: An Overview and Critique*. New York: General Learning Press.

Duncan, B. L. (1976). 'Differential Social Perception and Attribution of Intergroup Violence: Testing the Lower Limits of Stereotyping Blacks', *Journal of Personality and Social Psychology*, 34, 590–8.

Eagly, A. H. and Steffen, V. J. (1984). 'Gender Stereotypes Stem from the Distribution of Women and Men into Social Roles', *Journal of Personality and Social Psychology*, 46, 735–54.

Eagly, A. H., Wood, W. and Chaiken, S. (1978). 'Causal Inferences about Communicators and their Effect on Opinion Change', *Journal of Personality and Social Psychology*, 36, 424–35.

Edelman, M. (1977). *Political Language: Words that Succeed and Policies that Fail*. New York: Academic Press.

Edwards, D. (1978). 'Social Relations and Early Language' in A. J. Lock (ed.), *Action, Gesture and Symbol: The Emergence of Language*. London: Academic Press.

Edwards, D. and Mercer, N. M. (1987). *Common Knowledge: The Development of Understanding in the Classroom*. London: Methuen.

Edwards, D. and Middleton, D. J. (1988). 'Conversational Remembering and Family Relationships: How Children Learn to Remember', *Journal of Social and Personal Relationships*, 5, 3–25.

Eiser, R. (1986). *Social Psychology: Attitudes, Cognition and Social Behaviour*. Cambridge University Press.

Epstein, Y. M., Suedfeld, P. and Silverstein, S. J. (1973). 'The Experimental Contract: Subjects' Expectations of and Reactions to Some Behaviors of Experimenters', *American Psychologist*, 28, 212–21.

Erdelyi, M. H. (1974). 'A New Look at the New Look: Perceptual Defense and Vigilance', *Psychological Review*, 81, 1–25.

Ervin-Tripp, S. (1977). 'Wait for Me, Roller-skate' in S. Ervin-Tripp and C. Mitchell Kernan (eds), *Child Discourse*. London: Academic Press.

Ervin-Tripp, S. and Mitchell Kernan, C. (eds) (1977). *Child Discourse*. London Academic Press.

Essed, P. (1988). 'Understanding Verbal Accounts of Racism: Politics and Heuristics of Reality Constructions', *Text*, 8, 5–40.

Evans, R. I. (1980). *The Making of Social Psychology*. New York: Gardner Press.

Faranda, J. A., Maminski, J. A. and Giza, B. K. (1979). 'An Assessment of Attitudes toward Women with the Bogus Pipeline', cited in D. Meyers (1987), *Social Psychology*. New York: McGraw-Hill.

Fern, E. F., Monroe, K. B. and Avila, R. A. (1986). 'Effectiveness of Multiple

Request Strategies: A Synthesis of Research Results', *Journal of Marketing Research*, 23, 144–52.

Festinger, L. (1954). 'A Theory of Social Comparison Processes', *Human Relations*, 7, 117–40.

Fiedler, F. E. (1969). 'Style or Circumstance: the Leadership Enigma', *Psychology Today*, 2, 38–43.

Fiedler, F. E. (1972). 'Personality, Motivational Systems, and Behaviour of High and Low LPC persons', *Human Relations*, 25, 391–412.

Fincham, F. D. and Bradbury, T. N. (1987). 'The Impact of Attributions in Marriage: A Longitudinal Analysis', *Journal of Personality and Social Psychology*, 53, 510–17.

Fincham, F. D. and Jaspars, J. M. (1980). 'Attribution of Responsibility: From Man the Scientist to Man as Lawyer', in L. Berkowitz (ed.), *Advances in Experimental Social Psychology: Vol. 13*. New York: Academic Press.

Fishbein, M. (1982). 'Social Psychological Analysis of Smoking Behaviour' in I. Ajzen and M. Fishbein. (eds), *Understanding Attitudes and Predicting Social Behaviour*. Englewood Cliffs, NJ: Prentice Hall.

Fishbein, M. and Ajzen, I. (1974). 'Attitudes toward Objects as Predictors of Single and Multiple Behavioural criteria', *Psychological Review*, 81, 59–74.

Fiske, S. T. and Taylor, S. E. (1984). *Social Cognition*. Reading, MA: Addison-Wesley.

Freedman, J. L. and Fraser, S. C. (1966). 'Compliance without Pressure: The Foot-in-the-door Technique', *Journal of Personality and Social Psychology*, 4, 195–202.

Freedman, J. L., Sears, D. O. and Carlsmith, J. M. (1978). *Social Psychology*. Englewood Cliffs, NJ: Prentice Hall.

French, J. R. P. and Snyder, R. (1959). 'Leadership and Interpersonal Power' in D. Cartwright (ed.), *Studies in Social Power*. Ann Arbor: Institute for Social Research, University of Michigan.

Freud, S. (1930). *Civilization and its Discontents*. London: Hogarth.

Fromm, E. (1941). *Escape from Freedom*. London: Routledge.

Furnham, A. and Lewis, A. (1986). *The Economic Mind*. Sussex: Wheatsheaf.

Garfinkel, H. (1967). *Studies in Ethnomethodology*. Cambridge: Polity Press.

Garvey, C. and Hogan, R. (1973). 'Special Speech and Social Interaction: Egocentrism Revisited', *Child Development*, 44, 562–68.

Gelles, R. J. (1979). *Family Violence*. Beverly Hills, CA: Sage.

Gergen, K. J. and Gergen, M. (1981). 'Causal Attribution in the Context of Social Explanation' in D. Gorlitz (ed.), *Perspectives on Attribution Research and Theory*. Cambridge, MA: Ballinger.

Gibbs, C. A. (1969). 'Leadership' in G. Lindzey and E. Aronson (eds), *The Handbook of Social Psychology, Vol. 4*. Reading, MA: Addison-Wesley.

Gilbert, G. M. (1951). 'Stereotype Persistence and Change among College Students', *Journal of Abnormal and Social Psychology*, 46, 245–54.

Goffman, E. (1955). 'On Face-work: An Analysis of Ritual Elements in Social Interaction', *Psychiatry*, 18, 212–31.

Goffman, E. (1959). *The Presentation of Self in Everyday Life*. Harmondsworth: Penguin.

Goffman, E. (1971). *Relations in Public: Microstudies of the Public Order.* Harmondsworth: Penguin.

Gombrich, E. H. (1968). *Art and Illusion.* London: Phaidon Press.

Grady, K. and Potter, J. (1985). 'Speaking and Clapping: A Comparison of Foot and Thatcher's Oratory', *Language and Communications,* 5, 173–83.

Greenwald, A. G. (1980). 'The Totalitarian Ego: Fabrication and Revision of Personal History', *American Psychologist,* 35, 603–18.

Grice, H. P. (1975). 'Logic and Conversation' in P. Cole and J. Morgan (eds), *Syntax and Semantics 3: Speech Acts.* New York: Academic Press.

Hamilton, D. L. (1976). 'Cognitive Biases in the Perception of Social groups', in J. S. Carroll and J. W. Payne (eds), *Cognitive and Social Behavior.* Hillsdale, NJ: Erlbaum.

Hamilton, D. L. and Trolier, T. K. (1986). 'Stereotypes and Stereotyping: An Overview of the Cognitive Approach' in J. F. Dovidio and S. L. Gaertner (eds), *Prejudice, Discrimination and Racism.* Orlando, FL: Academic Press.

Haney, C., Banks, C. and Zimbardo, P. (1981). A Study of Prisoners and Guards in a Simulated Prison', in E. Aronson (ed.), *Readings about the Social Animal.* San Francisco: W. H. Freeman.

Harré, R. (1979). *Social Being: A Theory for Social Psychology.* Oxford: Blackwell.

Harré, R. and Secord, P. F. (1972). *The Explanation of Social Behaviour.* Oxford: Blackwell.

Harris, P. R. (1985). 'Asch's Data and the "Asch Effect": A Critical Note', *British Journal of Social Psychology,* 24, 229–30.

Hass, R. G. (1981). 'Effects of Source Characteristics on Cognitive Response and Persuasion' in R. E. Petty, T. M. Ostrom, and T. C. Brock (eds), *Cognitive Responses in Persuasion.* Hillsdale, NJ: Erlbaum.

Heider, F. (1958). *The Psychology of Interpersonal Relations.* New York: Wiley.

Heider, F. (1980). 'Perception and Attribution', in D. Gorlitz (ed.), *Perspectives on Attribution Theory.* Cambridge, MA: Ballinger.

Heritage, J. (1984). *Garfinkel and Ethnomethodology.* Cambridge: Polity Press.

Heritage, J. (1988) 'Interactional Accountability: A Conversation Analytic Perspective' in C. Antaki (ed.), *Analysing Everyday Explanation: A Case Book.* London: Sage.

Heritage, J. and Greatbatch, D. (1986). 'Generating Applause: A Study of Rhetoric and Response at Party Political Conferences' *American Journal of Sociology,* 92, 110–57.

Hewstone, M. (ed.) (1983). *Attribution Theory: Social and Functional Extensions.* Oxford: Blackwell.

Himmelweit, H. (1986). *How Voters Decide.* Milton Keynes: Open University Press.

Hollander, E. P. (1981). *Principles and Methods of Social Psychology.* New York: Oxford University Press.

Homans, G. C. (1951). *The Human Group.* London: Routledge and Kegan Paul.

Homans, G. C. (1961). *Social Behaviour: Its Elementary Forms.* New York: Harcourt, Brace and World.

Hovland, C. I., Janis, I. L. and Kelley, H. H. (1953). *Communication and Persuasion.* New Haven, CT: Yale University Press.

Hovland, C. I. and Sears, R. R. (1940). 'Minor Studies in Aggression: 4. Correlation of Lynchings with Economic Indices', *Journal of Personality*, 9, 301–10.

Howitt, D. (1982). *Mass Media and Social Problems*. Oxford: Pergamon.

Howitt, D. and Cumberbatch, G. (1975). *Mass Media Violence and Society*. London: Elek Science.

Hyman, H. H. and Sheatsley, P. B. (1954). 'The Authoritarian Personality – A Methodological Critique', in R. Christie and M. Jahoda (eds), *Studies in the Scope and Method of 'The Authoritarian Personality'*. Glencoe, IL: Free Press.

Jackman, M. R. and Senter, M. S. (1980). 'Images of Social Groups: Categorical or Qualified?', *Public Opinion Quarterly*, 44, 341–62.

Jahoda, M. (1959). 'Conformity and Independence', *Human Relations*, 12, 99–120.

James, W. (1950). *The Principles of Psychology*. New York: Dover (first published in 1890).

Jefferson, G. (1989). 'List Construction as a Task and Resource' in G. Psathas (ed.), *Interactional Competence*. Norwood, NJ: Ablex.

Jodelet, D. (1984). 'Représentation sociale: phénomènes, concept et théorie', in S. Moscovici (ed.), *Psychologie sociale*. Paris: Presses Universitaires de France.

Jones, E. E. and Davis, K. E. (1965). 'From Acts to Dispositions: The Attribution Process in Person Perception', in L. Berkowitz (ed.), *Advances in Experimental Social Psychology: Vol. 2*. New York: Academic Press.

Jones, E. E., Davis, K. E. and Gergen, K. J. (1961). 'Role Playing Variations and their Informal Value for Person Perception' *Journal of Abnormal and Social Psychology*, 63, 302–10.

Jones, E. E. and Sigal, H. (1971). 'The Bogus Pipeline: A New Paradigm for Measuring Affect and Attitude', *Psychological Bulletin*, 76, 349–64.

Kaitz, M. (1985). 'Role Conflict Resolution for Women with Infants', *Birth Psychology Bulletin*, 6, 10–20.

Karlins, M., Coffham, T. L. and Walters, G. (1969). 'On the Fading of Social Stereotypes: Studies in Three Generations of College Students', *Journal of Personality and Social Psychology*, 13, 1–16.

Kater, D. (1985). 'Management Strategies for Dual-career Couples', *Journal of Career Development*, 12, 75–80.

Katz, D. and Braly, K. (1933). 'Racial Prejudice and Racial Stereotypes', *Journal of Abnormal and Social Psychology*, 30, 175–93.

Kelley, H. H. (1967). 'Attribution Theory in Social Psychology', *Nebraska Symposium on Motivation*, 15, 192–238.

Kirscht, J. P. and Dillehay, R. C. (1967). *Dimensions of Authoritarianism*. Lexington: University of Kentucky Press.

Kniveton, B. H. (1986). 'Peer Modelling of Classroom Violence and Family Structure: An Experimental Study', *Educational Studies*, 12, 87–94.

Kniveton, B. H. (1987). 'Misbehaving Peer Models in the Classroom: An Investigation of the Effects of Social Class and Intelligence', *Educational Studies*, 13, 161–8.

Koestler, A. (1949). 'The God that Failed' in R. Crossman (ed.), *The God that Failed*. New York: Arno Press.

Kohlberg, L. (1968). 'The Child as a Moral Philosopher', *Psychology Today*, September, 25–30.

Kruglanski, A. W. (1979). 'The Endogenous–Exogenous Partition in Attribution Theory', *Psychological Review*, 82, 387–406.

Langer, E. (1978). 'Rethinking the role of thought in social interaction', in J. H. Harvey, W. J. Ickes and R. F. Kidd (eds), *New Directions in Attribution Research*. Hillsdale, NJ: Erlbaum.

Langer, E., Blank, A. and Chanowitz, B. (1978). 'The Mindlessness of Ostensibly Thoughtful Action: The Role of "Placebic" Information in Interpersonal Interaction', *Journal of Personality and Social Psychology*, 36, 635–42.

Lanzetta, J. T. and Kanareff, V. T. (1959). 'The Effects of Monetary Reward on the Acquisition of an Imitative Response', *Journal of Abnormal and Social Psychology*, 59, 120–7.

Latané, B. and Darley, J. M. (1970). *The Unresponsive Bystander: Why Doesn't He Help?* New York: Appleton-Century-Crofts.

Lederer, G. (1982). 'Trends in Authoritarianism: A Study of Adolescents in West Germany and the United States since 1945', *Journal of Cross-cultural Psychology*, 13, 299–314.

Lemert, E. M. (1972). *Human Deviance, Social Problems and Social Control* (2nd edn). Englewood Cliffs, NJ: Prentice Hall.

Leslie, A. (1987). 'Pretense and Representation: The Origins of "Theory of Mind" ', *Psychological Review*, 94, 412–26.

Levinson, S. (1983). *Pragmatics*. Cambridge: Cambridge University Press.

Lickona, T. (1976). *Moral Development and Behavior*. New York: Holt, Rinehart and Winston.

Linville, P. W., Salovey, P. and Fischer, G. W. (1986). 'Stereotyping and Perceived Distributions of Social Characteristics: An Application to Ingroup–Outgroup Perceptions', in J. F. Dovidio and S. L. Gaertner (eds), *Prejudice, Discrimination and Racism*. Orlando, FL: Academic Press.

Lippitt, R. and White, R. K. (1943). 'The Social Climate of Children's Groups' in R. G. Barker, J. S. Kounin and H. F. Wright (eds), *Child Behavior and Development*. New York: McGraw Hill.

Lipset, S. M. (1960). *Political Man*. Garden City, NY: Doubleday.

Lock, A. J. (ed.) (1978). *Action, Gesture and Symbol: The Emergence of Language*. London: Academic Press.

Lock, A. J. (1979). *The Guided Reinvention of Language*. London: Academic Press.

Locke, D. and Pennington, D. (1982). 'Reasons and Causes in Attribution Processes', *Journal of Personality and Social Psychology*, 42, 212–23.

London, P. (1970). 'The Rescuers: Motivational Hypotheses about Christians who Saved Jews from the Nazis' in J. MacCaulay and L. Berkowitz (eds), *Altruism and Helping Behaviour*. New York: Academic Press.

Lorenz, K. (1963). *On Aggression*. London: Methuen.

McArthur, L. A. (1972). 'The How and What of Why: Some Determinants and Consequences of Causal Attribution', *Journal of Personality and Social Psychology*, 2, 171–93.

McCauley, C. and Stitt, C. L. (1978). 'An Individual and Quantitative

Measure of Stereotypes', *Journal of Personality and Social Psychology*, 36, 929–40.

McCauley, C., Stitt, C. L. and Segal, M. (1980). 'Stereotyping: From Prejudice to Prediction' *Psychological Bulletin*, 87, 195–208.

McConahay, J. B. (1981). 'Reducing Racial Prejudice in Desegregated Schools', in W. D. Hawley (ed.), *Effective School Desegregation*. Beverly Hills, CA: Sage.

McConahay, J. B. (1982). 'Self-interest versus Racial Attitudes as Correlates of Anti-busing Attitudes in Louisville: Is it the Buses or the Blacks?', *Journal of Politics*, 44, 692–720.

McConahay, J. B. (1986). 'Modern Racism, Ambivalence and the Modern Racism Scale', in J. F. Dovidio and S. L. Gaertner (eds.), *Prejudice, Discrimination and Racism*. Orlando, FL: Academic Press.

McDougall, W. (1908). *Introduction to Social Psychology*, London: Methuen.

McGuire, W. J. (1985). 'Attitudes and Attitude Measurement', in G. Lindzey and E. Aronson (eds), *The Handbook of Social Psychology, Vol. 2*. New York: Random House.

Mann, R. D. (1959). 'A Review of the Relationship between Personality and Performance in Small Groups', *Psychological Bulletin*, 56, 241–70.

Manstead, A. S. R., Proffitt, C. and Smart, J. L. (1983). 'Predicting and Understanding Mothers' Infant-feeding Intentions and Behaviour: Testing the Theory of Reasoned Action', *Journal of Personality and Social Psychology*, 44, 657–71.

Maratsos, M. (1973). 'Nonegocentric Communication Abilities in Pre-school Children' *Child Development*, 44, 679–700.

Mead, G. H. (1934). *Mind, Self, and Society*. Chicago: University of Chicago Press.

Mervis, C. B. and Rosch, E. (1981). 'Categorisation of Natural Objects', *Annual Review of Psychology*, 32, 89–115.

Milgram, S. (1974). *Obedience to Authority*. New York: Harper and Row.

Milner, D. (1983). *Children and Race: Ten Years On*. London: Ward Lock.

Monson, T. C. and Snyder, M. (1977). 'Actors, Observers and the Attribution Process', *Journal of Experimental Social Psychology*, 13, 89–111.

Morris, D. (1968). *The Naked Ape*. New York: McGraw-Hill.

Moscovici, S. (1982). 'The Coming Era of Representations', in J. P. Codol and J. Leyens (eds), *Cognitive Approaches to Social Behaviour*. The Hague: Nijhoff.

Moscovici, S. (1984a). 'The Phenomenon of Social Representations', in R. Farr and S. Moscovici (eds), *Social Representations*. Cambridge: Cambridge University Press.

Moscovici, S. (1984b). 'The Myth of the Lonely Paradigm', *Social Research*, 51, 939–67.

Neisser, U. (1988). Five Kinds of Self-Knowledge. *Philosophical Psychology*, 1, 35–59.

Nelson, K. and Gruendel, J. (1986). 'Children's Scripts', in K. Nelson (ed.), *Event Knowledge: Structure and Function in Development*. Hillsdale, NJ: Lawrence Erlbaum.

Newcomb, T. M. (1961). *The Acquaintance Process*. New York: Holt, Rinehart and Winston.

Newcomb, T. M. (1963). 'Social Psychological Theory: Integrating Individual and Social Approaches', in E. P. Hollander and R. G. Hunt (eds), *Current Perspectives in Social Psychology*. New York: Oxford University Press.

Nicholson, N., Cole, S. G. and Rocklin, T. (1985). 'Conformity in the Asch Situation: A Comparison between Contemporary British and US University Students', *British Journal of Social Psychology*, 24, 59–63.

Nilson, R. B. (1980). 'Reconsidering Ideological Lines: Beliefs about Poverty in America', *Sociological Quarterly*, 22, 531–48

Nisbett, R. E. (1981). 'Lay Arbitration Rules of Inference', *Behavioral and Brain Sciences*, 4, 349–50.

Nisbett, R. E. and Borgida, E. (1975). 'Attribution and the Psychology of Prediction', *Journal of Personality and Social Psychology*, 32, 932–43.

Nisbett, R. E. and Ross, L. (1980). *Human Inference*. Englewood Cliffs, NJ: Prentice Hall.

Nisbett, R. E., Caputo, C., Legant, P. and Maracek, J. (1973). 'Behavior as Seen by the Actor and as Seen by the Observer', *Journal of Personality and Social Psychology*, 27, 154–64.

Orne, M. T. and Scheibe, K. E. (1964). 'The Contribution of Nondeprivation Factors in the Production of Sensory Deprivation Effects: The Psychology of the Panic Button', *Journal of Abnormal and Social Psychology*, 68, 3–12.

Pagel, M. D. and Davidson, A. R. (1984). 'A comparison of Three social-Psychological Models of Attitude and Behavioural Plan: Prediction of Contraceptive Behaviour', *Journal of Personality and Social Psychology*, 47, 517–33.

Perrin, S. and Spencer, C. P. (1981). 'Independence or Conformity in the Asch Experiment as a Reflection of Cultural and Situational Factors', *British Journal of Social Psychology*, 20, 205–9.

Pettigrew, T. F. (1958). 'Personality and Sociocultural Factors in Intergroup Attitudes: A Cross-National Comparison', *Journal of Conflict Resolution*, 1, 29–42.

Petty, R. E. and Cacioppo, J. T. (1986). 'The Elaboration Likelihood Model of Persuasion', in L. Berkowitz (ed.), *Advances in Experimental Social Psychology: Vol. 19*. New York: Academic Press.

Petty, R. E., Cacioppo, J. T. and Goldman, R. (1981). 'Personal Involvement as a Determinant of Argument-based Persuasion', *Journal of Personality and Social Psychology*, 41, 847–55.

Piaget, J. (1926). *The Language and Thought of the Child*. London: Routledge and Kegan Paul.

Piaget, J. (1932). *The Moral Judgment of the Child*. London: Routledge and Kegan Paul.

Plato (1956). *Protagoras and Meno* (trans. W. K. C. Guthrie). Penguin: Harmondsworth.

Pollner, M. (1987). *Mundane Reason: Reality in Everyday and Sociological Discourse*. Cambridge: Cambridge University Press.

Pomerantz, A. (1977). 'Compliment Responses: Notes on the Operation of Multiple Constraints' in J. Schenkein (ed.), *Studies in the Organization of Conversational Interaction*. London: Academic Press.

Pomerantz, A. (1984). 'Agreeing and Disagreeing with Assessments: Some Features of Prefered/disprefered turn shapes' in J. M. Atkinson and J. Heritage (eds), *Structures of Social Action: Studies in Conversation Analysis*. Cambridge: Cambridge University Press.

Potter, J. and Wetherell, M. (1987). *Discourse and Social Psychology: Beyond Attitudes and Behaviour*. London: Sage.

Potter, J. and Wetherell, M. (1988). 'Accomplishing Attitudes: Fact and Evaluation in Racist Discourse', *Text*, 8, 51–68.

Quattrone, G. A. (1982). 'Overattribution and Unit Formation: When Behavior Engulfs the Person', *Journal of Personality and Social Psychology*, 42, 593–607.

Quattrone, G. A. (1985). 'On the Congruity between Internal States and Action', *Psychological Bulletin*, 98, 3–40.

Rauch, C. F. and Behling, O. (1984). 'Functionalism: Basis for an Alternate Approach to the Study of Leadership', in J. G. Hunt, D. M. Hosking, C. A. Schriesheim and R. Steward (eds), *Leaders and Managers: International Perspectives on Managerial Behavior and Leadership*. New York: Pergamon.

Reeves, F. (1983). *British Racial Discourse:* Cambridge: Cambridge University Press.

Reich, W. (1975). *The Mass Psychology of Fascism*. Harmondsworth: Penguin.

Reicher, S. D. (1984). 'St Pauls: A Study in the Limits of Crowd Behaviour', in J. Murphy, M. John and H. Brown (eds), *Dialogues and Debates in Social Psychology*. London: Laurence Erlbaum.

Rosenbaum, M. E. and de Charms, R. (1960). 'Direct and Vicarious Reduction of Hostility', *Journal of Abnormal and Social Psychology*, 60, 105–11.

Ross, E. A. (1908). *Social Psychology: An Outline and Sourcebook*. New York: Macmillan.

Ross, L. D., Amabile, T. M. and Steinmetz, J. L. (1977). 'Social Roles, Social Control and Biases in Social-Perception Processes', *Journal of Personality and Social Psychology*, 35, 485–94.

Ross, L., Greene, D. and House, P. (1977). 'The "False Consensus Effect": An Egocentric Bias in Social Perception and Attribution Processes', *Journal of Experimental Social Psychology*, 13, 279–301.

Rothbart, M. (1981). 'Memory Processes and Social Beliefs', in D. L. Hamilton (ed.), *Cognitive Processes in Stereotyping and Intergroup Behavior*. New York: Erlbaum.

Russell, C. and Russell, W. M. S. (1957). 'An Approach to Human Ethology: Behavioural Sciences', *Behavioural Science*, 2, 169–200.

Sacks, H., Schegloff, E. A. and Jefferson, G. A. (1974). 'The Simplest Systematics for the Organization of Turn-taking in Conversation', *Language*, 50, 697–735.

Sagar, H. A. and Schofield, J. W. (1980). 'Racial and Behavioral Cues in Black and White Children's Perceptions of Ambiguously Aggressive Acts', *Journal of Personality and Social Psychology*, 39, 590–8.

Sahakian, W. S. (1982). *History and Systems of Social Psychology*. Washington, DC: Hemisphere.

Sanford, N. (1973). 'Authoritarian Personality in Contemporary Perspective' in

J. N. Knutson (ed.), *Handbook of Political Psychology*. New York: Jossey-Bass.

Sartre, J. P. (1954). *Refléctions sur la Question Juive*. Paris: Gallimard.

Schank, R. C. and Abelson, R. (1977). *Scripts, Plans, Goals and Understanding*. Hillsdale, NJ: Erlbaum.

Schonbach, P. (1981). *Education and Intergroup Attitudes*. London: Academic Press.

Schott, F. (1975). 'What is Aggression' in H. Selg (ed.), *The Making of Human Aggression. A Psychological Approach*. London: Quartet.

Sebeok, T. A. and Umiker-Sebeok, J. (eds) (1980). *Speaking of Apes*. New York. Plenum.

Seidel, G. (1988). 'Verbal Strategies of the Collaborators: A Discursive Analysis of the July 1986 European Parliamentary Debate on South African Sanctions', *Text*, 8, 111–28.

Selg, H. (1975). 'The Frustration-Aggression Hypothesis', in H. Selg (ed.), *The Making of Human Aggression: A Psychological Approach*. London: Quartet.

Semin, G. R. (1980). 'A Gloss on Attribution Theory', *British Journal of Social and Clinical Psychology*, 19, 291–300.

Semin, G. R. and Manstead, A. S. R. (1983). *Accountability of Conduct*. London: Academic Press.

Shatz, M., Wellman, H. M. and Silber, S. (1983). 'The Acquisition of Mental Verbs: A Systematic Investigation of the First Reference to Mental State', *Cognition*, 14, 301–21.

Sherif, M. (1936). *The Psychology of Social Norms*. New York: Harper and Row.

Sherif, M. (1966). *Group Conflict and Cooperation*. London: Routledge and Kegan Paul.

Sherif, M. and Sherif, C. W. (1979). 'Research on Intergroup Relations', in W. G. Austin and S. Worchel (eds), *Social Psychological Research of Intergroup Relations*. Monterey, CA: Brooks Cole.

Sherif, C. W., Sherif, M. and Nebergall, R. E. (1965). *Attitude and Attitude Change: The Social Judgement involvement Approach*. London: Saunders.

Sherwood, R. (1980). *The Psychodynamics of Race*. Brighton: Harvester Press.

Shotter, J. (1984). *Social Accountability and Selfhood*. Oxford: Blackwell.

Sistrunk, F. and McDavid, J. W. (1971). 'Sex Variables in Conforming Behaviour', *Journal of Personality and Social Psychology*, 17, 200–7.

Skinner, B. F. (1974). *About Behaviourism*. New York: Knopf.

Smith, J. L. (1987). 'Making People Offers They Can't Refuse: A Social Psychological Analysis of Attitude Change' in J. Hawthorn (ed.), *Propaganda, Persuasion, and Polemic*. London: Edward Arnold.

Snyder, M. (1981a). 'On the Self-perpetuating Nature of Social Stereotypes', in D. Hamilton (ed.), *Stereotypes and Intergroup Behavior*. Hillsdale, NJ: Erlbaum.

Snyder, M. (1981b). 'Seek and Ye Shall Find: Testing Hypotheses about Other People', in E. T. Higgins *et al.* (eds), *Social Cognition: Vol. 1*. Hillsdale, NJ: Erlbaum.

Snyder, M. and Uranowitz, S. W. (1978). 'Reconstructing the Past: Some Cognitive Consequences of Person Perception', *Journal of Personality and Social Psychology*, 36, 941–50.

Solomon, P., Kubzansky, P. E., Leiderman, P., Mendelson, J., Trumbull, R. and Wexler, D. (eds) (1961). *Sensory Deprivation*. Cambridge, MA: Harvard University Press.

Solomon, R. C. (1976). *The Passions*. New York: Doubleday.

Stockdale, J. E. (1978). 'Crowding: Determinants and Effects' in L. Berkowitz (ed.), *Advances in Experimental Social Psychology. Volume 11*. New York: Academic Press.

Storms, M. D. (1973). 'Videotape and the Attribution Process', *Journal of Personality and Social Psychology*, 27, 165–75.

Strodtbeck, F. L., James, R. M. and Hawkins, C. (1958). 'Social Status in Jury Deliberations' in E. Maccoby, T. M. Newcomb and E. C. Hartley (eds), *Readings in Social Psychology*. New York: Holt, Rinehart and Winston.

Swann, W. B. and Snyder, M. (1978). 'On Translating Beliefs into Action: Theories of Ability and their Application in an Instruction Setting', *Journal of Personality and Social Psychology*, 38, 879–88.

Tajfel, H. (1978). *Differentiation between Social Groups*. London: Academic Press.

Tajfel, H. (1981). *Human Groups and Social Categories*. Cambridge: Cambridge University Press.

Tajfel, H. (1982). *Social Identity and Intergroup Relations*. Cambridge: Cambridge University Press.

Tajfel, H., Billig, M., Bundy, R. P. and Flament, C. (1971). 'Social Categorisation and Intergroup Relations', *European Journal of Social Psychology*, 1, 149–75.

Tajfel, H. and Turner, J. (1979). 'In Integrative Theory of Intergroup Conflict' in W. G. Austin and S. Worchel (eds), *Social Psychology of Intergroup Relations*. Monterey, CA: Brooks Cole.

Tannenbaum, P. H. and Zillman, D. (1975). 'Emotional Arousal in the Facilitation of Aggression Through Communication', in L. Berkowitz (ed.), *Advances in Experimental Social Psychology, Vol. 8*. New York: Academic Press.

Taylor, S. E. (1981). 'A Categorization Approach to Stereotyping', in D. L. Hamilton (ed.), *Cognitive Processes in Stereotyping and Intergroup Behavior*. Hillsdale, NJ: Erlbaum.

Taylor, S. E. and Crocker, J. (1981). 'Schematic Bases of Social Information Processing' in E. T. Higgins *et al.* (eds), *Social Cognition*. Hillsdale, NJ: Erlbaum.

Thibaut, J. W. and Kelley, H. H. (1959). *The Social Psychology of Groups*. New York: Wiley.

Thurstone, L. L. (1928). 'Attitudes can be Measured', *American Journal of Sociology*, 33, 529–54.

Tisak, M. S. (1986). 'Children's Conceptions of Parental Authority', *Child Development*, 57, 166–76.

Turner, J. (ed.) (1987). *Rediscovering the Social Group*. Oxford: Blackwell.

Van Dijk, T. A. (1984). *Prejudice and Discourse*. Amsterdam: Benjamins.

Van Dijk, T. A. (1987). *Communicating Racism: Ethnic Prejudice in Thought and Talk*, Newbury Park, CA: Sage.

Vygotsky, L. S. (1987). *Thought and Language.* (edited by Alex Kozulin). Cambridge, MA: MIT Press.

Walster, E. (1966). 'Assignment of Responsibility for an Accident', *Journal of Personality and Social Psychology*, 3, 73–9.

Weigel, R. H. and Howes, P. W. (1986). 'Conceptions of Racial Prejudice: Symbolic Racism Reconsidered', *Journal of Social Issues*, 41, 117–38.

Wertsch, J. V. (1985). *Vygotsky and the Social Formation of Mind.* Cambridge, MA: MIT Press.

Wetherell, M. and Potter, J. P. (1986). 'Discourse Analysis and the social Psychology of Racism', *Social Psychology Newsletter*, 15, 24–9.

Wetherell, M. and Potter, J. (1988). 'Discourse Analysis and the Identification of Interpretative Repertoires', in C. Antaki (ed.), *Analysing Lay Explanation: A Case Book*. London: Sage.

Wetherell, M. and Potter, J. (forthcoming). *Mapping the Language of Racism: Discourse and the Legitimation of Exploitation*. Brighton: Harvester/Wheatsheaf.

Wicker, A. W. (1969). 'Attitudes versus Actions: The Relationship of Overt and Behavioural Responses to Attitude Objects', *Journal of Social Issues*, 25, 41–78.

Wieder, D. L. (1974). 'Telling the Code', in R. Turner (ed.), *Ethnomethodology.* Harmondsworth: Penguin.

Wimmer, H. and Perner, J. (1983). 'Beliefs about Beliefs: Representation and Constraining Function of Wrong Beliefs in Young Children's Understanding of Deception', *Cognition*, 13, 103–28.

Wood, W. and Eagly, A. H. (1981). 'Stages in the Analysis of Persuasive Messages: The Role of Causal Attributions and Message Comprehension', *Journal of Personality and Social Psychology*, 40, 246–59.

Word, C. O., Zanna, M. P. and Cooper, J. (1974). 'The nonverbal Mediation of Self-fulfilling Prophecies in Interracial Interaction', *Journal of Experimental Social Psychology*, 10, 109–20.

Zillman, D. (1971). 'Excitation Transfer in Communication Mediated Aggressive Behavior', *Journal of Experimental Social Psychology*, 7, 419–34.

SUBJECT INDEX

AUTHOR INDEX